THE POWER OF IP VIDEO

Unleashing Productivity with Visual Networking

Jennifer C. Baker, Felicia Brych Dalke, Michael Mitchell,
Nader Nanjiani

Cisco Press

800 East 96th Street
Indianapolis, Indiana 46240 USA

The Power of IP Video

Unleashing Productivity with Visual Networking

Jennifer C. Baker, Felicia Brych Dalke, Michael Mitchell, Nader Nanjiani

Copyright © 2009 Cisco Systems, Inc.

Published by:

Cisco Press

800 East 96th Street

Indianapolis, IN 46240 USA

Printed in the United States of America

First Printing December 2008

Library of Congress Cataloging-in-Publication Data:

The power of IP video : unleashing productivity with visual networking / Jennifer C. Baker . . . [et al.].

    p. cm.

Includes bibliographical references and index.

ISBN 978-1-58705-342-9 (paperback)

1. Multimedia communications—Industrial applications. 2. Digital video. 3. Labor productivity. I. Baker, Jennifer C. II. Title.

TK5105.15.P69 2009

658'.0567—dc22

2008049129

ISBN-13: 978-1-58705-342-9

ISBN-10: 1-58705-342-x

Trademark Acknowledgments

Warning and Disclaimer

Feedback Information

At Cisco Press, our goal is to create in-depth technical books of the highest quality and value. Each book is crafted with care and precision, undergoing rigorous development that involves the unique expertise of members from the professional technical community.

Readers' feedback is a natural continuation of this process. If you have any comments regarding how we could improve the quality of this book, or otherwise alter it to better suit your needs, you can contact us through email at feedback@ciscopress.com. Please make sure to include the book title and ISBN in your message.

We greatly appreciate your assistance.

Corporate and Government Sales

The publisher offers excellent discounts on this book when ordered in quantity for bulk purchases or special sales, which may include electronic versions and/or custom covers and content particular to your business, training goals, marketing focus, and branding interests. For more information, please contact:

U.S. Corporate and Government Sales 1-800-382-3419 corpsales@pearsontechgroup.com

For sales outside the United States please contact:

International Sales   international@pearsoned.com

Publisher	Paul Boger
Associate Publisher	Dave Dusthimer
Cisco Press Program Manager	Jeff Brady
Executive Editor	Brett Bartow
Managing Editor	Patrick Kanouse
Senior Development Editor	Christopher Cleveland
Project Editor	Seth Kerney
Copy Editor	Keith Cline
Technical Editors	Jose Leary, E. Brent Kelly
Editorial Assistant	Vanessa Evans
Book Designer	Louisa Adair
Cover Designer	Louisa Adair
Composition	Macmillan Publishing Solutions
Indexer	Tim Wright
Proofreader	Sheri Cain

CISCO

Americas Headquarters	Asia Pacific Headquarters	Europe Headquarters
Cisco Systems, Inc.	Cisco Systems, Inc.	Cisco Systems International BV
170 West Tasman Drive	168 Robinson Road	Haarlerbergpark
San Jose, CA 95134-1706	#28-01 Capital Tower	Haarlerbergweg 13-19
USA	Singapore 068912	1101 CH Amsterdam
www.cisco.com	www.cisco.com	The Netherlands
Tel: 408 526-4000	Tel: +65 6317 7777	www-europe.cisco.com
800 553-NETS (6387)	Fax: +65 6317 7799	Tel: +31 0 800 020 0791
Fax: 408 527-0883		Fax: +31 0 20 357 1100

Cisco has more than 200 offices worldwide. Addresses, phone numbers, and fax numbers are listed on the Cisco Website at **www.cisco.com/go/offices.**

About the Authors

Jennifer C. Baker attended Ohio University, where she majored in telecommunications. Her interest in video stems from this time, when she worked at both the local ABC affiliate and the local PBS station covering the news. She has 16 years of experience with voice and video applications, including telephony, contact center, unified messaging, video, and TelePresence. During her tenure at Cisco, she has been a consulting systems engineer, a senior marketing manager, and is now a senior product manager in the Cisco Worldwide Technology Practice. She is also a published author and the recipient of numerous industry awards. She lives in San Diego with her husband.

Felicia Brych Dalke completed a BComm in MIS from Memorial University of Newfoundland, and a master's degree in project management from the University of Quebec. She spent nine years in various IT development and planning positions with Revenue Canada in Ottawa before joining Cisco in 1999. During her term at Cisco, Felicia managed development and operation of several global IT services, including remote access, voice/web/videoconferencing, desktop video, instant messaging, and various voice services. Since 2006, she has worked with engineering organizations to promote adoption, new requirements, and integration for collaboration products. She currently manages an international consortium focused on collaboration. Felicia lives in Mountain View, California, with her husband and children. This is her second project for Cisco Press; she participated as an editor and contributor to *Troubleshooting Remote Access Networks,* published in 2002.

Michael Mitchell has been working with video at Cisco for more than 12 years. During this time, he has been uniquely positioned to witness the migration from traditional communication tools to the new paradigm of converged IP-based media. He is currently the director of the Collaboration Business Services team at Cisco. Team responsibilities range from global video production to connecting business processes with the latest Web 2.0 tools.

Nader Nanjiani has worked in the area of interactive media, IP telephony, communications, and marketing for more than a decade. Nader is currently a marketing manager at Cisco, where he has been specifically responsible for the marketing of IP phones, wireless phones, video endpoints, Unified Communications applications, and related call control applications. While at

Cisco, Nader has launched a series of award-winning online games, IP communication products, web applications, and communications solutions to boost awareness, revenue, and brand loyalty around Cisco technologies. In 2003, he launched the first-ever Cisco online community for certified engineers, which today supports the professional development needs of hundreds of thousands of Cisco customers, partners, and prospects. *The Power of IP Video* is Nader's second title with Cisco Press. He also co-authored *The Business Case for E-Learning,* published by Cisco Press in 2004.

About the Technical Reviewers

Jose Leary is a unified video specialist on the North America Business Video team for Cisco, and he is based out of Herndon, Virginia. He has worked in various technologies and positions since joining Cisco in 1999. He primarily focuses on Cisco Video over IP solutions and also has experience in network and unified communications technologies.

E. Brent Kelly is a senior analyst and partner at Wainhouse Research, specializing in unified communications applications and enabling infrastructure. Brent has authored numerous reports and articles on unified communications, migrating to IP communications, video network services, and the reseller channel. With 22 years of experience in developing and marketing highly technical products, Brent has served as an executive in a manufacturing firm, where he developed and implemented a manufacturing, marketing, and channel strategy that helped land national accounts at major retailers. Previously he was part of the team that built the devices Intel used to test its Pentium microprocessors. He has also led teams developing real-time data acquisition and control systems, and adaptive intelligent design systems for Schlumberger. Brent has worked for several other multinational companies, including Conoco and Monsanto. Mr. Kelly has a Ph.D. in engineering from Texas A&M and a B.S. in engineering from Brigham Young University.

Dedications

This book is dedicated to my husband, Shawn, who was incredibly patient and understanding while I spent many nights and weekends writing. Thank you for your love and support!

—Jennifer C. Baker

This book is dedicated to my mom, Maisie Brych, who taught me a strong work ethic and how to face life's challenges.

—Felicia Brych Dalke

This book is dedicated to my wife and kids. Thank you for putting up with me!

—Michael Mitchell

To my wife, Saba, for teaching many how to read through her work. And for inspiring me to write.

—Nader Nanjiani

Acknowledgments

The authoring team would like to thank many individuals within Cisco for inspiring and encouraging us to write this book. We particularly want to recognize Rick Moran, Jim Grubb, and Blair Christie for their ongoing management support.

We greatly appreciate the contributions from many leaders within Cisco who shared their experiences and success stories of how they used video within their business functions. A huge thank you to Jim Gould, Jeanette Gibson, Nahulan Buell, Lisa Magelby, Rune Olslund, Karen Bissani, Mike Fratesi, Laura Powers, Ann Swenson, David Butt, Josh Chase, Nancy Castillo, Phil Marechal, Kevin McMenamy, Randy Harrell, Jan Fandrianto, Denise Peck, Jeanne Quinn, Beata Mielcarek, Gale Lightfoot, Dave Cavanaugh, Oded Gal, Al Navas, Glenn Inn, Nate Mayfield, Adam Hessler, Bob Dennis, Brendon Hynes, Michael LaManna, Mohit Srivistava, Susan Monce, and Dawn Hayward. For their assistance, we want to thank Rami Mazid, Bob Gardner, John Williamson, Todd Scott, and Maryann Nguyen.

The Cisco on Cisco team, the Cisco Marketing organization, and the Cisco Public Relations team provided much of the case studies, white papers, video blogs, and press announcements that were summarized in this text as examples. Many thanks to Cisco's extended authoring teams.

We recognize and appreciate customer information shared in published materials from the University of California - Berkeley, Cleveland Metropark Zoo, 2Cimple Inc, Coracle Online Limited, the Institute of Chartered Shipbrokers (ICS), Grant Joint Union High School District, Magnet Bank, Mountain America Federal Credit Union, Wachovia, Alabama Department of Rehabilitation, Ontario Telemedicine Network, California's Healthcare Interpretive Network, Arras Hospital, Niagara Health System, the government of Afghanistan, InTouch Technology, SAP, Microsoft, Wipro Technologies, AT&T, British Telecom, Media-Saturn, Rogers Communications, Taj Hotels Resorts and Palaces, Pechanga Resort and Casino, Watford Football Club, Sports Museum of America, NBC Universal, Wal-Mart, and Verizon. We sincerely appreciated the contribution from Doug and Julie Thornton, who shared their experience about Operation Military Connect.

This book took almost two years to complete because of many other work and life priorities. Many thanks to Brent Kelly and Jose Leary, the technical editors, who provided valuable feedback and suggestions to improve the content. We especially thank the Cisco Press team for their patience and guidance during this process. Thank you, Brett Bartow and Chris Cleveland: You are true professionals!

Finally, we thank our families for their support and understanding as we spent many nights and weekends focused on researching, writing, and reviewing this text rather than spending time with them. We love you all!

Contents at a Glance

Contents

Introduction

Video changes everything!

When we think about the evolution of business communications, we first think about the telephone, text-based email systems, voice mail, text messaging, and voice conferencing. As businesses migrated to converged IP networks, we saw more integrated voice/web/videoconferencing, video streaming, instant messaging, and the start of integrated communications enter the business environment.

Today, we hear about quad-play technologies, Unified Communications solutions, TelePresence, IP video surveillance, video portals, Web 2.0 mash-ups, and various solutions developed to address a variety of business needs, all leading to visual networking. The use of IP video to transform business is a growing trend, and large companies or public institutions that want to remain competitive need to prepare for change!

What Is Visual Networking and Why Is It Important?

In the simplest terms, visual networking is the combination of digital video and social-networking (Web 2.0) technologies. It also includes various traditional video applications such as conferencing and streaming that enable communications, collaboration, and new business models. In terms of trends, IP video combined with interactivity promises to make the video experience measurably distinct and improved from the passive video viewing experience with traditional media. And the possibility of making video interactivity pervasive across web, mobility, and IPTV (next-generation TV) platforms promises even greater engagement and responsiveness for audiences.

So why is visual networking important? From a business perspective, the combination of Web 2.0 technologies and IP video means that your teams will be able to interact and collaborate in a meaningful way from anywhere in the world. Thus, businesses can have an unprecedented level of agility. Teams can form dynamically around an opportunity, rapidly build rapport, begin developing solutions, and then be repurposed to a new opportunity. Physically "being there" is no longer a requirement.

A few Internet video trends highlight the growing acceptance of this form of communication. In 2005, 9 billion video streams were served over the Internet, and in 2006, that number rose to 31 billion streams. By December 2007, in only 1 month, 10 billion video streams were served— (more than all of 2005)! Video now accounts for 60 percent of Cisco internal network traffic; and although we are an obvious early adopter of these technologies, it is a sign of changes to come.

In 2008, another video trend was established. NBC Universal captured more than 3600 hours of video from the 2008 Olympic Games (more video than all other Summer Games combined)! Viewers were able to watch video recordings online via the Internet of events that had never been broadcast before. By 2010, corporate TelePresence traffic is expected to generate more traffic than the entire Internet backbone in 2000. All of these trends demonstrate the growth of IP video and indicate a need for even greater Internet bandwidth.

From a product perspective, these trends keep Cisco focused on video as a strategic priority, and require a next-generation platform to manage the expected demand. The network is the platform to provide new video experiences; and content creators, aggregators, service providers, and consumers are all stakeholders in creating these experiences.

What Is This Book About and Why Are We Writing It?

The purpose of this book is to share with you potential business value from the use of IP video and visual networking in enterprise and public sector environments. Examples, case studies, and quotations are used throughout the text to describe the Cisco experience, or in some cases the Cisco evolution, in our use of IP video to engage employees, partners, and customers. We also describe how IP video is changing customers' businesses or services within several industries. The examples demonstrate how visual networking is used to increase agility, cut operational costs, improve communications, grow revenue, and create new competitive advantages.

Besides the examples and case studies, we also provide an introduction to quad-play technologies (voice, video, web, and mobility applications) and describe how they are changing today's workplace. Employees are able to conduct business, regardless of location, as long as there is an Internet or appropriate smartphone connection. In the summary chapters, we cover many visual networking use cases and discuss the future of visual networking, particularly as it relates to green initiatives (the new global priority).

As authors, our experience crosses many viewpoints about video as product managers, marketing experts, business sponsors, IT managers, end users, and teleworkers. We have either planned, developed, deployed, or used all Cisco video or video-related products, and we see how the integration with social-networking applications is changing how we do business.

As an authoring team, we make use of visual networking wherever we can, whether contributing to a blog about the book or conducting a review session with our Cisco Press team members. We've included here a recent picture of Jennifer, Mike, Felicia, and Chris using our USB cameras and WebEx Meeting Center to conduct a meeting about this book and share our video. Jennifer and Chris are both full-time teleworkers, but by using visual networking tools, they are just as connected to their team members as if they were sitting in the next cubicle. Chapters 1 and 2 explore this concept of enabling remote work and more efficient communications through quad-play solutions.

Who Should Read This Book?

The focus of this book is on the business value created from IP video in an enterprise or public sector environment. It does not cover the technology considerations for implementing the individual technologies. Based on this business focus, CxOs, business decision makers, managers, business process experts, communicators, and strategic planners from any functional discipline, within any industry, will benefit from the examples and best practices shared in this text.

We assume you will be able to apply these examples to your business and identify how you might be able to improve communications, cut costs, or even transform your business to grow revenue. At the very least, the examples will show you what Cisco and other companies are experiencing and might spark some new thinking.

Visual Networking to Transform Business

Across many industries, visual networking is creating positive opportunities to improve business. The most natural example is improving communications within a corporation, which can be as simple as deploying video blogs to enable one-to-many communications, or can be more complex such as deploying video telephony to enable better one-to-one communications. Either way, the visual queues available through video provide a richness to the communication that is not present through audio or text alone. Video increases the impact and retention of the message and helps build trust.

In the education space, organizations are globally deploying video technologies to transform learning and education management. The current use of IP video has enabled innovation of learning for career advancement and to enrich the classroom. The University of California - Berkeley uses it to reach dispersed learners via podcasts, delivering content to students both on and off campus. IP video is also being leveraged to secure campuses and schools, thus fostering safer learning environments.

With regard to the financial services sector, we discuss how a major U.S. bank implemented IPTV as a new training method, accelerating new product revenues by nearly 25 percent. This initiative achieved a return on investment in less than one quarter! The bank also uses the IPTV solution to improve corporate communications and share best practices among its sales associates. Several other

U.S. financial institutions are also using IP videoconferencing and TelePresence to improve business relationship, extend expertise to customers, grow revenue, and reduce travel.

Besides the traditional use of video to improve communication and collaboration between staff and hospitals, the healthcare industry is finding innovative ways to improve patient care by increasing access to medical expertise. The University of California Los Angeles (UCLA) and Johns Hopkins medical facilities are using InTouch Remote Presence Robots to enable doctors to project themselves to another location via remote-controlled mobile robots: to move, see, hear, and talk as though they were actually there. In Canada, the Ontario Telemedicine Network (OTN) uses a dedicated IP network to link nearly 400 sites in rural northern Ontario to large urban teaching hospitals. They conduct more than 32,000 video consultations per year, and use the infrastructure to deliver educational broadcasts.

In 2008, the use of TelePresence made significant advancements. More than 40 global service providers have deployed Cisco TelePresence in their networks. Several providers, such as AT&T and British Telecom, have already started to grow their business by offering TelePresence services to their customers. Even the real estate and hospitality sector is buying in to this new business offering. Taj Hotels Resorts and Palaces have started to offer public TelePresence services between global locations on a pay-by-the-hour basis to customers. This offering is definitely a competitive advantage for Taj over other global luxury hotels.

Two Cisco vertical solutions provide the opportunity to change real estate and sports industries through Cisco Connected Real Estate and Cisco Connected Sports. The solutions incorporate a combination of Unified Communications, TelePresence, IP video surveillance, digital media, wireless, and other applications to transform the management and operations of buildings and sports complexes. The benefits associated with these solutions include lower operating costs, improved security, new and improved customer experiences, and new revenue opportunities. Pechanga Resort and Casino and the Watford Football Club are two organizations in this sector that are taking advantage of the power of IP video.

Overall, the use of IP video and visual networking are transforming business in many industries. Within Cisco, the application of video is evident within each functional line of business. From key delivery organizations such as product development, marketing, and sales to corporate support organizations such as human resources and finance, IP video is improving communications, enabling knowledge transfer, growing revenue, and reducing costs, particularly through travel reduction.

Visual Networking to Influence Public Opinion

Cisco began studying trends in visual networking earlier this year by sponsoring research for and application of a Visual Networking Index (VNI). A VNI Forecast was first introduced to provide projections for global IP network growth and usage. It is based on analysis from independent analysts' forecasts. You can read more about about VNI in Appendix B.

As part of this VNI focus, regular installments of a VNI Pulse are planned to provide quantitative views of network-based consumer behavior through direct data collection. The first Pulse study, which was released just before this book went to print, describes the influence of visual networking in the 2008 U.S. presidential campaign. Participants in the Cisco VNI Pulse study included more than 1800 registered U.S. voters, who identified themselves as Democrat, Republican, Independent, or undecided. Some of the key findings included the following:

- Traffic to popular online video websites increased fivefold in 2008 from 2004.

- The Internet was identified by 62 percent of respondents as a regular source of election information, surpassed only by television (82 percent).

- Online video was used by 30 percent of voters to follow election coverage, and 75 percent of these users thought that watching online video enabled them to follow the election news and events more closely.

- Online video users appear more engaged than non-online video users; 62 percent stated they follow the election closely, in comparison to only 37 percent of non-online video users who said they are not following the election closely.

The Internet and visual networking are playing a key role to provide voters with election information and news coverage. One need only browse the content posted on YouTube, Wikipedia, or various news sources to learn about the campaigns, investigate issues, and form an opinion. And more than ever, citizens are using these tools to express their own opinions and have them heard.

How Is This Book Organized?

Although this book is intended to be read cover to cover, it is organized to allow you to focus on only the content that is most relevant to you. Part I of the book, Chapters 1 to 3, provides an introduction to the topic and dscribes why video and quad-play technologies are playing such a crucial role in communications today. These chapters also describe how the workplace is changing into work moments. Part II, Chapters 4 to 9, covers the Cisco experience with visual networking, organized by business function: CxO, finance, marketing, engineering, human resources, and sales.

Part III, Chapters 10 to 13, covers the external customer experience with visual networking, from several vertical markets making the greatest use of video: education, financial services, healthcare, high tech, real estate and hospitality, and sports and entertainment. Part IV, Chapters 14 and 15, describes the many use cases of visual networking and demonstrates how the future of video will impact business and the environment. If you do intend to read all chapters, the order outlined in the book is an excellent sequence to follow.

Chapter Summary

- **Chapter 1, "Quad-Play and the Curse of Interesting Times":** Business is evolving to enable employees to work differently and do more with less. The workplace is being altered by a combination of integrated voice, video, web, and mobility applications, also known as quad-play technologies. This chapter explores the key trends driving the need for change: virtualization, globalization, and consumer-led entry of applications.

- **Chapter 2, "The Way We Work":** Quad-play technologies enable employees to conduct business any time, from any location, using any device. They are transforming the traditional work environment and enabling employees to achieve better work/life balance. This chapter describes a real-life scenario that demonstrates their use, and the chapter describes the potential benefits from the use of quad-play technologies.

- **Chapter 3, "Beyond Workplaces: Video in Collaborative Workspaces":** As the workspace evolves, we will find all aspects of communication benefit from quad-play collaboration tools. This chapter discusses how "work" is no longer a location we go to, but the activity we engage in regardless of where we are. Work can exist anywhere collaboration is possible, which is nearly anywhere with access to a network.

- **Chapter 4, "Scaling the CxO":** Traditional forms of executive communication cannot keep pace in today's global business environment. IP video is the key to allowing the CxO to scale in this new world. The expected benefits to the CxO from IP video are scalability, consistent communication, and increased global collaboration.

- **Chapter 5, "Cisco Finance and Investor Relations: Transforming Processes, Partnerships, and Public Perception":** This chapter discusses how video is used with the finance and investor relations functions to improve internal and external working relationships, improve training and knowledge transfer, provide real-time access to information and subject matter experts, improve the Cisco public image, and reduce travel cost.

- **Chapter 6, "Cisco Marketing: Video Accelerates Communications, Collaboration, and Time to Market":** The marketing organization uses visual networking for both internal and external communications. This chapter demonstrates how IP video is used to improve communications and collaboration, to accelerate global go-to-market of new products and services, and to connect with customers in many new, high-impact ways.

- **Chapter 7, "Optimizing a Global Engineering Organization":** The Cisco Development Organization uses video to improve communications, knowledge transfer, and the product-development process. This chapter describes various use cases from engineering executives, technical leaders, and program and project managers.

- **Chapter 8, "Maximizing Your Human Resources Through IP Video":** This chapter concentrates on the increased productivity that IP video can add to the employment process: recruiting, ramping up new hires, knowledge transfer, and change management. It also covers the benefits of IP video in a company's childcare efforts, and how it can help companies execute better during rough market fluctuations.

- **Chapter 9, "Save More, Make More: Increasing Sales Productivity with IP Video":** Enterprises should look to revenue generation and not just cost avoidance when measuring the ROI of IP video. This chapter explores benefits experienced by the sales function to drive both cost savings and top-line revenue growth from making the sales force more efficient, conducting product launches faster, and making subject matter experts available sooner.

- **Chapter 10, "Transforming Educational Paradigms with IP Video":** This chapter demonstrates how video is being used in education to generate increased value for students, administrators, and communities. With increased adoption of mobile video, we expect even greater innovation in meeting the need for anytime-anyplace instruction.

- **Chapter 11, "Financial Services and Video: Accelerating Revenue, Relationships, and Much More":** Financial services institutions tend to take a more conservative approach toward technology adoption (to ensure security and reliability before deployment). However, even these companies are looking at the potential of new technology to help them do business more effectively. This chapter discusses how video makes a measurable impact on collaboration, training and relationship building, new product rollout, customer service, and regulatory compliance.

- **Chapter 12, "The Doctor Will See You Now: Transforming Healthcare with Video":** Video solutions provide hospitals, medical groups, and even governments with improved access to support and expertise, and thus improve the delivery of healthcare. This chapter discusses how healthcare organizations are using video to build and extend medical expertise, improve staff communications, transform patient care, reduce the cost of care, and improve patient experience with new and innovative services.

- **Chapter 13, "The Influence of IP Video on Other Industries":** This chapter explores the use of video in the high-tech, real estate and hospitality, and sports and entertainment industries to improve communications, reduce operating costs, and create competitive advantages. A cross-industry example to give back to the community is also shared.

- **Chapter 14, "Opportunities in the Era of Visual Networking":** This chapter examines how organizations may benefit when all things Web 2.0 are embedded into video to unleash the era of visual networking. The opportunities and applications for e-commerce, advertising, business-process improvements, and collaboration are extensive and varied. Besides businesses, other segments such as entertainment, education, and public communications also stand to benefit from visual networking applications.

- **Chapter 15, "Collaboration Like Never Before: To Make a Difference":** When combined with other collaboration and conferencing tools, IP video empowers organizations to address the environmental challenges stemming from climate change. This chapter discusses how the use of these technologies can improve remote collaboration and productivity, leading to several benefits that protect the environment.

- **Appendix A, "How Cisco Uses Streaming Video for Worldwide Corporate Events and Training."**

- **Appendix B, "Cisco Visual Networking Index: Forecast and Methodology, 2007–2012."**

PART I

WHERE ARE WE HEADED?

CHAPTER 1

QUAD-PLAY AND THE CURSE OF INTERESTING TIMES

Executive Summary

In this chapter, you will learn how businesses are evolving to enable employees to work differently and do more with less. The workplace is being altered by a combination of integrated voice, video, web, and mobility applications (commonly referred to in the industry as quad-play technologies). Some key trends driving this need for change include the following:

- **Virtualization**: The capability to replicate our desired environment anywhere, anytime using communication technologies such as voice, video, web, and mobility through any device

- **Globalization**: The need to enable multinational project teams that span geographies, and to understand how communications is impacting financial interdependencies in the world economy

- **Consumer-led entry of applications**: The trend of Web 2.0 and visual networking technologies being introduced in the enterprise by individuals and business functions, rather than IT

It was still early in the day for some of us in the year 2000 when we filed into a conference room at the Cisco headquarters in San Jose, for a new-hire orientation event to learn about: Cisco Culture and Processes. As we reflect today, many of the details from those sessions have now faded from memory; however, a particular question that Cisco Chairman and CEO John Chambers posed to the group that day remains just as relevant, not only for Cisco, but for any individual or organization.

During his presentation, he turned to the audience and asked the following:

What if I doubled your workload and halved your resources? How would you do work?

Audience responses ranged from working smarter to refusing to work at all. After a few moments of back and forth, Chambers offered up the answer himself:

You'd choose to work differently.

He went on to elaborate how when faced with a perpetual challenge of doing more with less, as individuals or workers, we tend to prioritize differently, allocate resources differently, and design our work processes differently. It's about how we as humans adapt to our situations. And that's exactly what has been evident over the years, not only at Cisco, but across many organizations around the world.

Doing more with less has become not just a mantra for downtimes or tough times or belt-tightening times, it has now become an accepted way of doing business at all times, largely because it is now indeed possible to do so with emerging technologies, including video. It is now possible to revamp, upgrade, or fine-tune our business processes on a continuous basis. It has kept us in the constant hunt for more innovative communications tools.

When we observe how businesses have evolved (not only as workers at those businesses, but also as customers or owners of those businesses), we can identify three key trends that have propelled that "work differently" phenomenon in recent years:

- Virtualization (anytime, anywhere capabilities)
- Globalization
- Consumer-led entry of applications

Let's take a closer look at how these underlying trends and their relationship to IP video are influencing productivity across the board.

Virtualization: A Common Modus Operandi

Simply put, virtualization is the ability to replicate our desired setting anywhere, anytime using communication technologies such as voice, video, web, and mobility through any device.

Many simple examples help to clarify the concept of virtualization:

- We all have probably responded to critical business emails or executed online transactions while attending a kid's soccer game or a family event. And it was better than missing the personal event.

- We have probably used our home at times for work, viewing video on demand or a live broadcast about the latest corporate or product announcement.

- We may have listened to podcasts while sitting in traffic during commute hours or while on an airplane, extending our productive time.

- Some of us have probably decided to dismiss an agent or a stockbroker because we can now virtually enable those services right at our fingertips without the need to hire an intermediary.

The sections that follow explore how virtualization is enabled through quad-play technologies, including video.

Quad-Play in Virtualized Environments

A host of voice, video, web, and mobility applications (commonly referred to in the industry as quad-play technologies) are altering the workplace. A user's personal space and workspace is less distinct today as a result—with the definition of what comprises a workspace being more dependent on the situation rather than a specific location. We now have the option to choose between work moments and relaxing moments at any given place. We can choose the commute to work to be a working moment when we take a conference call in the car. Or we can view a video training course at home late in the evening. Or we can choose to count a morning jog as a work moment when we have our own eureka moment about a business problem.

Quad-play capabilities turn multiple time zones into a single time zone: real time. Project teams with members from locations in North America, Asia, and Europe are familiar with collaborating at odd hours. Ours is a generation that might go down in history as having blurred the boundaries between personal life and work life. The use of quad-play technologies has evolved the traditional work model to a virtual model; there's hardly a dull moment these days.

Why Video?

Internally, through effective use of video, web, voice, and mobility, Cisco has benefited from virtualizing many of the face-to-face events and deriving significant savings in the areas of e-learning, business meetings, sales communications, and product introductions. The power of IP video remains central to the discussion about the future of communication technologies at Cisco, because it not only stimulates an insatiable demand for bandwidth at work and home, it also offers an irreplaceable level of intimacy, detail, and texture to the interaction. According to the famous anthropologist Ray I. Birdwhistell, body language and facial expressions deliver 65 percent of the communication.[1] Whether it's for learning, working, relaxing, or playing, video, when unified with web and high-quality voice, delivers richness to the interaction, making a virtual experience that much closer to reality. Over other media, video has always offered the best return on our time in terms of quantity of content delivered in a given moment. It also adds a dimension of trust, increasing the impact of the communication. With the interactivity of the web and the ubiquity of mobile phones alongside strides in online video, the quad-play offers a virtual experience not witnessed before.

Video is changing the way companies are doing business. It enables collaboration both internally between employees and externally with customers and partners. Video also increases operational efficiencies and creates new competitive advantages. We share many examples in Part II, "Cisco in Play," and Part III, "Show Me the Money," of how Cisco and our customers are using video to achieve these benefits.

Globalization 3.0 at Our Doorstep

A natural outcome of the quad-play environments remains our interdependence on people, places, and services we might never see, touch, or influence. The world of work has shrunk, bringing co-workers located across nations and continents to common teams, projects, and conference calls on a regular basis. Quad-play environments might have in some cases contributed in making the workplace a bit more complicated, competitive, and culturally nuanced, requiring the workforce to be equipped with new skills and processes to overcome such challenges.

Globalization is also demonstrated through the financial interdependencies from one economy to another. These dependencies have more of an impact now because of global access to information and an ability to immediately react.

A Rocky Ride

Global stock markets have always been in transition, but they seldom made front-page news for the reasons they did on February 27, 2007. It was a day when the Chinese stock market slid, and over the next 20 hours the sliding frenzy caught on to the rest of the world as markets opened in other time zones.

Here's how it went: Former Chairman of the U.S. Federal Reserve Alan Greenspan (a tribal elder of the free market global village) stepped up to a podium in Hong Kong a day before and pronounced that a U.S. recession in the second half of 2007 was likely. Those comments were followed by rumors that the Chinese ministry was contemplating greater regulation of capital gains.

Having witnessed the financial crisis of September 2008, with near thousand point gyrations on the Dow Index of the stock market, we may now think of the February 2007 evens as a mere blip in the larger context. But there was something different about this day when the news of the day rattled the Chinese stock market investors, who began to fret about whether America would be able to sustain buying from China at the same rate (all the shoes, slacks, and sundries that it had been importing). Either way, in February 2007, Chinese stock market speculators, who had pulled money out of their homes to earn a living off of the stock market, weren't taking any chances. The blessing of interesting times (a term often attributed to Confucius, an elder sage from China) was about to take effect on Wall Street a few hours after the Shanghai Index dropped 270 points, or 8.8 percent, in one day. U.S. investors who experienced several years of superior returns on international stocks were about to find the globalization ride a tad queasy.

This was not the first time Asian markets were going to impact the global economy, but this was the first time the Dow slid more than 400 points in sympathy with the Shanghai market index. The preceding year, 2006, was the first time in history when net outflow of investments from the United States had exceeded investment inflow to the United States. This was also the first time that we collectively watched, gasped, and heaved as the market fell 200 points in two minutes. That fall resulted because of a server backlog of sell orders on the New York Stock Exchange that were exercised almost simultaneously, inside of a few minutes, as a backup server took effect, causing a precipitous drop in the index.[2] Real-time access to global financial information and the ability for individual investors to respond immediately from any communication-enabled location and device contributed to this situation.

But the questions lingered for days after the event. Since when has what happened on Main Street USA had such an impact on the Chinese investors that their decisions in turn had an adverse impact on Wall Street? Was the interdependence that we now felt with other world economies a direct outcome of how communications technologies over past several years have changed the way we work, live, play, learn, and invest?

Has It Really Gotten That Flat?

As authors with the task of writing a book on IP video, we collectively wondered what the financial interdependence of world markets we were witnessing really meant. Was this the phenomenon that Thomas Friedman, the Pulitzer Prize winning *New York Times* columnist, had described as Globalization 3.0 in his bestselling book *The World Is Flat*. We heard him speak to a Cisco audience about terms such as "ten flatteners," "triple convergence," and "Globalization 3.0." We followed his logic through the speech and dutifully reviewed our respective copies of the bestseller on planes and in airport lounges.

Of course, we understood offshoring and outsourcing, but we had also grown up with the metaphor that the world economy catches a cold when the American economy sneezes. So, we weren't sure if the interdependence of an underperforming and underrepresented Chinese stock market could potentially shake anything up on Wall Street. Was this really Globalization 3.0 in action?

We remembered Tom Friedman defining Globalization 3.0 as a phenomenon driven by power being in the hands of individuals to create and collaborate, as opposed to Globalization 1.0 where the power was mainly concentrated in the hands of nations, and Globalization 2.0 where multinational corporations held sway. The ability of the individual to participate was built on what Friedman likes to call a "platform" that enables a new age of creativity and a new age of connectivity. His thesis argues that one of the more significant distinctions of Globalization 3.0 is that it has allowed talent from developed and developing nations to compete on a level playing field with little relevance to nationality, color, geographic boundaries, or heritage.[3]

Offshoring, outsourcing, productivity improvements, the personal computer, network capacity, workflow software, communities, and mobility appliances, according to Friedman, have all contributed to the creation of Globalization 3.0. As we thought through it further, we realized that the platform that Friedman kept referring to was the vast information superhighway that provides tremendous value for organizations all around the world (and will continue to do so for the foreseeable future).

So, we went back to the text for a closer look, and there it was: Companies such as Cisco, Microsoft, Sun, HP, Oracle, and many others had indeed contributed in creating the "platform" to enable this global interdependence. The cycle of increased data, mobility, voice, and video applications has indeed stoked greater economic interdependence across continents and now further drives the need to remain connected. Our collective economic well-being now remains tied to countries we might never visit, within cultures and languages we struggle to understand, and with companies whose names we might find hard to pronounce (thanks to Globalization 3.0).

We always understood that stock gyrations, oil futures, and commodity price ups and downs will remain a constant in international markets. From gas prices to both manufacturing and IT jobs to the kitchen table, the effects of Globalization 3.0 permeate. With an increased reliance on international stocks for gains, international commodities for consumption, and international team members for projects, investors, consumers, and workers will seek greater visibility, understanding, and insight into other regions.

The need to know, with granularity and texture, more about where and how our collective economic futures are handled will keep us tuned in for greater collaboration within our global village. And that need to know more about others, which we all share, partly explains why we chose to write about IP video, the most efficient medium of our time and with the ability to transfer the greatest amount of information in the least amount of time. Also, IP video is the only medium that builds the necessary relationships and trust for team members and partners to compete successfully in this global village.

Consumer Led: When Work Emulates Social Networks

The drive for innovation in business process has it roots in workflow and workforce optimization. Organizations understand the tools available and respond in an opportunistic way to improve collaboration, reduce costs, and increase profits.

The collaboration in today's world using voice, video, and web tools over expanding mobile platforms is being driven increasingly by the users. Because consumer-focused communication tools are plentiful and affordable, users can integrate them into their daily repertoires and personal networks with increasing ease and confidence. With a generation that grew up on technologies such as IM, SMS, Skype, and now Facebook and YouTube about to hit the workplace, these users are not about to let up anytime soon.

Users are continuing to drive this trend at work, which is often referred to as consumer-led entry of applications in the enterprise. The trend refers to rogue applications finding their way into the workplace and bolstering productivity under the radar (that is, without explicit knowledge or permission from the IT department). Eventually, these rogue applications become identified and integrated into the work life as innovation.

However, unlike the model of IT-recommended solutions being adopted by employees, as with typical enterprise software and applications, *consumer led* suggests an employee recommended solution being adopted by the IT organization. Examples include employees using Google Talk or Skype before the IT department recognizes the need for enabling softphones on employee desktops. This trend first occurred within Cisco in early 2001, when users of commercial IM systems began rapidly using these products to conduct business, reducing the time to make decisions. Unfortunately, this usage did not comply with internal security policies and created a business priority for a secure internal IM service, which was then launched by IT later that year.

The tools that are not necessarily as much a part of the workflow, but more a part of workforce behavior, have begun to influence productivity. For decisions about productivity applications, instead of looking to innovative ideas from IT vendors, IT organizations need only to check with their knowledge workers on what mash-ups, social networking, or online game tools they are using to come up with the next enterprise or business innovation.

From Web 2.0 to Visual Networking

With mobility technologies so far along among consumers in Europe and Asia, we daresay that innovation might well find its way into the palms of an average Asian teenager before it reaches the desk of a Fortune 500 CEO. Even the advent of Apple iPhone, so hailed as a breakthrough in the U.S. consumer markets in offering next generation of mobility applications, faces tough competition in Asia and Europe. On those continents, many of the capabilities offered by the Apple iPhone have long existed on mobile phones, thanks to a more sustained investment and development of advanced 3G networks.[4]

In its December 18, 2006, edition, while reporting on Best of 2006 business ideas, *BusinessWeek* wrote the following:

> Maybe it was seeing how easily their kids amassed hundreds of friends on MySpace. Or watching the blogs go all viral on bad news about their companies. Whatever the reason, managers discovered social-networking tools en masse this year.[5]

Notice how the text attributes consumers influencing innovation in the workplace, not IT.

The trend continued in the July 2008 McKinsey Quarterly survey on Web 2.0, in which they reported an adoption rate of 2.5 Web 2.0 tools per company this year. The main reasons provided for this adoption was the business functions identifying new technologies, and then either working with or without IT, to deploy them in the enterprise. Companies that were more successful with their deployments achieved this by integrating the tools with business processes, aligning with strategic initiatives, or getting senior managers to be role models.[6]

Within Cisco, Web 2.0 solutions are in various stages of deployment, and the majority of efforts are a result of IT reacting to the consumer-led trend and priorities identified by business units. Wikis, blogs, RSS, podcasts, and the remaining suite of social-networking tools all enable collaboration, and are now being incorporated into business processes.

From a video perspective, this trend of Web 2.0 and social networking has evolved to become visual networking, a term now widely used within Cisco to indicate the integration of social networking and video. Two examples of these tools are video blogs and YouTube. Video blogs are now heavily used at Cisco, both internally and externally, and it is now John Chambers's favorite way to communicate to employees. C-Vision is the Cisco version of YouTube, enabling employees to easily create and post videos, pictures, and other content for viewing and comment by other employees. Where traditional adoption of applications was measured in quarters, most of the Web 2.0 and visual networking solutions are measured in months, because of the viral nature of these tools.

Viral Video: The Edward R. Murrow of Our Times?

Let's use the aftermath of Hurricane Katrina in September 2005 as a case in point. The images were in sharp contrast. On one side, the president of the United States praised his political appointee Commissioner Michael Brown, the then-head of the Federal Emergency Management Agency (FEMA), with his famous words, "You're doing one heckuva job, Brownie." On the flip side, the American public witnessed video clip after video clip on TV and the Internet of people suffering the effects of the hurricane in New Orleans, with no help from the government or FEMA in sight. The video images fueled a blogging trail, and news sites and reporters began to pick up on the national sentiment to build a chorus of protest against government apathy. The president's sound byte, commending Michael Brown's performance, in the midst of a fiasco, personified that apathy.

The juxtaposition of those video clips and sound bytes, and the subsequent noise around the event, formed a contrast that dealt a crucial blow to the U.S. administration's credibility. Not only did it cost the Department of Homeland Security and FEMA tremendous embarrassment and Commissioner Brown his job, it might have even been responsible for the president's party losing control of the U.S. Congress in the 2006 midterm elections. Those events also triggered a mistrust of Washington D.C. within the US electoral population which eventually helped propel Senator Barack Obama—with his message of change—to the presidency in November 2008.

With YouTube and Google Video opening the doors for anyone to place favorable or unflattering video evidence about an entity, organization, product, or business in plain sight of the public, the opportunities or risks are that much greater. IP video available to users today is a leveler: Those with big budgets for sophisticated productions and those on a shoestring budget and who can only afford homemade movies can compete head to head on the strength of their substance. If a popular political party of the most powerful head of the state in the world is not immune from its effects, all others should look out. Actions or statements expressed in an obscure location, captured through the innocuous lens of an unassuming cell phone and then shared virally over the web, can hold the speaker accountable for those actions elsewhere in the world.

We all took notice when YouTube was purchased for $1.6 billion by Google. We were also intrigued by the developments when Viacom sued YouTube for $1 billion for copyright infringement. And then other organizations launched their own video portals to stake a claim in the emerging market for Internet video. The democratization of video has intrigued many bloggers, social networkers, and online enthusiasts. Already, YouTube-like services are finding their way into business organizations that are setting policies on how and what to post from external sites.

And with the added ability to push these videos to mobile phones, video players, and video iPods on-the-fly for viewers, business communications are enabled with a vista that has never existed.

Ultimately, it boils down to the compelling nature of IP video, whether on our TV sets, desktop, or mobile phones, that makes it more potent as a communications vehicle. Of all the communication technologies, video enables persuasion, negotiation, and exposition in a virtual setting that few other technologies can match. To borrow the words of an illustrious broadcast journalist, Edward R. Murrow, we know that video "can teach, it can illuminate, and yes, it can inspire."[7]

What Next?

In the following chapters, we discuss in greater detail how different technologies, especially IP video, have helped productivity, revenue generation, and empowerment for individuals and organizations. We provide examples from Cisco and its customers to illustrate the point.

Use of web, voice, video, and mobility applications at Cisco assumed a level of adoption that demonstrated not only a positive return on investment (ROI) and a set of best practices for Cisco to share with the industry, but also a series of solution offerings for other organizations to take advantage of (as discussed in Chapter 2, "The Way We Work"). Web conferencing, voice over IP, security, and wireless solutions have offered multifaceted services to make work life rewarding and productive for knowledge workers all over the world. Along the way, the industry has rewarded Cisco efforts by acknowledging that converging voice, video, data, and wireless over a single network within an organization is now considered a foregone conclusion.

Summary

In July of 2008, YouTube alone received 11 billion video views. The sheer volume and speed with which video content is generated, posted, and shared virally has altered the shape of debate, accountability, politics, and policies in today's wired societies around the globe. IP video has the potential to empower individuals largely through the speed with which it allows us to share, assimilate, and process information. The power of IP video is becoming evident in our personal lives already, and as most other recent innovations, is fast finding its way into our work lives also.

It stands to reason that organizations will also benefit from the instant collaboration enabled through IP video. If managed well, the resulting innovation will benefit organizations in the long run. Increased IP video and visual networking among coworkers should lead to improved collaboration—resulting in eventual efficiencies and increased effectiveness for the organization. The following chapters will explore in greater detail the opportunities for increased organizational productivity and collaboration resulting from IP video and associated communications technologies.

End Notes

1. Roger Crockett, "The 21st Century Meeting," *BusinessWeek*, 26 February 2007, 72–79.

2. Jessica Dickler, "Technical Glitches Plague the Wall Street," *CNN Money*, 27 February 2007.

3. Thomas Friedman, *The World Is Flat*, New York, 2006.

4. Ian Rowley, "Coolest Mobile Phones in the World," *BusinessWeek*, 12 December 2006.

5. Michelle Conlin, "Web 2.0 Goes Corporate," *BusinessWeek*, 18 December 2006, 101.

6. "Building the Web 2.0 Enterprise: McKinsey Global Survey Results," The McKinsey Quarterly, (http://www.mckinseyquarterly.com/Information_Technology/Management/Building_the_Web_20_Enterprise_McKinsey_Global_Survey_2174), July 2008.

7. Edward R. Morrow, Keynote Speech to Radio-Television News Directors Association (RTNDA) Convention, 15 October 1958.

CHAPTER 2

THE WAY
WE WORK

Executive Summary

This chapter discusses how the quad-play technologies of voice, video, web, and mobility are transforming the traditional work environment by enabling collaboration and employees to conduct business any time, from any location, using any device. This chapter discusses two main topics:

- A real-life example of quad-play technologies (that is, Unified Communications, TelePresence, mobility, presence, and video streaming) used to prepare and deliver (within a matter of hours) an effective communication to the Cisco sales force.

- Management considerations to enhance work/life balance and their associated benefits (that is, greater employee satisfaction and productivity, reduced real estate requirements, and reduced travel expenses and reduced carbon emissions)

Chapter 1, "Quad-Play and the Curse of Interesting Times," discussed how the world around us is changing as a result of quad-play technologies: integrated voice, video, web, and mobility applications, with video being a central application. Let's now discuss specific and practical examples of how video and other quad-play technologies translate into business benefits through effective collaboration.

The practical examples in this chapter demonstrate that video in conjunction with voice, web, and mobility applications will help create an environment conducive for productivity in organizations. Similarly, on the technology side, a combination of powerful servers, astute software, intelligent networks, clever devices, and nifty applications drives the creation of coveted quad-play environments. However, to say that one or the other of the components offers a silver bullet to innovation is selling the innovation process short.

Use of Video in Organizations

Organizations use both live (synchronous or real-time video) and archived (asynchronous or on-demand) video to support collaboration internally.

Two popular options for using real-time video as a means of communications and delivery are as follows:

- **Broadcast video (single source to multiple recipients)**: Broadcast video involves participants watching a presentation and asking questions via text, while following along with presentation slides or any additional screen shots or graphics.

- **Videoconferencing (two or more individuals collaborating on a video call)**: The use of real-time video for conferencing involves two or more participants connected over IP or ISDN to conduct a face-to-face conversation at a distance.

On-demand video offers anytime-anyplace (asynchronous) access to the video, audio, and accompanying slide presentation. The content might include archives of past live broadcasts, presentations, or sales support. For instance, sales and sales support personnel might receive an email alert with a short (30 second to 5 minute) video that demonstrates a specific solution, appropriate use of a specific feature, or troubleshooting of a technical problem. Longer-duration video on demand (VoD) training modules offer an efficient way to learn in 10- to 15-minute chunks of lectures, anytime-anyplace.

IP video content does have its own constraints, not the least of which is the audience attention span. The attention span of a participant viewing a video presentation, for example, begins to taper after 5 to 7 minutes and becomes nonexistent soon after 15 minutes.[1] Content creators also face challenges. For example, without live feedback reinforcing the speaker, presenters who might excel when presenting face to face might find the delivery experience a bit wanting.

IP Video and Collaboration at Work: An Illustration

In this section, we describe a scenario from a day in the life of the co-authors of this book to make the point about how video works to scale the delivery of a message. In short, we were tasked with preparing a briefing for the Cisco 8000-person sales force (about new opportunities to promote the benefits of IP video).

The example that follows is based on true capabilities; it underscores how organizations can leverage IP video, along with the other quad-play technologies for voice, web, and mobility. Any business can thus improve mobility, instant communication, and rich media to save countless person hours, while tapping the best of a dispersed talent pool without the cost of travel or relocation.

Find Them Now

[8:15 a.m. PT—Monday, April 30]

Mike Mitchell sends a meeting request for a quick conference call in 15 minutes with the other 3 authors of this book. Mike has to step into the Executive Briefing Center shortly to present at a client meeting. After he sends the meeting invite, he finds each of us accepting the invite from different locations.

Jen Baker is getting ready to step into her car when she sees the meeting invite on her mobile handset. She is about to set out on a two-hour drive from her home in San Diego to the sales office in Irvine. She is meeting an analyst to demonstrate the latest Cisco capabilities in Irvine in the afternoon. Jen decides to join the conference call from her car. With a few voice commands, she is able to access the conference bridge.

Felicia Brych has taken the week off from work to use her personal time to tie up some loose ends with this book from her home in Mountain View. She has just settled down with a cup of coffee at her kitchen table to start writing on her laptop when she sees the meeting invite from Mike. Felicia decides to use the softphone on her PC, which emulates her desk phone at work, to join the conference call.

Nader Nanjiani is based in Richardson, Texas. Being two hours ahead of the others, he is already at the office and has just returned from a product management discussion when he notices the meeting invite on his desk phone and calls in.

Softening the Edge of Fast Turnarounds

[8:30 a.m. conference call]

We have a bit of a good news, bad news situation [says Mike]. We have an opportunity to speak with thousands of our sales force over a live broadcast today on the topic of the power of IP video. The bad news: The broadcast is at noon today, and I am in customer meetings from 9 to 11 a.m. We'll need slides and script for a 12-minute talk. Can we still pull this off or better to pass?

The team decides not to pass up the opportunity. Jen will conduct research by contacting Cisco Public Relations and Cisco Marketing research for customer testimonials and marketing data. Felicia will organize the slide deck. And Nader will take those talking points to write up a 12-minute script and a draft of host questions.

A face-to-face rehearsal is set for 11 a.m. for 30 minutes via TelePresence, during which Mike will familiarize himself with the slide deck and the script. Mike agrees to offer input on the draft script during the one 10-minute break he expects to have during his client meeting at 10 a.m.

Mobility: Productivity on the Go

[9:00 a.m. PT—Jen's car]

Work begins in earnest. Jen starts by making calls from her car. Because her mobile phone is part of a Unified Communications solution, she can use speech to text to locate the right people from the internal Cisco directory and call contacts around the company to gather the required information.

While on the phone, if she misses a call, she can view callers' presence information (displayed next to their numbers), which indicates whether a party is available to receive a call or is currently busy. From a quick look at the display, she can see how many voice mails she has received. She can quickly distinguish the personal ones from the work ones. She selects to listen to the messages about customer testimonials first.

She also calls the email server from her car to read attachments back to her, using text to speech, from the contents of her latest emails on the testimonials. She also receives links to a couple customer YouTube videos about their experience. Always a proponent of safe driving, she uses a few voice commands to forward all voice mails and emails on customer testimonials, received during the course of her drive, to Nader and Felicia.

Click to Call from Anywhere

[9:30 a.m. PT—Felicia's kitchen]

Felicia makes great progress on the slides. She receives the emails from Jen on customer testimonials in her Microsoft Outlook inbox. She embeds a short video clip into the presentation material. Felicia then receives an instant message from Nader: "We might need more clarification on the last customer quote about the post-sale experience."

Through instant messaging capability in WebEx Connect, Felicia finds the Cisco account manager responsible for that customer is online and available. Using the WebEx One-Click capability, she launches a videoconference, complete with web conference, to gather additional details.

Follow Me Around

[10:00 a.m. PT (noon CT0—Nader's office]

Nader sends the first draft of the script to Mike for his review and steps away for a short lunch break. Mike then calls Nader's desk number; but no problem, both his desk phone and his mobile phone ring at the same time. "The words are fine, but I need some nonverbal cues in the script, as well, just so the producer knows how to cover it," says Mike. Nader conferences in Felicia and agrees to review with her in 30 minutes.

As Nader finishes the call and enters the elevator, a flat-screen digital sign on the elevator wall "senses" his presence from the RFID tag on his badge. Recognizing that Nader had participated in last summer's "Bring Your Child to Work" day, the display shows an announcement about the current year's event. A quick swipe of the badge and Nader is registered for the volunteer event before he has even stepped out of the elevator.

From Voice to Video to Web

[10:30 a.m. PT (12:30 PM CT)—Nader's office/Felicia's kitchen]

On the way back from lunch, Nader instant messages (IM)s to Felicia from the hallway. "Ready to chat?" Felicia calls Nader's desk phone. Because both his desk phone and mobile phone are synced as he walks back to his desk, Nader transfers the call seamlessly from his mobile phone to the desk phone with the touch of a button.

"How about I see you deliver it over video so that I can suggest visual cues?," asks Felicia at one point during the call. In a moment, they click and transfer the call into a desktop video session, without dropping the call or redialing. Felicia reads the questions, and Nader "answers" from the script. They make notes about where to add emphasis to the presentation.

Felicia then clicks her software client for an ad hoc web conference to review the slides with Nader. They quickly make the necessary changes to finalize the presentation.

Virtual Collaboration

[11:00 a.m. PT—TelePresence room(s)]

Mike, Nader, and Jen call into a Cisco TelePresence multipoint meeting from San Jose, Richardson, and Irvine. "Your shirt looks a lighter shade than the producers generally like on the broadcasts," says Jen Baker on the call. The three can view each other in high definition as they virtually sit across from each other in a life-size video meeting. Felicia, being at home, decides to join by voice call, and Nader shares the slides in a web conference. "I have a sports coat in the office that I'll put on," replies Mike.

Mike and Nader go through a quick rehearsal. "Mike, instead of pointing to the flat panel, if you would soften the gesture with just a nod or a glance at it, that might work," comments Jen after observing the run. "Let's do that line one more time." Mike delivers the line with a softer gesture. "Okay. Changed that in the script, as well," says Nader. "We're good to go."

One to Many in a Matter of Moments

[Noon PT—Cisco studios]

Mike delivers a flawless presentation as part of a large sales webinar, with other panelists delivered from the Cisco TV studio. The live broadcast is delivered as a webinar, along with slides, to the Cisco sales force. More than a thousand people from the sales team join live to listen to the presentation. Those unavailable or in other time zones have the option to view the recorded VoD later. Audience questions are handled over a question manager system in real time to address any queries.

After the broadcast, Felicia will create an emphatic three-minute video clip from the broadcast, post it on an internal YouTube-like video portal, and circulate the link to her team by email. Mike sees a host of emails with follow-up questions and interest in the "the power of IP video" messages. The team accomplished their objectives!

Moral of the Story

Our previously described experience helps to highlight how video and quad-play capabilities enable teams to work more effectively from any location, while leveraging the benefits of their IP communications infrastructure. A pervasive end-to-end IP infrastructure is essential, and this underlying network architecture makes collaboration environments possible in today's organizations.

This example also demonstrates how a team can prepare an effective communication and deliver it to thousands of employees within a few hours. These quad-play tools eliminate a lot of the human latency involved in executing a business process or just completing a tactical project.

In the not-too-distant past, a similar exercise might have taken weeks, if not months (and cost a fortune). And even then, the impact of the message would be lost with each subsequent rendition from notes and memory. In addition, those not present at the event would have just their notes to rely on. Today, they can access over the Internet the video recording at their own convenience from their workplaces or homes.

Besides the increased productivity and reduced travel expenses, these tools enable a level of cross-functional collaboration and agility that is nearly impossible to accomplish with traditional communications. Playing phone-tag, dealing with missed calls, plowing through multiple voice mails sequentially to find one, and locating co-workers are some of what Sage Research describes as pain-points of communication and collaboration between teams. According to Sage Research, more than two-thirds of enterprise employees report difficulty reaching their colleagues on the first attempt.

Making a Difference

Now that we have outlined some of the uses for video and quad-play technologies in an organization, let's discuss what else is possible. The hard dollar savings in travel and productivity is part of the conversation, but managers also need to consider the soft benefits of improved morale attributable to a better work/ life balance.

Why should senior management care about communication tools? Short answer: Because workers aren't happy. Of workers under 25 years of age surveyed by the U.S. Conference Board, just 40 percent say they are satisfied with their jobs. Of workers surveyed in all age groups, only 52 percent of those making more than $50,000 per year reported job satisfaction. And only 36 percent expressed satisfaction with work/life balance, growth prospects, workload, and communications channels. The sections that follow present some compelling reasons why management teams might want to leverage the latest technologies, to stack the deck in the employer's favor when it comes to job satisfaction, work/life balance, and environmental support.

Productivity When Away from the Office

Remote-work arrangements offer a solution for business continuity in times of crisis (for example, snow days or other natural or man-made disasters). They also offer an alternative to the mandatory office environment, which might be a constant source of chatter, stress, and productivity loss for workers.

According to a Manpower study from June 2006, a large part (80 percent) of the U.S. workforce would like the option to work remotely rather than commute to the office. Would it be unrealistic to expect workers to be more productive from a more convenient remote setting, such as a home office? As long as workers have the latest communication technologies, they should be able to complete projects as efficiently remotely as at the office.

A Family-First Workplace

Employees want to be there when their children score their first goals (and not have to miss out on an important conference call to be there, either). They want to be home (not at a client site) on Valentine's Day. Look around next time you're at a children's sporting event. Most likely, you'll see a number of parents checking their emails (while still following the game). Such behavior suggests neither an exploitative employer nor a slacker employee.

Employers and employees reach an understanding on a case-by-case basis, through a mature outlook about work effectiveness/efficiency. If the work/life balance discussion is left put off for too long, the competitiveness of companies in knowledge-intensive industries might become compromised (especially during a talent shortage).

Environmentally Friendly Workplaces

We all have witnessed steeply rising oil prices, and most of us are concerned about our carbon footprint. But, how often do we hear employers propose programs to help reduce energy consumption and to reduce greenhouse gas emissions? What if, in the interest of work/life balance, U.S. organizations allowed about 20 percent of their workers to work from home twice a week? Policymakers debate options as if the United States must follow the commuting patterns of the mid- to late-twentieth century for the rest of eternity.

As a matter of social responsibility, what if organizations were to introduce videoconferencing and TelePresence programs to replace travel? Besides being good for worker morale and productivity, these programs would be good for our environment and the economy in general.

Even Cisco has significantly reduced its carbon footprint by using TelePresence. Since the original deployment, almost 35,000 meetings have avoided travel, with an estimated $137 million in savings (and almost 69,000 metric tons of greenhouse gas emissions avoided).

Rationalizing Real Estate

Companies have been rationalizing office space since the 1990s, creating shared "hoteling" space. Such spaces provide a temporary workspace at the office for employees who work part time from home or who are regularly out of the office on business. In a shared workspace environment, any desk can feel like it is yours as long as your laptop works and the phone can be personalized with your individual extension number.

As companies continue to cut operating costs, reducing office space (particularly when renting) is an option worth exploring. Much has been published about how to manage this transition from a policy and technology perspective. It just takes a corporate vision and strategy to make it real. Chapter 13, "The Influence of IP Video on Other Industries," discusses the Cisco Connected Real Estate solution.

All About Nuance

When we are on the phone and must make a yes or no decision, we often wonder whether the silence on the other end is a smile or a grimace. As a result, workers in negotiation or persuasive discussions usually prefer to fly out to meet colleagues and customers in person.

What if employees were to have tools that capture the nuance of words remotely through a lifelike communications experience? What if the communications experience could ensure that even a slight gesture by either party does not go undetected during the course of a conversation? If a credible alternative for travel were available, would the hours at the airport, the middle seat, the day away, and the airfare still be worth it?

Video is immersive and enables face-to-face relationships. Thus, it helps to build trust among participants involved in the communication, even though they might be anywhere in the world. The life-size, high-quality video and audio from TelePresence provides this lifelike communications option.

Summary

Collaboration technologies enable employees to conduct business at any time and from any location and using any device. They truly enable a workforce to choose between work moments and personal moments, providing options to achieve work/life balance.

A pervasive end-to-end IP infrastructure is essential to leverage the host of quad-play and communications technologies described in this chapter. Communications and media offer the user experience, but it is the underlying network architecture that delivers the flexibility and the capacity to manage bandwidth-intensive applications, particularly video. This architecture makes collaborative environments possible in today's organizations.

An application-rich environment is not a silver bullet of technology. Instead, a host of discrete factors contribute to sustained collaboration within an organization, factors such as applications, networks, platforms, management policies, and corporate culture. Potential benefits derived from remote-work arrangements include improved work/life balance, greater employee satisfaction and productivity, reduced real estate requirements, and reduced travel expenses (and the associated reduced greenhouse gas emissions).

End Note

1. Patricia Galagan, "Delta Force," *Training Magazine*, May 2002.

CHAPTER 3

BEYOND WORKPLACES: VIDEO IN COLLABORATIVE WORKSPACES

Executive Summary

This chapter discusses how

- Organizations need to collaborate for effective operations.

- Today's collaboration tools (that is, video, audio, mobility, and the web) allow work to take place where the worker is located rather than where the employer is located.

- Video enhances the collaboration experience and, with other technologies, helps to increase understanding, trust, and relationships between individuals at work.

We discussed in earlier chapters that today's workspace has become as much a concept of time as of place. We can divide our daily life into working or nonworking moments, irrespective of whether those moments occur at the office, while waiting at the theater box office, or lounging at the swimming pool. What distinguishes work from nonwork is not so much the physical location but the predisposition of the individual. With ever-increasing video-, audio-, and web-conferencing capabilities, individuals can now work from anywhere they have network connectivity. If a worker completes a conference call while at her child's soccer practice, the soccer field constitutes the workspace for that moment in time.

A knowledge worker workspace could best be described as any location where an individual's workflow tools are readily available; for many people, this includes collaboration tools. Simply put, to collaborate is to tap into the expertise of others when performing work. An individual's expertise on a topic might be limited, but being able to pull in the skills of others, who might be remote, preferably in real time, could improve both the efficiency and the effectiveness of our work.

The embedding of real-time communications capabilities such as voice, mobility, video, and conferencing in our day-to-day work will enable greater productivity by reducing travel and the time required to make decisions and by increasing teamwork. As real-time video, voice, mobility, and web communications permeate through all aspects of work and become pervasive across all types of workspace devices, such as conferencing units, PCs, handsets, and MP3 players, we stand to unlock the full potential of collaboration.

Consider for a moment how we work. Consider, for instance, the functions we perform within our workspace on a daily basis. We can classify them into four distinct categories (in no particular order):

- **We devise**: Devising relates to all the "figuring things out" tasks that we do at work, such as planning, assessing, searching, or strategizing.

- **We transact**: Transactions, on the other hand, relate to tasks around negotiation, buying, payment processing, ordering, pricing, selling, or acquiring.

- **We interact**: Interaction refers to talking, conferring, or meeting other colleagues for advice, approval, input, or guidance.

- **We produce**: Production refers to creation of content, whether that content is documents, deliverables, widgets, or services.

Collaborative technology tools have always played a role in these activities, but so far it has not permeated through those work categories.

How Might Collaboration Really Play Out at Work?

Imagine while processing payroll (a desire to transact), you come up with a question (a desire to interact). To pull away from that transaction session to set up a separate conferencing session seems inefficient. But that is exactly what happens currently. What if the ability to interact in real time were embedded right into the payroll-processing tool? Similarly, an individual creating artwork (a desire to produce) should be able to seek input (a desire to interact) on her in-progress masterpiece from mentors or colleagues, no matter how remote they might be, in real time without having to interrupt the creative process. She should be able to just launch an application that shares her artwork with others in living color (using video/web conferencing).

Imagine the savings in time that could be easily achieved by embedding video with web collaboration into the daily workflow, and imagine the improved quality of decision making. Doing so would eliminate the need for meetings with action items.

As seamless sharing of communications becomes more prevalent while devising, transacting, interacting, or producing, without the risk of delays, more of us will choose to collaborate. Let's consider an example of how embracing video in her day-to-day work altered the life of one executive assistant at Cisco.

"Virtual Margaret"

Margaret Hooshmand lived in the Bay Area for 10 years, and has worked at Cisco Systems for the past 5 years. She loved her job, her supervisor, and her team in San Jose, California. As the years passed, however, Margaret began to wonder whether the Bay Area was the best place for a single mother to raise her daughter and whether the cost of living in the area was worth it. Margaret began looking for alternatives; in spring 2006, she decided to relocate to Dallas, Texas.

When she informed her supervisor, Marthin De Beer, vice president and general manager of the Emerging Markets Technology Group (EMTG) at Cisco Systems, of her intention to relocate, he genuinely felt conflicted. Although he did not want to lose a valuable Cisco employee, he did want her to enjoy life and feel comfortable about raising her daughter under good circumstances. Over their first three years working together, Margaret and Marthin had built a solid, successful working relationship. He really did not want to lose her because of the move. They needed a solution that would allow Margaret to work with her team, but in another Cisco office location in Texas.

Because of the nature of her job as his executive administrator, whatever solution they chose had to enable them to communicate and collaborate effortlessly, despite their geographic disparity. In her position, face-to-face contact with team members was critical, as was immediate accessibility. As Marthin's executive assistant, she engaged with all levels of employees in the San Jose office, and the need for her to maintain that constant interaction with anyone who approached her desk throughout the day was essential. Besides communicating with her own team members, she needed to remain a valuable resource to any employee who needed help or direction. Any alternative selected had to allow for her to continue working as if she were still seated at her desk in San Jose, and enable her to perform her everyday duties as effortlessly as possible.

Enter TelePresence

Margaret opted to try the new Cisco TelePresence solution, which her team was planning to release shortly after Margaret's planned move. The timing was right. The solution offered the life-size, high-definition video to create that feeling of being "in person" that the team was looking for (see Figure 3-1):

> Every morning that I dial in, I think to myself, is this really happening? I can live where I want, work at a company that I love, and still have a full-time presence. That's amazing.
>
> Margaret, executive administrator, Cisco Systems

Figure 3-1   *Virtual Margaret*

According to Margaret, the transition was easy after her move. She and Marthin were able to continue working together as a team:

> Marthin and I read each other really well, which is key to a successful relationship between administrator and supervisor.
>
> I thought that we would lose that connection and interaction when I moved to Texas, but with the Cisco TelePresence solution, we are able to see each other in life-size proportions, look each other directly in the eye, and speak naturally without any audio delay. We can still read each other's body language, which is critical in our particular business relationship. We joke now that Marthin can still clearly see me smirk while raising my eyebrows in typical Margaret fashion; nothing has changed.

This solution has worked so well that there are now two systems installed at the San Jose office. One is at Margaret's old desk in San Jose, and the other one is in Marthin's back conference room, which they use for one-to-one meetings, other weekly meetings that she must attend with Marthin, and for quick discussions and decisions that need to occur throughout the day. With one push of a button, Margaret vanishes from her location outside of Marthin's office, and then instantaneously reappears in his conference room. It is fast, reliable, and truly amazing. Margaret continued with this:

> I love the fact that I can still actively participate in any and all meetings required. If I were forced to dial in via audio only for such meetings, I would feel remote and disengaged. With this solution, I am virtually present, as if I were there with the team in person.
>
> In the beginning, there were a lot of people stopping by. Mouths would drop open when people saw me, as if in disbelief and amazement of what they were seeing. Now, as folks get used to seeing me day in and day out, it is business as usual. One interesting thing that I noted in the beginning was that I felt like I was on camera all the time, and it made me feel a little self-conscious. Now, I don't even remember that I'm on camera. It feels like I'm still in San Jose; for eight hours a day, I'm fully engaged in the business at Cisco headquarters. If it were not for the clock on my back wall here in Richardson indicating central time, I would completely forget that I'm in Texas!

Business Implications

Both Marthin and Margaret are reaping the benefits of TelePresence. Marthin was able to keep a key member of his team, and Margaret was able to keep the job that she loves at the company that she loves while living in and bring up her daughter in a more affordable area. Margaret's happiness with the arrangement is obvious:

> It is the best of both worlds. Not many companies would take a chance like this.

Since adopting the technology, Margaret Hooshmand has earned the moniker "Virtual Margaret." Her story has been featured in business periodicals, on CBS, and in major publications. Margaret finds the video experience natural and intuitive. The story strikes a familiar chord with workers around the world (perhaps sooner than it does with management), and for good reason, too.

With the trends in offshoring and teleworking, more and more managers face the reality of managing remote employees. Video provides one way to stay connected with these dispersed employees. A video deployment could be life-size, high-definition video as Margaret and Marthin use or a web camera attached to a PC running videoconferencing software. Video (and the potential of working remotely it promises) offers useful alternatives when businesses are retaining existing talent, attempting to recruit Millennials, or dealing with workforce relocations.

Too Many People, Too Many Trips

Traffic congestion challenges us all. At the turn of this century, the number of people living in urban areas surpassed those living in rural areas for the first time. We can hardly expect this to be a reversible trend. With that increased urbanization comes the associated problems of urban congestion, dilapidated infrastructure, and environmental degradation.

According to an urban mobility report issued by the Texas Traffic Institute, an average driver in the United States spends about 38 hours a year in traffic delays.[1] That totals 4.2 billion person hours in 2005, up 5 percent over the previous year. The traffic delays eat up 2.9 billion gallons of fuel (at an estimated cost of $78.2 billion). For a 50-mile round-trip commute, we can expect the average U.S. commuter to use from 500 to 800 gallons worth of fuel each year depending on vehicle efficiency. Although high gasoline prices have reduced some travel, commuting (and its attendant delays) remains a necessary evil for the vast majority of workers. The study attributed the situation to "too many people, too many trips over too short of a time period on a system that is too small."

Boosting "Engagement" at Work

Employee engagement will also positively impact productivity, but it is seldom discussed in the context of communications. Use of electronic tools by senior management, such as webinars and voice mail, has been shown to positively impact employee engagement.[2] Broadcast video or video-on-demand (VoD) sessions aim to further increase the sense of proximity among employees and senior leadership within organizations.

According to a global workforce effectiveness study released by the consulting firm Towers Perrin in the fall of 2007, only one in five workers around the world report being engaged on the job. That statistic is reinforced by the nearly two out of five employees who report that they feel disenchanted or disengaged about work.[3] The numbers are serious because studies have shown that those organizations with highly engaged workers demonstrate a positive correlation with growth and profitability, whereas those with low levels of employee engagement are negatively correlated to financial performance.

Simply put, *engagement* indicates whether employees are willing to go the extra mile for their employers. The term *engagement* refers specifically to the degree to which employees feel emotionally tied to the company, have a clear sense of how to add value to the company's performance, and are willing to take steps to add that value. The study also suggests that senior leadership within an organization can positively influence engagement levels among workers by clarifying policies, roles, expectations, and organization direction.[4]

Business leaders who conduct regular informal discussion forums over video or participate in electronic town-hall meetings are more likely to increase the engagement levels within their teams. The cost of boosting engagement through increased communication is greatly reduced with tools such as videoconferencing and streaming video over the Internet. And, there are intangible benefits: An engaged workforce within an organization will feel more empowered to contribute and add value to the organization's goals.

Workplace Flexibility to Reduce Healthcare Cost

As employee wellness programs become more prevalent in Fortune 500 companies,[5] those programs may be missing a key component: workplace flexibility to encourage healthful behavior among employees. Whereas video helps boost productivity by enabling greater collaboration, the greater flexibility for employees (that is, less travel or fewer commutes) could potentially help reduce healthcare costs for organizations.[6]

Rising healthcare costs are creating pressures on organizations to take proactive measures. Discussions about making wellness programs mandatory are occurring, and organizations are also considering penalizing unhealthful behaviors such as smoking.[7] Organizations may soon consider workplace flexibility as a contributing factor to enable healthful behavior.

According to a study by Wake Forest University School of Medicine, workplace flexibility (such as flextime, job sharing, and remote working or telecommuting) leads to healthful behaviors and positive lifestyle changes.[8] Facing a challenge from healthcare costs, organizations offering workplace flexibility or telecommuting in parallel with a comprehensive wellness program might derive even greater value from their efforts. Offering workers an option to offset "time on the road" with "time at the gym" could encourage healthier lifestyles for employees (and subsequently reduce the cost of healthcare for the organization).

Employees frequently traveling for face-to-face meetings with co-workers could opt to replace the windshield time with an appropriate video solution that delivers virtual face-to-face meetings. Besides making more productive use of employee time, flexibility in their work life enabled through use of video would also help employees more effectively telecommute. Whether as a result of reduced travel or a reduced commute, workplace flexibility will leave employees with more time on their hands to adopt "positive lifestyle habits."[9]

Summary

Video cannot replace every nuance of interaction that occurs when people are in the same room. However, we can maintain productive work relationships and sound organizational communication with remote workers using video as a tool.

As the workspace evolves, we will find all aspects of communication benefit from video-, voice-, mobility-, and web-based collaboration tools. A desire to improve the quality and depth of content will drive us to increase our use of rich media during conferencing sessions; context will ensure that the nuance and the decision inputs into our conversations are readily accessible (a grimace or smile sometimes speaks more than words). "Work" is no longer a location we go to, but the activity we engage in regardless of where we are. Work can exist anywhere collaboration is possible, which will be almost anywhere with access to a network.

End Notes

1. "Drivers Lose Entire Work Week per Year to Traffic Congestion," Associated Press, 18 September 2007.

2. Andrea Coombes, "Fewer Workers Are 'Engaged' at Work and Most Want More from Execs," *MarketWatch*, 21 October 2007.

3. Ibid.

4. Ibid.

5. Michelle Conlin, "Get Healthy—Or Else," *BusinessWeek*, 26 February 2007.

6. Andrew Swinton, "Study: Telecommuting Is Healthy For You," *ZDNet News*, 15 October 2002.

7. News release, American Heart Association, 10 May 2007.

8. Michelle Conlin, "Get Healthy—Or Else," *BusinessWeek*, 26 February 2007.

9. News release, Wake Forest University Baptist Medical Center, 10 December 2007.

PART II

CISCO IN PLAY

CHAPTER 4

SCALING THE CxO

Executive Summary

In this chapter, you will learn how corporate leaders can use IP video to communicate more efficiently and effectively, across geographic expanses, to all employees:

- Traditional forms of executive communication cannot keep pace in today's global business environment.

- IP video is the key to allowing the CxO to scale in this new world.

- The expected benefits to the CxO from IP video are scalability, consistent communication, and increased global collaboration.

Anyone who has managed employees knows the frustration of translating new ideas into employee action. You can have a clear concept of what needs to be done, and who needs to do it, but the real trick is getting everyone aligned to the new direction. How many times have you sent out a "brilliant" email outlining a new direction and then sat back in amazement as nothing is realized. You think, "Didn't they get the email? How come nothing changed?" So, you start the time-consuming process of meeting with everyone one on one, and then you start to see some movement in the right direction.

Time passes, and you notice a need to adjust the concept, or perhaps the team starts falling back on the "old ways." So, you send another email and book more one on ones.

Your employees are not incompetent or out to thwart your genius. This is just the messy reality of dealing with human beings. We are a social bunch, and communication is what we thrive on. What makes human beings even more difficult to deal with is that communication is most effective when we hear the voice and see the face of the person we are interacting with. You can't just upload some new parameters or upgrade our firmware. Dealing with humans takes, well, a "human touch."

Communicating with everyone one on one is inefficient, but manageable within a small group. However, CxOs who need to reach out to 50, 500, 5000, or 50,000 has a real dilemma on their hands.

Unfortunately, some CxOs try to handle communications in much the same way as a line manager or the owner of a small business. They send out the email and hope for the best or, if it is important enough, start booking one on ones with their VPs. Then, the CxO's direct reports communicate with their direct reports, and then to the next level, and so on down the line.

This approach presents several problems:

- It is time-consuming for the CxO personally.

- Messages can get distorted. Each line manager who communicates the message "customizes" it.

- Even if directives or vision are ultimately communicated accurately, the human latency in disseminating the message can lead to business inefficiencies given today's pace of business.

- Little or no feedback reaches the CxO from the people who actually do the work.

To help mitigate the ineffectiveness of this hierarchical style of communication, CxOs have traditionally typically responded in one of two ways. They either increase their time "managing by walking around" or hold more "all-hands" meetings to get everyone together to hear the same message.

The first mechanism is usually the most popular with employees. Corporate legends are filled with the "Average Joe" executive who spends a good deal of time walking around and speaking directly to the employees.

In the early days at Cisco, CEO John Chambers used to walk around with a little red wagon full of candy. He would walk through a section of cubes and hand out a piece of candy to get a conversation going with an employee. This openness was extremely endearing to the employee and, more important, helped set the tone for open communications that is still part of the company today.

However, an obvious problem with walk-around, skip-level communications is that it does not scale. Even if your employees are located in the same place geographically, it is still a huge drain on the CxO's time. John, with his little red wagon, simply could not see enough employees in the time he had. One response to this was the creation of a monthly employee breakfast with John. Any employee who had a birthday that month was invited to breakfast with John in a large meeting room. John would take questions for an hour or two and get feedback from employees. Yet this, too, had some obvious scalability limits. The worst of which was being limited to those employees physically located at our headquarters in San Jose, California.

The next response to the ineffectiveness of traditional hierarchical communications is the ever-popular All Hands meeting, where everyone is required to gather in person. It comes in a mind-numbing variety of flavors. You have your group All Hands, your divisional All Hands, your manager's All Hands, your company All Hands, and so on, and so forth. Although it is great to get everyone together from time to time, these All Hands meetings are rarely 100 percent attended and are a huge time commitment for all involved. Employees in geographically distributed companies are either excluded, have to call in, or have to travel to attend, which greatly increases the impact the meeting has on their personal productivity.

What the CxO needs is a tool with the scalability of email that carries the weight of an in-person meeting. Recognition of this need is why we see so much interest in video from the executive level.

To be sure, this interest is not new. For the past 30 years or more, we have seen companies experiment with ISDN videoconferencing and satellite-based video broadcasts. Despite the costs and the complexity of these systems, companies recognized the need to have the capability. At Cisco, for example, we used to happily pay hundreds of thousands of dollars to produce conventional satellite broadcasts. It was not cheap or easy, but was still an improvement over other forms of communication.

Your Broadcast Network

In recent years, video has become much more accessible to the CxO. The foundational enabler of the new *video-friendly* enterprise is the ubiquity of the IP network. All forms of communication are converging on to the IP network, and video is just the latest application to hit. For the CxO with an IP network, this means that you already have the basis for a private video-communications network.

The IP network has dramatically lowered the cost of transporting the video signal, but it is still important to know the capabilities of your current network before using IP video. For a videoconference, IP video means no more ISDN-per-minute fees or installation costs. For a video-broadcast system, it means no more private satellite networks. The broad availability of IP networking has exponentially reduced the cost of using video.

The ubiquity of IP has also made video much easier to use. For example, we use the Cisco Unified Video Advantage product for internal desktop videoconferencing. It integrates with our IP phones, and videoconferencing is truly just as easy as making a phone call. The integration between the phone and a video camera would not be possible without the convergence to an IP network. In fact, myriad vendors make applications that facilitate the use of video over the network.

Finally, the CxO is addressing a workforce that has become increasingly accustomed to communicating via video. With the huge popularity of video on the public Internet, employees are no longer surprised by the use of video on the company intranet.

Direct Employee Interaction

Within Cisco, the use of video has become a regular part of how executives communicate with employees and with each other.

The evolution of John Chambers's Birthday Breakfast is one of the best examples of how video has become integrated into a corporate tradition.

As Cisco continued to grow, John Chambers needed a way to keep the Birthday Breakfast tradition alive while recognizing our growing employee base outside of our headquarters in San Jose. We began to experiment with using an IP video broadcast of the in-person event to reach the larger employee base. It was immediately accepted and appreciated by the remote audience, many of whom never had access to the event in the past. With little extra effort or cost, John was suddenly able to scale the event around the globe.

Today, the Birthday Breakfast also includes integrated IP videoconferencing. Videoconferencing units are wheeled in to the large meeting rooms of major campuses outside of San Jose. In the San Jose meeting room, the remote locations are projected life size onto the side walls. The effect is that the San Jose room appears to be expanded with the employees from locations all around the world. It is a wonderful, visual example of the global nature of our company. The videoconferencing feeds are then mixed in to the live broadcast so that remote employees viewing at their desktop get the full effect.

The entire event is focused on direct employee-to-CEO interaction. There is no formal presentation, and John takes questions the entire session.

On any given month, more than half of the total attendees are viewing the Birthday Breakfast via IP video. However, not all of these viewers are remote employees. The scalability of IP video has allowed employees who are "not invited" to the event to nevertheless attend. Although we could easily block those viewers, John has instead chosen to allow access to anyone who wants to get his latest thoughts. In this way, the Birthday Breakfast has become a powerful way for John to squash rumors before they get out of control or to share information on the major events of the day.

Of course, one thing that we still have to take into account is the time difference between San Jose and the rest of the world. It is the middle of the night for many employees during our Birthday Breakfast. IP video can help here, too.

Each Birthday Breakfast is recorded as a video on demand (VoD) that is segmented by question for easy access. An additional 1000 or so employees watch the VoD version every month.

Kelly Lang, director, Strategic Communications, puts it like this:

> Video is an amazing and effective medium to deliver a message, and we believe it is one of the best communication tools we have to scale John's voice. We love video for the simple fact that John could never physically be in all the locations and time zones that he is requested. How else could we retain a constant "touch" and main-tain consistency in key messaging? When being "live" is not possi-ble, we use video for everything imaginable.

John's use of video is becoming even more frequent, casual, and accessible. In addition to the Birthday Breakfast, John does a monthly video blog or "vlog" (see Figure 4-1).

John records this vlog once every month or so when he has time between meetings. He is able to use his Cisco Unified Video Advantage to record it himself without any production support. The file is then uploaded as a blog so that employees can comment directly back to John.

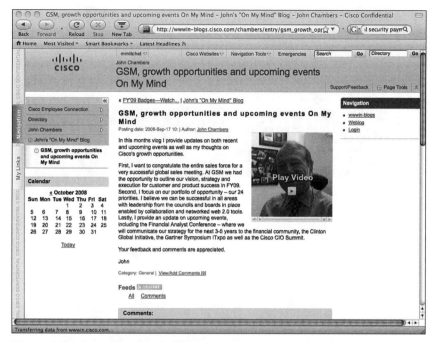

Figure 4-1   *John Chambers's Vlog*

John's vlog was cited by employees as one of the reasons they nominated Cisco to the sixth spot in *Fortune* magazine's "100 Best Places to Work" award (see Figure 4-2). This new form of executive communication was also recognized by the International Association of Business Communicators (IABC) with their 2008 Silver Quill award.

John's approach of driving an open forum for employee interaction has also trickled down the management chain. Because of the low cost of IP video communications, the average All Hands meeting can now be broadcast out to global employees. Each broadcast includes a Q&A session and is recorded as a VoD for employees who cannot be physically present. The heads of large or highly dispersed divisions also regularly record vlogs to keep their teams aligned on common goals, recognize accomplishments, and even just to keep rumors from propagating.

Figure 4-2 *Cisco Number 6 in 100 Best Places to Work* (Fortune *magazine*)

Open Access

Another meeting that is regularly broadcast on IP video is the quarterly Estaff meeting. This is a two-hour meeting for VPs and above to receive strategic updates on the direction of the company. The premise for the broadcast is to allow global executives to attend the meeting without traveling. The broadcast can be, and occasionally is, password protected to allow free interaction between executives on potentially controversial topics.

What is more interesting, however, is that the broadcasts are most often *not* password protected. Any employee, anywhere in the world, can potentially choose to receive the same update as a senior executive. IP video can allow for various levels of security, but when queried, senior management did not see any reason to restrict the data from the average employee. Including the individual employees requires no extra effort, so why not give them direct access to the same information?

For the next rung down the management ladder, there is an annual executive All Hands for directors and above. This event is the Strategic Leadership Offsite and is scheduled toward the end of each fiscal year to set the strategic direction of the company for the coming fiscal year.

The format has leaders from each of the major business groups presenting on their focus areas and goals for the coming year. The directors in the room can then leave the event with an idea about how they can align their own divisions with the goals of the company.

However, the VoD version of each of the presentations is made available to the entire employee base. Individual employees can select a particular area relevant to them and receive the strategic direction for the company directly from senior management.

The key advantage to the CxO is that a consistent message can be delivered throughout the process and to each level of the organization.

Accountability

All this openness from senior management has both overt and subtle implications for the communication environment at Cisco.

Table 4-1 outlines the problems with historical hierarchical communications that opened this chapter and the effect that IP video has had on them.

Table 4-1   *Effect of IP Video on Communication*

Historical	IP Video
Effective communication is time-consuming for the CxO. One-on-one communication is often required.	Video is more effective than email, but just as scalable. A message can be delivered once and relayed to the entire team.
The message gets "customized" as it is relayed down the management chain.	Employees can get their strategic information directly from senior management. A line manager can still explain the relevance to the employee's day-to-day work, but the core message remains intact.
Little or no feedback reaches the CxO from the people who actually do the work.	Every employee has access to any executive in open sessions. Remote employees can submit questions during the broadcast via text or even two-way video. Executives can publish vlogs that allow employees to comment directly on a subject. Every broadcast also includes a survey so that trends can be analyzed.

In short, IP video is more effective, scalable, and interactive than traditional forms of business communications.

There is also a more subtle effect on the executive ranks. Every VP who presents is recorded, and what the VP says becomes a record of intentions. This is not necessarily used in performance reviews or to catch someone in an embarrassing situation. It does, however, make senior management commit and align with each other.

This can be a powerful tool for CxOs to make sure their VPs are aligned with the overall company strategy. When the VPs are asked to present on their team's direction, they are making a public testimonial to the entire company.

From Innovation to Requirement

The benefits of using the tools for any large, global enterprise are now so blatant that to not use the tools may put your company at a competitive disadvantage. IP video, along with networked communications in general, is one of the chief enablers of both the pace and the global scope of business today. Like email in the 1990s, video communication in this decade is becoming a baseline capability in a large company.

Jennifer Mitchell, event manager in the Cisco Corporate Communications Department, adds the following:

> As a global company, we were always looking for ways to incorporate remote offices and make them a part of our employee events, celebrations, and meetings. Cisco's IP video solution has given us a platform to extend our in-person birthday chats, company all-hands meetings, and "take our children to work" events to our remote sites, and at times offering two-way communication to truly embrace the "in-person" experience. With its reliability and ease of use, IP video has become an intricate part of planning programs; so no matter where one sits, every employee has the opportunity to not only hear it, but see it first hand.

For the CxO, IP video is clearly the most effective way to communicate in a global enterprise. Whether it is using TelePresence to manage and communicate with a subsidiary in Europe or using an IP video broadcast to set a strategic direction in Asia, IP video tools enable CxOs to efficiently exert their influence globally.

As an example at Cisco, video tools are an integrated part of how we are managing our expansion in India. A new CxO office was created: chief globalization officer. A long time Cisco leader, Wim Elfrink, was appointed to the position. To demonstrate his commitment to the role, Wim volunteered to move to India while still maintaining his responsibilities around the world. From India, Wim will continue to manage a large division headquartered back in San Jose.

Wim will be will equipped with an IP video toolkit to enable his global strategy. Cisco is installing a basic video-broadcast capability in the Bangalore office to enable Wim to continue to communicate with every employee at Cisco. He will be able to use TelePresence from Bangalore to attend senior staff meetings without having to travel.

In announcing the move, Wim said:

> Cisco's globalization strategy, which takes advantage of our own collaboration technologies, will radically change how people interact and share information. This is a bold step in reshaping the way companies approach the global marketplace.

Whereas a move to India might not be a requirement for most CxOs, it is also no longer a hindrance to being successful in a global enterprise.

From Requirement to Innovation

While a baseline IP video capability has become a requirement in today's large enterprise, innovative uses of the technology continue to manifest themselves. For example, entire company events are becoming virtual. Gone are the company meetings where thousands of employees gather in a convention hall in San Jose, while remote employees watch an IP video broadcast. This forum has been replaced with a "hub site" defined by a round, central stage, surrounded by a modest 200+ local employees, and further encircled by mammoth high-definition screen projections of "remote sites" where hundreds of other employees now participate from Cisco offices around the globe. Employees not attending from the hub or remote sites can still watch an IP video broadcast of the event, and can view the interactions of employees attending virtually. You can grasp just a slight understanding of the experience by looking at Figure 4-3.

Figure 4-3   *Company Virtual Meeting*

Cisco switched to this company meeting format in August 2007, with rave reviews from participants. A selection of feedback from employees follows:

> "I do want to tell you it was AWESOME! Very, very cool! It was like we were right there in the room in San Jose."

"I've been here over 10 years. I think this was the best company meeting ever."

"The format was outstanding, and I look forward to this going forward. This format should allow John Chambers to 'host' from any location around the world."

"Using TelePresence takes the meeting to the next level. Thanks for making it real."

"I liked seeing the high-definition screens and audience in the background while watching via IPTV. It was much more interesting than just viewing the stage."

This format helps address communication and inclusion gaps that remote employees usually encounter for traditional events, and it boosts morale in the remote-site locations. An additional indicator is the client satisfaction ratings from these virtual events, which are above average from past events.

Patrick Conboy, project manager and one of the visionaries of the company virtual meeting, describes it as follows:

The original concept was to create windows into other parts of the world. The design was based on this concept with seven sites participating in the first virtual company meeting. We knew going in that this was going to be the right virtual solution, and it was!

The new format also won its share of awards, including the League of American Communications Professionals (LACP) 2007 Magellan Awards "Gold Award" for Excellence.

A second example of pushing the innovation envelope for company events is the recent opening of the Cisco Globalisation Centre East in Bangalore, India. During the opening ceremonies, John Chambers demonstrated the next-generation display of Cisco TelePresence to "transport" a life-size holographic image of Marthin DeBeer, SVP emerging technologies, virtually onto the stage in Bangalore. Those in the audience were in awe when Marthin appeared on the stage to congratulate the Bangalore team and talk about this next generation "on-stage" experience. Figure 4-4 is a picture from the VoD, with John and Marthin virtually on stage together in Bangalore, even though Marthin was really on the other side of the world presenting from San Jose.

Figure 4-4   *On-Stage Experience*

Beata Mielcarek, Bangalore campus IT program manager, who attended the opening ceremonies, described it like this:

> I had two impressions of the event. First, if you blinked when Marthin was "transported" on stage, you would never have known he was virtual. Second, his image was so crisp that you really thought he was there in real life. This was definitely not the old *Star Trek* imaging, it was so much better.

The buzz about these latest innovations create a greater sense of company pride, and demonstrate that the innovation culture is still burning bright within Cisco. The technology investment to implement such events is high, but to the many CxOs involved, the resulting impact is well worth the effort. From a video perspective, we are excited to see the use of TelePresence and high-definition video evolve as part of large-scale events.

Customer Interactions

Now that the CxO can communicate more effectively internally by using IP video, what is he or she going to do with all that free time?

Unfortunately, the golf course might have to wait. The increased effectiveness that IP video gives the CxO internally can free up time for customer interaction. This is one of the most underrated value points for the tools. Every company wants its senior executives to spend as much time as possible with the customer base. IP video can help improve day-to-day internal interactions to allow the CxO to spend more time analyzing customer needs and trends.

John Chambers, for example, is able to meet with at least 50 additional customers per quarter because of Cisco TelePresence. Not only is he available more often because he is traveling less, but he can meet with multiple customers in the same day or even in the same session.

In one recent focus group, for example, 18 different companies from 12 different TelePresence locations around the world met with John to review a particular topic.

IP video has an even more direct role to play with the customer, and we concentrate on this in the coming chapters.

Summary

Today's CxO is presented with more leadership challenges than ever before. Companies are more diverse and geographically distributed, while the speed of business continues to accelerate.

IP video and the visual network allows the CxO of a large organization to maintain the same consistent corporate messaging and employee-to-executive feedback that you expect in a much smaller company.

Visual networking and the human intelligence that is part of any organization can be combined to provide a company with unprecedented agility and productivity.

CHAPTER 5

CISCO FINANCE AND INVESTOR RELATIONS: TRANSFORMING PROCESSES, PARTNERSHIPS, AND PUBLIC PERCEPTION

Executive Summary

In this chapter, you will learn how video helps the Cisco Finance team and the Investor Relations team to

- Improve internal and external working relationships and collaboration while driving down travel cost

- Improve training and knowledge transfer

- Drive corporate alignment behind major initiatives

- Improve group productivity

- Provide real-time access to information and subject matter experts

- Improve Cisco's public image with investors, financial partners, and the press

This chapter discusses two major finance organizations within Cisco:

- The structure under the chief financial officer, the Finance team, which is largely concerned with internal finance activity

- Investor Relations, which is a vehicle to reach financially-oriented external groups, including press, analysts, and shareholders

The finance function within Cisco has 6 divisions with approximately 1200 employees worldwide: Finance and Business Operations, Corporate Finance, Sales Finance, Tax and Treasury, Internal Controls, and Cisco Capital, which offers financing options to Cisco customers.

Meanwhile, Investor Relations, part of the umbrella Corporate Communications group (including Analyst Relations and Public Relations), is a much smaller group, consisting of approximately a dozen employees worldwide.

Both groups are strong users of video, and have evolved and increased its use in their organizations over the past 8 to 10 years. Let's look first at each group's organizational goals, and then explore how each has used video to help meet them (and, of course, take a look at their lessons learned).

Cisco Finance

Cisco Finance has several overarching goals and objectives:

- Improve alignment across functions, including improved working partnerships and support
- Provide for greater depth and skill development of the team
- Ensure Finance speaks with one voice
- Facilitate sales and optimize productivity by reducing time spent checking sales data for compliance and by reducing the number of groups involved

With this in mind, the Finance team leverages a variety of video solutions in support of day-to-day operations, planning, training, and executive communications: live IPTV, video on demand (VoD), integrated desktop video, videoconferencing, and TelePresence. Finance first began using video in the year 2000 as a way to reduce travel costs, especially for large group meetings. Naturally, its first application was for quarterly All Hands meetings, but it has evolved over time to include more activities, more subjects, and greater frequency. Business benefits include the following:

- The ability to build strong working relationships globally
- The ability to train more effectively
- Providing consistent messaging across all groups
- Ensuring regulatory compliance and more efficiently handling of change management

The sections that follow provide some examples.

Improving Organizational and Cross-Functional Alignment: Video Improves Day-to-Day Working Relationships and Operations

With so many Finance personnel around the world, the team uses audio and web conferencing (Cisco Unified MeetingPlace) on a daily basis to meet and collaborate. Commonly, team members participate in five to six such conferences daily. The team also uses MeetingPlace to collaborate on monthly/quarterly/yearly close procedures, and for yearly planning and budgeting. MeetingPlace enables them to include video of the individual participants too, and because most team members possess a desktop camera, they can see and be seen by other team members as they collaborate.

Desktop video is also used in one-to-one interactions within the team. One controller in Global Inside Sales regularly uses the desktop video product (Cisco Unified Video Advantage [CUVA]) during calls with his team. He has a number of teammates around the world, many of whom he interacts with on a daily basis, but may only see in person one to two times a year. The desktop video helps him establish and maintain great working relationships. It also helps him get to know new team members quickly to accelerate their working effectiveness.

Developing Team Depth and Skills: Video-Enabled Training

Video has also been a critical factor in Finance's "40 Hours Take or Teach Program," a core part of the development strategy within Cisco Finance. In this program, employees can take any type of training (finance related or not), and they can teach others in an area of their expertise. Under this program, each Finance employee completes 40 hours of training by the end of each fiscal year, thus improving both their exposure and job readiness. Jim Gould, vice president of Finance, noted the following:

> There is actually a fair mix of both take and teach, with much of it done using audio/web/videoconferencing, live IPTV broadcasts, and video on demand.

Because so many presentations and training classes are now done using video or recorded media, Jim mandates that his entire team take presentation skills and media training courses as part of the Take or Teach program. He believes that communications is a core competency, as much as any financially oriented skill. Even though they might never speak publicly on behalf of the company, this communications training teaches employees how to sell an idea, exert influence, and clarify their messages. An offshoot of this is that the leaders of the organization have to become even better at communicating to stay ahead, raising the depth and skill set of the entire group.

When it comes to training cross-functional teams on financial topics, Jim points out that it is also important to get executive sponsorship from the leaders of those functions. The leadership can mandate training and compliance with initiatives that salespeople, for example, would not normally prioritize or see the immediate benefit of. By using VoD, prerecorded messages from the functional executives can be included right at the top of the content, underscoring their expectations and follow-up steps, including tracking and reporting for a level of compliance. In the case of the Sarbanes-Oxley Sales Empowerment initiative (discussed later in this chapter), Finance requested that Rick Justice, Cisco's executive vice president for WW Sales, record an opening introduction to their sales training, which was very successful in gaining the attention of the account teams. He also indicated that reports would be run to track completion rates and post-training test scores, helping to further ensure audience attention.

For the audience themselves, Jim noted the following:

> Video allows you to still be interactive, as well as do Q&A, with a
> potentially global audience.

Live broadcasts of everything from 30 minutes to 2 hours have been very effective, often garnering between 100 and 500 active viewers. If video is prerecorded instead as a VoD, breaking the content into 15-minute blocks enables it to be more effectively absorbed by the audience, providing them good grounding in the material. One offshoot is that VoDs often will get tens of thousands of viewings because the global audience can view them at their convenience. Whether live or recorded, users also get the benefit of being able to track it for reporting back up to the heads of functional groups about completion rates, success rates on post-training tests, and information about how to refine for future improvement. Surveys following the broadcast or VoD can also provide immediate feedback on successes and areas of improvement.

Ensuring Finance Speaks with One Voice: Executive Messaging, Global Communications

The Finance team takes advantage of video to convey executive messages at its own meetings and to effect consistent, inclusive global communications across large functional groups. The major benefit has been that executive video keeps messages on point and keeps the continuity and momentum of the team constantly moving forward. This medium also provides another venue for executives to really connect with their teams in a personal way, even allowing them to display a bit of humor. The team has found it so successful that they average three live broadcasts per month, everything from All Hands meetings, to training, to online seminars on a wide range of finance topics.

Providing Consistent Messaging Across Groups: All Hands Meetings

All Hands meetings, generally held quarterly, bring together the entire Finance team and provide updates on current progress and on upcoming initiatives (see Figure 5-1).

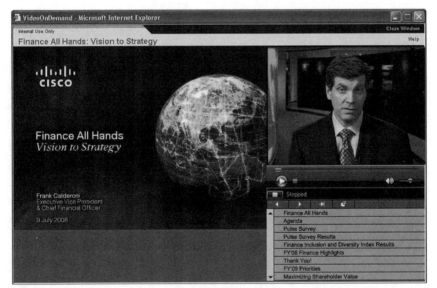

Figure 5-1   Example Finance All Hands Meeting Broadcast over IPTV

In holding these meetings over the past six to seven years, the team found that a mix of media is actually more effective to the overall presentation. The team used a live broadcast of the meeting slides for years, but also began to include short-form videos among the presentations. Over the past several years, the team found presentations that include videos actually score higher, on average earning a satisfaction rating of 4.4 out of 5 versus a 4.1 for slides alone. The videos provide powerful messaging that tends to stick with viewers, particularly when it includes both their peers and executives and not just executives alone. This lends a credibility and reality that executive messaging alone cannot.

Jim Gould shared his experience:

> A mix of media really helps get your point across quickly and easily. You can also take some risks with humor in video, for example, or perhaps use music or effects that you can't do live. It's also a great chance for your personality to really come through. In fact, using music and video changes the atmosphere of the room. If you have a "theme" song of sorts, you can get across impressions and messages, and hit different nerves than what people normally bring to work. People also tend to remember your message long afterward because of that association.

Facilitating Sales While Ensuring Compliance: The Sales Empowerment Initiative

> Without a doubt, video has been an enormous help with change management.
>
> Jim Gould

Rather than let Sarbanes-Oxley corporate-compliance requirements weigh down on the Finance and Sales team, Cisco undertook an initiative to spread out authority on sales decisions but still retain the ability to track account activity in detail. This, of course, required a lot of training, both within the Finance team and cross-functionally with Sales to work effectively.

Internal preparation among the Finance team for this initiative was done using audio/web conferencing powered by Cisco Unified MeetingPlace and a mix of video technologies: videoconferencing, live video broadcasts, and VoDs. The Sales training was conducted using live broadcasts, which were recorded into VoDs for later playback.

Jim Gould's global Finance and Operations team led this effort over a period of more than 12 months. He provided the following comments:

> We have to do and manage more things globally now, such as Sarbanes-Oxley compliance, and these have to be uniform *globally*. Video helps us to roll out these initiatives and operationalize them. We have to communicate more, but also across more functional groups and in greater detail. Sarbanes-Oxley taught us more about how everything works together as a solution, product and services, as well as functional groups from Sales to Support to Finance to Manufacturing. This understanding allows us to be proactive, not reactive, and video is a major tool in staying on the offensive.
>
> Video enables us to now roll out major initiatives quarterly, instead of just two times per year. Not only do we save a lot of time and hassle from not sending people around to do in-person training, but the overall quality is actually better and more uniform. We're also able to track how people do on post-training tests, which gives us great feedback on shaping and presenting the content for the next time. Another great benefit of video is that we can actually roll things out just by individual regions if we need to. We now have more of a command and control function from corporate, which helps us cut back on the lost productivity, stress, and cost of travel.

Looking Ahead: Next Steps for Finance

The Corporate Finance team, particularly the Sales Finance function, is now adopting TelePresence. TelePresence is a new technology that enables users to meet with remote participants who might be thousands of miles away, yet feel as if they are all face to face, seated around the same table. TelePresence combines advanced audio, ultra high-definition video, and a specially designed environment that creates the "face to face in the same room" meeting experience. TelePresence is enabling account teams to work more closely with Finance on deal management and to build cross-functional relationships with teams in the field.

The Tax and Treasury team is one of the teams beginning to use TelePresence. The Treasury Investment team's main objective is to prudently invest surplus cash while managing the investment risk of Cisco's financial assets. Responding to constantly changing market conditions requires real-time risk assessment and sometimes instantaneous strategic implementation. This is a daunting challenge, considering that the company's cash portfolio contains more than 1800 positions and 700 different issuers, and 80 percent of the total investments are managed in offshore locations. To meet the challenge, the team needed a way for its 3 dozen distributed staff members across 15 external banking partners to communicate more effectively and frequently. In addition to portfolio management, they rely on their partner financial institutions to forecast market and economic conditions, consult on the overall portfolio strategy, and provide the highest level of operational service. David Holland, senior vice president and treasurer, noted the following:

> Collaboration and partnership on this scale require an ongoing
> high-touch relationship.

The team is transforming the way it does business by using Cisco TelePresence to conduct face-to-face meetings both with global banking partners and within its own team. Taking it one step further, they are also using it for portfolio performance reviews, relationship management, and even global recruiting.

Quarterly Performance Reviews

In the past, Cisco conducted face-to-face portfolio reviews with bank relationship managers only once or twice a year because of the costs and logistics of travel. Attendees were generally limited to the banking partner's relationship manager and other members of the account team, often excluding other experts who were best positioned to review the portfolio and prevailing market conditions.

Now with TelePresence, the Investments team is meeting more frequently "face to face" with portfolio managers and other experts to review their performance and receive market and economic updates. With broader participation, the dialogues are richer, more productive, and more convenient because experts and partners can now also join the discussion.

Cisco and its bank partners have already saved more than $100,000 annually in travel costs. Through more-effective communications with its partners, the Investments team expects it could enhance the Cisco portfolio's annual performance. By just earning a fraction of a percentage point on its annual return, the team would generate millions in additional value.

Executive Relationship Management

Previously, existing or prospective banking partners flew senior leaders and subject matter experts to Cisco locations to meet face to face with the Cisco Treasury team. The combined pressure of lengthy travel time and conflicting executive schedules frequently resulted in postponed or canceled meetings with partners, many of whom are based in financial centers in New York or across Europe. Today, TelePresence enables the entire Treasury leadership team to interact more frequently with its incumbent and potential banking partners, both for relationship management and to evaluate new proposals. Meeting with Cisco TelePresence maintains the personal touch of a face-to-face relationship, frees up time that would otherwise be spent hosting a traveling guest, and still enables the clear communication required to transform a relationship into incremental business. Roger Biscay, vice president and assistant treasurer of Cisco, says, offered this insight:

> It used to take too much time to schedule face-to-face meetings with our global partners. But with Cisco TelePresence we can plan, schedule, and meet within just a couple of days, and at a small fraction of the cost.

Three key business benefits derive from this application:

- **Faster engagement cycles**: The ability to conduct more face-to-face meetings is important for evaluating and selecting partners in the banking sector.

- **Cost savings**: Cisco and its business partners are saving more than $200,000 annually by avoiding travel.

- **Faster decision making**: The Treasury Investments team used Cisco TelePresence during the 2007–2008 credit crunch to increase the speed and quality of decision making and ultimately reduce risk across the portfolio.

Treasurer David Holland shared his experience:

> With the markets suffering under an unprecedented amount of pressure, we needed to make informed decisions in an incredibly short turnaround time. With TelePresence, we could very quickly schedule face-to-face sessions with our trusted bank partners, which gave us access to the right people and information to navigate through this difficult period. Traditional face-to-face meeting methods can't measure up to Cisco TelePresence in terms of low cost, responsiveness, or access to the right people.

Global Recruitment

Cisco used to fly candidates for top-level finance positions based outside of headquarters to various interviewing locations. Now, candidates are invited to drive to a nearby Cisco office, where they can use the local TelePresence room to interview "in person" without leaving their home city. This has already reduced recruiting costs and accelerated the speed of interviews. In addition, it has given and continues to give Cisco an advantage in that prospective employees save time and are impressed to witness Cisco's advanced green technologies in action.

Finance: Lessons Learned

This section examines various business benefits that Finance has realized from its use of video:

- Reducing travel costs while building strong working relationships globally.
- Training is more effective.
- Messaging is more consistent across all groups and teams.
- Ensuring regulatory compliance and efficiently dealing with change management.

The Finance team also shared a few overarching lessons learned:

- Have a communication strategy in mind for the entire year, rather than just event by event, and consider what is appropriate for each event:

- What can be communicated by voice mail or email, live or recorded video, audio/web conference, or even a TelePresence session?

- What can be done centrally, and what can or should be done locally?

- Consider cultural norms. Humor, in particular, can vary widely by theater and needs to be considered.

- Have people on the extended team who can act as "experts" in available video offerings, schedule or organize them, and possibly develop different strategies and processes for when various needs arise.

- Use video when appropriate to the situation. Jim Gould explained this concept:

> One place that we don't use video, deliberately, is what we call "Executive brown bags," where teams can meet in small numbers with an executive over either lunch or dinner. The goal is for these to be really personal, almost off-the-record conversations where people can ask anything. If they knew they were being recorded, they wouldn't be nearly as candid.

Video Applications in Investor Relations

In contrast to the extremely large corporate Finance team, the Investor Relations (IR) team is made up of only about a dozen employees worldwide. Alongside Analyst and Public Relations, IR is a key group within Cisco Corporate Communications. The goal of this group is to help shape the perception of Cisco and the role of the network to external groups, including individual investors and institutional entities. Video is key to both the teams' internal operations and their external outreach, and what follows are some examples of each.

Internal Uses

The majority of the IR team is based in San Jose at headquarters, but a few team members are distributed around the globe to cover activity in other theaters and key cities. For internal meetings, Cisco Unified MeetingPlace conferencing is used daily to help meet and share information and to plan and react to swiftly changing market dynamics. For many team members, it is not uncommon to be on five to seven MeetingPlace sessions per day. The team has added desktop video cameras (CUVA) to the audio- and web-collaboration tools to help team members lend a personal touch to their communications, especially with those at a distance.

Two other principal internal uses of video are driven by IR. One is the weekly "investor recap." This has grown out of daily internal market updates that are done via voice mail to everyone in the company. The weekly recap VoD is an average of three to five minutes in length and has a host/interview format to make it more interesting to viewers and less like a "talking head." The other principal activity is a recap of the quarterly earnings call, which is a five- to eight-minute VoD. These VoDs are recorded and available to all employees the same afternoon that earnings are announced to provide immediate messaging from executives to employees on quarterly performance. What's great about VoD is that it is oriented toward quick response, high impact, and can be done for low cost. In fact, a VoD can cost as little as $15 to produce, and can be done directly from a user desktop just as easily as it can be done in studio.

External Applications

On the external front, use of video in IR goes back eight years, when the company began to webcast earnings calls. At first, it was an audio-only webcast. Over time, more and more interested parties began to tune in via the web, resulting in a significant cost savings to the company over the dial-in audio bridge. Although an audio bridge is still available today, the majority of listeners actually tune in via the webcast to both hear and see slides. In fact, response was so positive that the company began to regularly offer a speaker series via webcast. These "tech talks" often feature a third-party expert as a moderator, and are generally offered two to three times per quarter (see Figure 5-2). The tech talks are a great educational tool for customers, and IR is now adding video to the existing audio/web capabilities to make the experience even more dynamic.

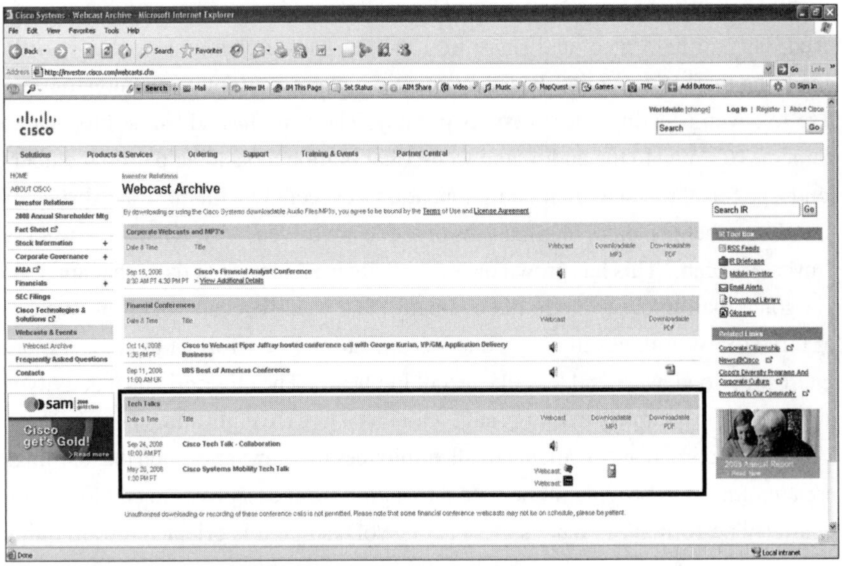

Figure 5-2 *Cisco.com Site Highlighting Tech Talks for Investors*

Today, another prominent external use of video in IR is for the annual analyst conference held in December. This practice started back in 1999. The analyst conference is an expensive event to hold, and requires interested parties to travel to San Jose. By broadcasting the event (speakers, slides, and demonstrations are all available), the cost of the physical event goes down, and more people can participate globally. An example of the real power of this global reach came in 2001 following the 9/11 attacks. The analyst conference fell just two months afterward, and no one particularly wanted to travel at that time. Understandably, remote attendance for the event that year was the highest it has ever been. The technology behind this has also changed over time, from satellite originally in the first year to IPTV, providing similar quality, but at a 70 percent to 80 percent cost reduction.

In addition to its annual report, Cisco publishes a Corporate Citizenship Report (see Figure 5-3) that addresses stakeholder concerns for Cisco citizenship governance practices and its commitment to employees, the environment, and society. It reflects Cisco thinking and progress to date on the issues that affect the sustainability and health of our business and society, and describes the tangible benefits of citizenship activities. The full printed report is available at Cisco.com, but a video summary is now available with it that features various executives addressing major points and putting a more human face on these types of activities.

Figure 5-3 *Cisco Corporate Citizenship Report with Video Summary*

Press-Related Activity

Although not driven directly by Cisco, quarterly earnings also generate requests for TV interviews with Cisco executives by business-oriented media such as CNBC and Bloomberg. Following these interviews, replays are available indefinitely on the News@Cisco website (see Figure 5-4). Powered by the Cisco Digital Media System, the site provides an easy way to create and manage video content, readily viewable within a web browser. In fact, the site has more 500 videos available at any given time.

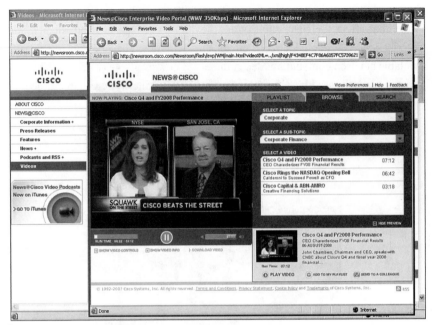

Figure 5-4   *News@Cisco Site Featuring Media Coverage*

In an interesting twist on IR activity, in August 2005, Cisco made history when it virtually opened the NASDAQ stock exchange from the San Jose headquarters. Senior executives and about 200 employees were on hand for the live television broadcast back to New York and to various media outlets. There was also live streaming on the web. One NASDAQ official offered the following comment:

> It's truly fitting that we're doing this virtual opening with Cisco because it is Cisco technology that makes this opening possible.

Web Presence

Cisco has been using video on the web since 2000, the time of the bust in the dotcom era. Jeanette Gibson, a director on the Cisco Corporate Communications team, recognized that change was imperative:

> The bust meant we had to do things differently, to streamline, share, and be more consistent in our messages, and also to realize that our audience had changed.

When video was first made available on Cisco's online newsroom (http://newsroom.cisco.com), the team immediately noticed a spike in web traffic and interest and positive feedback to the videos that were posted. It was obvious that visitors were interested in video and that the company should try to provide information in this format as much as possible. In fact, by 2006, the number two reason people visited News@Cisco was to watch videos.

It was also obvious that the team needed to come up with some guidelines to help make that easy to do. The following are two such rules:

- Keep content to around two minutes.

- Assume every piece is being watched by the press, and therefore keep content press friendly.

Over time, the guidelines have evolved to consider that most content may be shared with a consumer-focused audience, and therefore should be straightforward, less technical (fewer acronyms), and if appropriate, be more fun or have a lighter tone. It is also acceptable to use longer-form video, but with the recommendation to take a full topic and break it into individual chapters, making it 5 to 15 minutes for each chapter for it to be more digestible.

Gibson, who focuses specifically on New Media applications, explained the reasoning behind the use of video:

> The general belief is that people tend to retain five times better what they see and hear. Video is a great way to get your message out, and to do so consistently across internal and external audiences. Customers also expect video now on our website, and they further expect the ability to share them with others. There is definitely a viral quality even with corporate video.

One consideration for any organization using video is that *anything* could end up on YouTube and should therefore be treated accordingly. (For example, part of one bank's company meeting was captured on a cell phone camera and then replayed on YouTube more than 300,000 times.)

Gibson shared her thoughts about the power of video:

> Video is a great way to leverage content in multiple formats, too. A live meeting can be broadcast, recorded, and played back later in VoD format, and then we can take sections from it and turn that into

a five-minute podcast [see Figure 5-5]. This is a great way to continually distribute content in more places and give it longer life. Within Corporate Communications, we're always discussing the content that we're producing because it's likely that we can use it for multiple purposes. This helps to keep it fresh, maximizes our budget, and provides a constant stream of content that we can use.

Figure 5-5   *News@Cisco: Video Portal with Videos, Podcasts, New Media*

Latest Applications: Looking Ahead

Always looking to add video in new ways, IR has also begun to use Cisco TelePresence for investor meetings (see Figure 5-6). Since the product introduction in October 2006, the team has held a few investor meetings this way, and already the company and the investors are seeing TelePresence as a powerful, effective tool to scale expertise and respond rapidly to investor needs. IR also sees this as a great way to do more investor meetings in less overall time.

It also helps with sensitive situations, such as when a CEO of a major bank wanting to meet with either the Cisco CEO or CFO. With every executive's schedule being so busy, there is limited time to allow for urgent travel on short notice. With TelePresence, both parties can now schedule 30 to 60 minutes and meet quickly, without anyone getting on a plane. As a side benefit, using the technology in this way shows financial services firms how great an impact TelePresence can have in their own businesses.

Figure 5-6   *Cisco TelePresence*

Gibson added:

> In Corporate Communications, we are also now starting to use TelePresence to meet face to face with our consulting partners. For example, we have a large web vendor based in New York who we have recently started to meet with using TelePresence. They liked the experience so well that they now want to meet more frequently.

Another practice within IR is to do benchmarking with other companies in the industry. These meetings are also starting to be done via TelePresence, enabling Cisco to do benchmarking with more companies without ever leaving corporate.

Investor Relations: Advice and Considerations

Initially, the goals for IR were to be leading edge in terms of use of video and other multimedia applications, and to share best practices with others. This has changed and grown over time from the initial webcast of analyst calls to the annual shareholder and analyst meetings. In fact, access to the annual shareholder meeting could eventually become entirely virtual, with it being broadcast over the web and yet still allowing for open question-and-answer sessions.

Lisa Magleby, a business manager on the IR team, offered the following advice on the use of video:

> The benefits of using video always outweigh the risks. These applications enable you to rapidly have global reach, and often result in significant cost savings and productivity gains. However, it is important to do your research. There are a lot of options out there, offering different tools and levels of functionality.

It is therefore important to consider several things as you decide on a video-delivery mechanism:

- What are your goals today, long term?
- What is your audience willing and able to use?
- What is your budget now and over the long term?

If you focus on only what you really need today, you might find that you have to completely replace it just a short time from now. At the same time, there is no need to pay for functionality you will never use. Always look for something that is modular enough to grow and change with your needs.

Cisco Corporate Communications suggests organizations that are considering using video more frequently should benchmark with those who do it well. Jeanette Gibson suggests media companies, such as CBS.com (which also has partnerships with YouTube, Second Life, and Sling Media), E! Online, ESPN, and other news sites, are great examples from which to model both web design and the content, length, and format of their communications. Each of these sites has a robust video player, with an appropriately large watchable format, and search capabilities to make content easy to find.

It is also important to look at organizations that work extensively with the media or have a broad mobile audience seeking information. Sports leagues are great examples, such as Major League Baseball (MLB.com) and the National Football League (NFL.com). They attract both individual consumers (seeking real-time information, game playback, and the ability to interact and comment) and media (seeking real-time stories, statistics, and comments from the newsmakers).

Within an organization, Gibson also suggests creating a video committee to help drive the use of video, urge departments to use it and share content, provide guidelines for successful use, and provide funding and tracking to make it easy to deploy and evolve. It is important to remember there can be a self-funding model. Expenses reduced by one department's use of video can fund the deployment for another. This is, in fact, how the deployment within Cisco began.

Summary

Cisco found executive involvement is often the key to broad adoption and successful use of video, and the Finance team reaching out to the Sales team to help drive process change is a great example of this being done well. It is also critical to understand the organizational culture and both how and why video is being used.

As with any technology, it is about the product, the business process, and the application all coming together to meet a compelling business need. The Finance and Investor Relations teams have clearly put a lot of thought into their goals and into when and how the technology can help them to achieve them.

It is also important to focus on end users and how/where they can access video content. After all, the mix of live and recorded media can be a great way to ensure that everyone can view the material on his or her own time. And, in the case of IR, the adoption of the web, and the user-friendly Digital Media System, was a good choice because it requires nothing more from an external viewer than a browser to operate. This eliminates any barriers to getting their messages across outside the company.

Both Finance and IR, within Cisco, have carefully examined their budget and funding model in an effort to maximize results. Although travel-cost reduction is certainly a major driver for both groups, the efforts of the Finance team with the Sales team in particular also have the power to drive revenue for the company, whereas IR efforts have an impact on stock price. When employees see that technology can not only improve daily business process and reduce cost, but also drive revenue and improve public perception, broad adoption is generally the result. And, if done properly, a self-funding model can be implemented, where the benefits of one deployment (that is, travel reduction) fund successive implementations or the addition of new technologies.

CHAPTER 6

CISCO MARKETING: VIDEO ACCELERATES COMMUNICATIONS, COLLABORATION, AND TIME TO MARKET

Executive Summary

In this chapter, you will learn

*   How the marketing team uses video to interact with employees and partners to improve communications and collaboration
*   How the team uses video to accelerate global go-to-market of new products and services
*   How video helps the marketing team connect with customers in many new high-impact ways

The Cisco marketing team consists of approximately 1000 employees and is responsible for corporate, solution, product, segment (enterprise, service provider, commercial, small-to-medium business [SMB]), and industry marketing. Many of these employees are distributed globally because of theater-focused coverage, acquisitions, and the simple geographic location of the employees. As a result, regular internal collaboration, such as staff meetings and even executive communications, relies heavily on video. The marketing team uses a mix of video tools to interact with employees, partners, and customers, both effectively and frequently. This chapter explores examples of how marketing uses video for both internal and external uses.

Internal Uses

Internal uses of video by the marketing team include everything from small group collaboration and staff meetings to larger-scale events, such as All Hands meetings, and coordination of product launches. The goal is to reduce travel, while improving the speed of communications and collaboration across a global team.

One-to-One and Small Group Collaboration

Each Cisco product family has a small marketing team associated with it, and these groups interact on a weekly, if not daily, basis. Often, these teams are based in multiple locations, and they interact with colleagues globally. Therefore, the teams commonly use Cisco MeetingPlace audio and web-conferencing capability for meeting and sharing information effectively. In 2004, the company also began to roll out desktop video cameras associated with the desktop IP phone (Cisco Unified Video Advantage [CUVA]). CUVA enables video to pop up in a window on the employee's PC display when he answers a call on his IP phone. At first, only about 750 employees had these cameras; but over time, more than 40,000 have been rolled out internally. CUVA's video capability has also been integrated into Cisco "softphones" that are loaded on employee laptops. Therefore, video can follow employees even while they are on the road. Furthermore, teams can include video along with the existing audio and web functionality from wherever they might be.

MeetingPlace provides individual marketing team members with a powerful, portable collaboration environment. When collaboration calls for an increased level of face-to-face video or image quality, TelePresence can take small group collaboration one step further. With its 1080p high-definition video, life-size images, rich audio, and collaborative sharing tools, TelePresence helps small groups augment their ability to share incredibly detailed visuals, body language and facial cues, and other subtle nuances that could be important to the meeting.

Regardless of which tools are used, both MeetingPlace video and TelePesence enable teams to build and maintain face-to-face relationships, and it allows them to make better decisions based on real visual cues, including designs, photography, and packaging, rather than verbal descriptions alone.

A great example of an executive who takes advantage of the power of video meetings is Jan Fandrianto, a vice president with Linksys, who has part of his team based in San Jose and part in Irvine, California. Jan and his team have begun to use TelePresence for product reviews. When a new product is designed, there is often only one prototype available. If they had to ship a product prototype back and forth between locations for examination, development teams would lose work time and incur the expense of overnight shipping each time. Instead, they meet in their respective TelePresence rooms, and can jointly discuss and demonstrate products at the same time in the same meeting. Meeting using TelePresence saves the company significant time and expense, and enables the team in possession of the prototype to continue working with it as soon as the meeting concludes. It also ensures that the prototype is not lost or damaged in transit.

Staff Meetings

Because Cisco is rolling out more than 200 TelePresence rooms globally, many distributed teams are now using these rooms on a weekly basis for their staff meetings. This is also proving to be a great way to bring in outside speakers to present to the team without requiring travel, and TelePresence helps build relationships with other marketing teams at the same time. There is also a cultural benefit to using TelePresence. Just as some cultures prefer live conversations to voice mail or email, many also prefer face-to-face meetings to simple audio/web conferencing. TelePresence can bridge the distance and cultural gap nicely by making globally distributed teams feel as if they are all seated together at the same table. The effect is so natural and positively received that many teams are even bringing in outside partners and vendors to review contracted projects, particularly for videos/advertising, web design, and visual tools for the sales force.

Larger Group Meetings

Video clearly works well in one-to-one and small group meetings. However, it works equally well on a larger scale to a broader audience, improving executive communications, facilitating planning and operations, and accelerating product launches and competitive response. The sections that follow examine a few examples.

Executive Communications

Executive communications are a regular part of Cisco culture. In the case of Cisco Corporate Marketing, the leadership of the organization uses video on demand (VoD) to communicate out to all employees at the beginning of the year about major initiatives, and then again at the halfway point to communicate progress of those initiatives. These VoDs are typically only 10 to 15 minutes in length, but they help to provide consistent communications and to build a bond between employees distributed around the world and their leadership. In addition to these semiannual VoDs, quarterly All Hands meetings are held (see Figure 6-1). These are attended in person by everyone based in San Jose, but broadcast using Cisco IPTV to the several hundred remote employees. Typically, these broadcasts are 90 minutes to 2 hours in length, and feature multiple presenters, related video content, and a question-and-answer period. The marketing team has found that a mix of presentations and videos help to keep audience attention and get key messages across more powerfully. Most presenters incorporate 1 or 2 videos (customer case studies, a look at past year achievements, and so on) into their presentation.

Figure 6-1 *All Hands Meeting*

Planning Meetings

In late 2005, Hurricanes Katrina and Wilma struck the southern United States, preventing several Cisco marketing executives from traveling to an important planning meeting in Florida. Using multipoint IP videoconferencing capability, however, they were still able to participate and actually conducted the meeting more swiftly than they would have in person. Denise Peck, vice president of Marketing Operations, described the experience:

> We actually set aside six hours for the meeting, but because you
> don't have some of the same in-person socializing on video, we

were able to get the meeting completed in just four hours, and we skipped the plane flight, as well. I also felt that people were more attentive, spending less time on their laptops doing email. In fact, afterward people said that we should conduct more meetings using video.

Competitive Response

In April 2005, a competitor made a series of product and marketing announcements that warranted a direct, rapid response by Cisco executives to the global sales force. However, many of the ideal presenters were in different locations at the time. To get around this issue, the presenters went instead to their closest Cisco production studio (there are five globally), and were able to participate in a joint video broadcast. Their respective portions were encoded and sent across the Cisco WAN to the central San Jose studio for multicast out to the sales force. In this way, Cisco executives were able to get timely, accurate information out to the sales force, maximize productivity, and save more than $25,000 in expenses that would have normally resulted from travel and the use of other media (for example, satellite transmission) to get the message out.

Product Launch

In 2005, the Solutions Marketing Team decided to undertake a fairly massive product launch consisting of approximately 40 new communications products, services, product names, and pricing. Introducing so many new products and services simultaneously was a very different practice from the norm, but it was done for a variety of strategic reasons. This was also to be a global launch, involving all theaters, which meant nearly 1000 employees in total would be involved. Clearly, communications and easy collaborative capability would be critical in making the launch successful.

Initially, the extended team met a few times in person so that appropriate relationships would be formed among members. For subsequent meetings, however, the decision was made to use collaborative tools, specifically Cisco MeetingPlace audio/web/videoconferencing capability for regular weekly and monthly meetings (see Figure 6-2). The launch was also set to occur during a busy travel season, and marketing executives would need to be able to jump into meetings from wherever they were around the world to actively participate and to provide guidance and approval.

Figure 6-2   *Cisco Unified MeetingPlace with Integrated Video*

Rick Moran, vice president of Unified Communications Solutions Marketing, paints a compelling picture of the motivation behind using collaborative tools for the launch:

> Our message to the market is that Unified Communications solutions enable you to communicate more effectively and therefore streamline business process. We build these tools, we market them, so it only makes sense that we should use them ourselves in our own business processes, and they do have a huge impact!

One other consideration was that the Cisco internal MeetingPlace solution is integrated directly with Microsoft Outlook, which enabled employees to schedule and update meetings rapidly. Before the integration with Outlook, Cisco found that scheduling a meeting for both web and audio conferencing took employees nearly 19 minutes; however, the time dropped to just 5 minutes after multiple tools were integrated into a single scheduling interface. This efficiency alone saved the company almost $14 million in the first year of use.

Using MeetingPlace rather than in-person meetings significantly reduced travel time and expenses, while helping employees work effectively from wherever they were based. MeetingPlace users often comment that meetings start on time, finish earlier, and have fewer disruptions because users can see who is speaking and sharing right on their web browsers. In addition, the ease of sharing desktop applications enables users to avoid having to email material to other participants or preload content before the meeting.

The extended team met weekly for short status meetings and to review deliverables, and it met monthly for half-day and full-day planning meetings. Because meetings occurred regularly over a period of more than seven months, the monthly meeting times were altered each month to be fair to all theaters, sometimes occurring at 8 a.m. Pacific time and other times at 5 or 6 p.m. Pacific time. Individual subteams met daily to keep project pieces moving, often using integrated desktop video to keep that "face-to-face" feeling among remote team members.

One of the benefits of collaborating using audio/web conferencing is that team members can have input into the materials as they are being developed rather than only reviewed after the fact. This shortens overall review cycles. Jeanne Quinn, marketing communications manager, offered the following:

> Cisco Unified MeetingPlace allowed us to collectively review large files, including flash and voiceover, discuss our thoughts, recommend changes in real time, and make changes on the spot to ensure our production deadlines were met.

In any global launch, marketing materials need to be produced that reflect cultural differences and language translation needs. Normally, theater marketing teams need time to translate initial collateral into locally appropriate messaging and positioning. By participating in the actual development of the collateral through team MeetingPlace sessions, the theater marketing teams had early input to the materials while they were being developed, which meant less translation and rework later. This also helped them to reduce their costs by tens of thousands of dollars, making good use of limited local marketing budgets.

As the internal preparation came to a close, it became important to focus on training various audiences. First, the focus was on the Cisco internal sales force. A 15-minute VoD was recorded by the executives involved with these groups and made available the week before the actual internal launch. This helped build an understanding of the strategy behind the new launch format, and to build excitement and awareness of the new products themselves. A week later, a two-hour live IPTV broadcast was held, featuring both product marketing and management representatives. It provided an in-depth overview of the new products and services, and enabled the audience to ask questions of both those on camera and of a group of "question managers" taking questions via chat. This was also rebroadcast later to accommodate other time zones, and made available as a VoD. A few days later, a similar IPTV broadcast was done for Cisco channel partners, providing them with the same product information, with messaging tailored to the partner community. In this way, the product marketing team was able to train thousands of salespeople globally in a matter of just a few days and for less than $25,000. (Keeping costs down is important not just per event, as in this case, but also because Cisco does more than 80 live events per month.)

The external launch to customers consisted of two distinct video-based events. The first was a live customer event hosted by Cisco executives, recorded at the VoiceCon trade show in Florida. This recording was then added to the beginning of a prerecorded webcast event, also featuring Cisco product experts. This webcast was "simulated" as live, allowing customers to feel as if they were participating in the product unveiling at VoiceCon and to get in-depth exposure to the products and be able to ask questions of experts via chat. The webcast had more than 6000 registrants, which is nearly 4 times the normal high, and nearly 2500 actually attended for the full length of the program.

External Uses

We have covered a wide range of internal uses of video by the marketing team, and there are an equal or greater number of external applications for it. External uses by the team include everything from webcasts to case studies to video datasheets and new media. Regardless of the use, the goal is always to create a high-impact connection between the customer, the company, and its solutions. The sections that follow provide a few examples.

Webcasts and Bannercasts

The Cisco marketing department conducts frequent webcasts, typically 6 to 12 per month. These are often a mix of topics and aimed at a variety of segments from small business to service providers. Cisco has found that the most effective webcasts are often those featuring an outside moderator, such as a third-party market analyst or a customer presenting their own case study, and a Cisco product expert. Audio and web conferencing are often used at a minimum, and video may also be used if the situation and budget allows. Typically, video can add thousands of dollars to the cost of the event, but can be well worth it when the speaker is trying to make a more personal connection with the audience.

Webcasts enable the marketing teams to reach hundreds to thousands of prospects and customers alike on a round-the-clock basis, and to do so at less than half the cost of an in-person event. It is small wonder then that the number of webcasts produced year over year has increased more than 30 percent, and that more webcasts now include video as one of their key elements. In fact, more people sign up for and attend video webcasts than audio-only or audio/web. Original live broadcasts account for approximately 85 percent of the webcasts done today,[1] but they can also be rebroadcast later with live question managers to accommodate various time zones and languages in which questions might be received. Interestingly, the average attendee stays longer on a live broadcast than an on-demand event. It is therefore important to load up key content within the first 30 minutes of the program. And of course, the webcast can be posted indefinitely as a VoD, extending the life of the content, allowing it to be seen by many more people, and generally making good use of the marketing budget. Reports indicate that approximately 70 percent of those who attend these webcasts are the desired decision makers, and approximately 50 percent of the time, they have a pending project (0 to 4 months away) that motivated their attendance. This provides an immediate result and helps to build longer-term interest. Best of all, lead generation from such events runs at a cost of just a few dollars per lead, making it a very affordable marketing tactic.

A new variation on webcasting is known as *bannercasting* (see Figure 6-3). Bannercasts include the ability to link live streaming video (webcasts, other video content) to a web banner ad. By capturing attendees via a banner ad, it provides improved customer targeting, but still enables interested parties to interact as effectively as they can through any standard webcast. Cisco started to adopt this methodology in late 2006; it produced good results in terms of attendance and customer feedback.

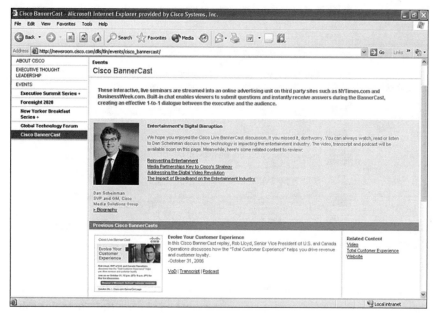

Figure 6-3   *Cisco Bannercast Events Page*

Video on the Web: News@Cisco Portal

The News@Cisco portal (see Figure 6-4) was originally started as an online press room, but has evolved to become a marketing tool as well. Featuring more than 500 videos and numerous podcasts at any given time, it allows prospective customers to watch product demonstrations, hear executive messaging about technology trends, and view other customer case studies. Because it is powered by the easy-to-use Digital Media System, users can watch videos with nothing more than their standard browsers.

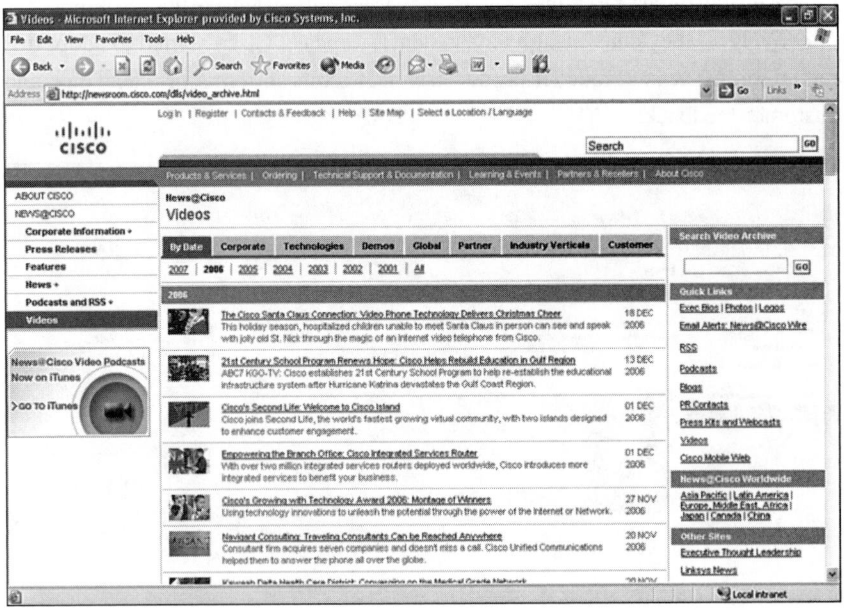

Figure 6-4   *News@Cisco Portal*

The video portal within News@Cisco (see Figure 6-5) is also organized such that users can search for content by product and by industry. Built-in tools enable visitors to create their own playlists for rapid location of their content later on and to email content quickly and easily.

One outgrowth of having a strong video player and search capability such as the Cisco video portal is that marketing strategies can also be extended on the web using video. For example, TV series can be replayed in their entirety on the network's website. This allows viewers to become acquainted with a series online and then become regular weekly viewers, improving ratings and advertising revenues. A powerful example is video on Apple's iTunes store. NBC's program *The Office* was a critical darling, but struggling in the ratings until it was released on iTunes. In just one month, it accounted for nearly one-third of all of NBC's downloads on iTunes, and then delivered its highest-ever ratings on the regular network showing. NBC clearly attributes the increase to the marketing synergy with programming available on the iPod.

Figure 6-5 *Video Portal*

Video Datasheets

Datasheets are an important part of the technical marketing around each product that Cisco brings to market, enumerating the features and functions available. Over time, however, there has been a desire to add media so that the technical features and benefits of an offering truly come to life. One great way to do this "in person" is by demonstrating the product. Therefore, the product marketing team has created video datasheets (see Figure 6-6) in addition to the printed material. This allows a demo to be done online at any time for prospective customers, and customers are up to five times more likely to remember the product as a result. Although the use of video datasheets is still somewhat new, it has been so well received that even Cisco partners have begun to embrace it as part of their marketing collateral (see Figure 6-7).

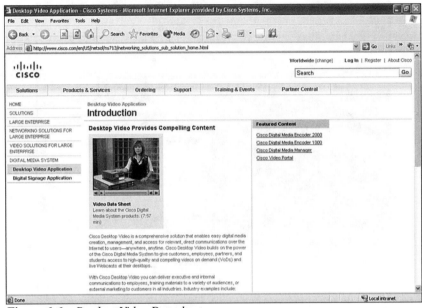

Figure 6-6 *Product Video Datasheet*

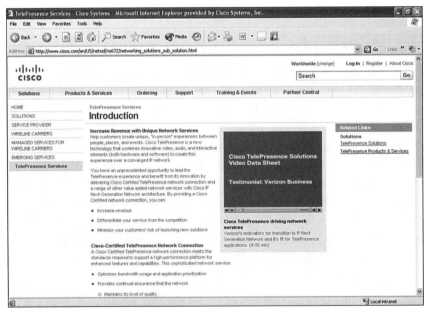

Figure 6-7 *Partner Video Datasheet*

Embedded Video in Websites: External Product Launches

Increasingly, solutions from Cisco are moving from the wiring closet to something that business users would see on their desktops. Therefore, it becomes important to reach out to a business audience directly, familiarize them with Cisco, and address how a particular product or solution can benefit them. In the case of Cisco TelePresence, it is a new collaborative meeting solution that can significantly impact the way organizations communicate and impact the productivity of executives, business leads, and individual employees. When the product was announced in October 2006, CEO John Chambers wanted to get personally involved in reaching out to customers and share his vision for how TelePresence could transform business processes. So, the marketing team involved him not only in launch-day activities and the product webcast, but also embedded a short video message from him in the product website (see Figure 6-8). This enables him to reach out in a personal way to every new visitor to the site and encourage them to watch some of the embedded demonstration videos. Since the product launch, TelePresence videos have become some of the most-watched content at Cisco.com, and users tend to stay on the site longer than on any other Cisco.com solutions page. Other Cisco.com pages now have similar embedded executive messages within them.

Figure 6-8 *Cisco TelePresence Website with Embedded Video from John Chambers*

Exploring New Places to Use Video: Second Life

Cisco is also exploring new places on the web in which to insert video. Cisco has a new presence in the virtual environment known as Second Life (see Figure 6-9), the fastest-growing online virtual community. It has 1.2 million residents as of October 2008, and opens up new possibilities for marketing to and interacting with customers. There are two Cisco "islands" in Second Life, one public and one for Second Life members. Both islands offer ways to receive training, technical support, and executive/product briefings, with video incorporated so that users can learn more about items of interest in a high-impact manner.

Figure 6-9   Cisco Second Life Presence

Summary

The Cisco marketing team has found video-, audio-, and web-conferencing to be powerful ways to connect internal teams and to connect partners and customers. Video's flexibility, ready availability, and low usage cost make it an easy choice among all the collaborative tools available to a globally distributed marketing team. Video is also a constantly evolving medium that can adapt to changing needs, and it encourages experimentation in selected places, such as an individual web page or targeted marketing campaign. Finally, video can be rapidly scaled to an entire organization to maximize impact and create a powerful, lasting connection with employees, partners, and customers.

End Note

1. http://www.On24.com.

CHAPTER 7

OPTIMIZING A GLOBAL ENGINEERING ORGANIZATION

Executive Summary

In this chapter, you will learn how the Cisco Development Organization uses video to improve communications, knowledge transfer, and the product-development process:

- Executives use IP video broadcasts and video on demand to communicate messages to employees distributed across the globe. This consistent message ensures a common strategy and method of execution.

- Technical experts use video on demand, live broadcasts, and videoconferencing to transfer knowledge. These methods prove particularly useful when managing acquisitions.

- Program and project managers use web conferencing and videoconferencing to run effective review meetings with distributed teams. These same tools are used by technical staff for effective brainstorming sessions, by engineers focused on testing, and by customer support to optimize their processes.

The Cisco Development Organization (CDO) consists of almost 30,000 employees from more than 30 business units, within 7 technology groups. Because of the number of acquisitions over the years and investment in strategic locations, CDO staff are now located in more than 180 locations in 46+ countries around the globe. The majority of organizations consist of dispersed teams that span several sites globally. Effective collaboration and teaming are paramount to ensure that product schedules stay within the committed dates and that quality solutions are produced.

As with most technology companies, staff from CDO communicate regularly with their cross-functional technology peers, in addition to partnering closely with other internal functions, including manufacturing, marketing, sales, and customer advocacy (support and professional services). Building and maintaining effective working relationships is key to the success of any individual business unit.

Figure 7-1, which shows the 12 largest engineering facilities around the globe, illustrates the distributed nature of the CDO.

Cisco Major Development Locations

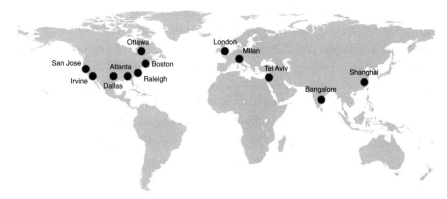

Figure 7-1   *Cisco Major Development Locations*

Developing and manufacturing solutions, when most team members are spread across multiple countries and time zones, is a challenge for any engineering organization. This chapter discusses how the Cisco engineering teams use video and related communication tools to successfully release dozens of products every year.

Technical Strategy and Execution

CDO employees and leaders are accustomed to change to leverage technology transitions and build a next-generation company. Change is part of our culture. To create that next-generation company, the management style within Cisco is evolving from a *command and control* approach to *collaboration and teamwork*, which enables Cisco to execute on the many strategic initiatives it has prioritized. A recent example of this evolution of CDO is the formation of the Cisco Development Council, composed of seven technology groups and led by senior vice presidents (each reporting to the CEO). These large engineering organizations are responsible for all Cisco core technologies, including routing, switching, security, IP communications, wireless networking, storage networking, network management, and many other emerging technologies.

It is impossible to listen to any CDO executive presentation these days without hearing the word *video*. Video is a cross-company priority and a core component of the innovation focus within Cisco. Development or support of video-related technologies can be found across each of the seven technology groups. With so much cross-functional development occurring, one wonders just how Cisco can successfully achieve its objectives, when teams are so drastically dispersed.

True to Cisco culture, CDO executives use video as much as possible as a medium to communicate with employees, management teams, peers, customers, and partners. The sections that follow provide examples of how these executives use various video solutions to reach a distributed community of engineers and to integrate new acquisitions into the Cisco family.

Employee Communication

Obviously, the effort that goes into preparing employee communications is not worthwhile unless the majority of employees see/hear/read it and the intended result is achieved. Within Cisco, IP video has been used to deliver employee communications for more than 10 years, and it is a key delivery medium in any communication planning.

Quarterly Meetings

Part of Cisco culture is open communication, and to support that philosophy, quarterly All Hands meetings are conducted by all executives from director level to executive vice president. CDO executives are no different and conduct All Hands meetings using different approaches. Depending on the organization, locations with the largest number of employees usually gather locally in a large facility, and all other employees participate via a Cisco TV broadcast using our IP network and the Internet. Employees receive an Outlook meeting invitation with information about how to attend locally or remotely using Cisco TV. The remote employees can view the presentation slides, watch the presenters, and ask questions through an online question manager, just as if they were physically present in the room. This ability for anyone to ask questions is what helps to keep communication open between employees and executives. It is a great medium to ensure employees hear a consistent message about the organization's direction and how it will be executed.

Employees based in distributed locations can attend this meeting from the comfort of their own homes or any Internet-enabled locations, using a Cisco virtual private network (VPN) software client or hardware device. Even those employees who have access only to a low-bandwidth dial-up connection can listen to the audio via a 20-kb/s broadcast stream. The broadcast can be viewed by engineers using either a Windows or UNIX/Linux desktop.

A significant benefit of this All Hands format is that all employees, no matter where they are in the world, can participate in the meeting and hear key strategy (and its execution) messages. Each All Hands event is automatically recorded into a video on demand (VoD) and is accessible by employees who missed the live meeting to watch at their leisure. The VoD is segmented based on the presenter so that viewers can select just the content they want to see.

Another benefit of this type of Cisco TV event is the reporting and survey capabilities. IP communications enable the specialists managing events to view reports that identify how many viewers watched an All Hands meeting and what most interested them. Cisco TV reports cover viewing statistics of both the live event and the VoD. A survey is also issued to viewers to capture feedback about the meeting content; this survey also provides the communication team with timely information about how they can adjust future events.

Executive Announcements

Throughout the year, various announcements from CDO executives are communicated to employees using VoDs over our IP network. These videos are either professionally recorded in an internal studio or recorded from any desktop using a standard video-capture and -editing application. When the VoD is posted, it is accessible from appropriate CDO websites or on related internal news sites. The VoDs are stored and managed on the corporate VoD infrastructure, which supports the entire Cisco organization. The VoD recordings can cover content such as organizational change, messaging on CDO focus areas such as innovation and performance culture, and presentations delivered during recent conferences. Cisco

IT recently deployed an internal YouTube-like service, which will also be used to share executive announcements with employees via video.

Based on internal Baseline Communication Surveys conducted in 2007, CDO employees prefer to receive executive announcements via multiple mediums and not just email. This is especially true for video when the employees are based in remote locations; they want to see the presenter rather than just read text.

Another form of video communication used by some executives is externally recorded content from TV interviews. Links to these interviews are shared internally and are posted on various news websites. Employees hear and understand that executive messaging shared externally is consistent with what is shared internally.

Effective Integration of Acquisitions

Since 1993, Cisco has successfully acquired more than 125 technology companies. Acquisitions are used as a strategy to enter new markets and extend internal research and development capabilities, and to speed time to market of new products for markets Cisco is already in. However, there is only a "match" when there is a shared vision, long-term and short-term wins and, most important, a shared culture.

Integrating the employees from acquired companies with Cisco processes, tools, and culture is critical to the acquisition's success. A lot of focus is placed on continually optimizing the acquisition processes, to make it as seamless as possible and increase the probability of a successful integration.

Knowledge Transfer

When Cisco acquired Scientific Atlanta (SA) in 2006, it was one of the largest acquisitions for Cisco to date. From a strategic perspective, it gave Cisco an advantage in the video-technology space because of the intellectual capital within SA. The problem is how to share that knowledge among hundreds of engineers at SA and hundreds specializing in video within Cisco. Gale Lightfoot, senior staff program manager from SA, shares his experience:

A great example of knowledge transfer between the employees from SA and Cisco was the creation of the Video Architecture Summit, which connected some of the most valuable "Video/IP Thinkers" in our company. Many of these people would not have been able to participate without the "connecting" capabilities of video. In 3 days, the Cisco network brought together over 750 people simultaneously during some periods, for live discussions around topics critical to our future business, and that of our customers.

About 50 percent of the participants in the Video Architecture Summit attended via a conference facility in San Jose, California, or via a conference facility in Atlanta, Georgia. Large screens in each facility displayed the remote site. The remaining 50 percent of participants, from around the globe, attended via a live IPTV broadcast. Most presenters were in the San Jose and Atlanta locations, but several others presented via videoconference from several other Cisco offices. Remote participants could ask questions either through traditional videoconferencing or through a question manager as part of the IPTV broadcast.

Gale, who was also a co-chairperson of the Video Architecture Summit, had this to say:

Beyond this live audience, the VoDs of the event were viewed by many others who have since connected with the casting of vision and addressing challenges. This impressive access to our valuable resources to meet challenges, and accurately cast vision, is made possible only by looking to the network for ways to bring people together, virtually!

The sharing of knowledge between Cisco and newly acquired companies is critical. The Video Architecture Summit is a great example of how this occurred successfully between many large engineering organizations. A survey conducted by Greg Thompson, a co-chairperson for the event, captured an overall rating of excellent from 61 percent of respondents, and a rating of good by another 34 percent. There was also significant feedback documented to be incorporated in the next event. This represents an amazing result considering there were more than 750 participants and, based on the survey, 89 percent spent $0 on travel. They were able to optimize knowledge transfer, while definitely minimizing travel expenses.I

Engineering Training Day

As part of the acquisition process for engineering teams, an Engineering Training Day is organized to provide an overview of some of the Cisco business fundamentals to enable and empower engineers in their day-to-day work. The focus is also to promote consistent, repeatable processes through a set of common standards and terminology. Much of the content involves VoDs, which allows the training to be repeatable and scale.

A website is dedicated to this topic and provides links to all the relevant sources of engineering standards and processes. The website covers hardware, software, development methodology, intellectual property, case management, and much, much more.

Dave Cavanaugh, director of engineering learning, provides this example of video use during the acquisition training process:

> Training on the Defect Tracking System involves the newly acquired employees watching a video and taking VoD-based training before a site visit. Once the subject matter expert is there in person, he/she can then have an in-depth discussion with the new employees about how the process applies to the new company's business process, making better use of everyone's time.

Multisite Product Development

Although engineering teams are highly technical, their communication skills and use of communication tools can vary significantly. The communication preferences of team members can also differ depending on the type of communication they receive. Therefore, it is important to understand these preferences and usage patterns, to ensure you use the most appropriate medium, or combination of media, to communicate within distributed teams.

Because several CDO organizations place such a high value on the use of video and other rich media tools for remote communications, their resulting adoption rate is four times higher than the Cisco corporate average. The following sections describe communication preferences within CDO, the successful use of video and rich media by distributed engineering teams, and the correlation of video with travel avoidance.

Team Communication Preferences

Baseline Communication Surveys were issued to several CDO organizations during the first half of 2007. The results of these surveys identified preferences and usage of available communication tools by engineering teams. The surveys also enabled employees to provide feedback and input about all aspects of communications. Results were used to help focus adoption efforts for effective use of the tools, primarily as a way to reduce travel budgets.

Based on the responses related to communication preferences, about 50 percent of respondents preferred email as a means of communication within their teams and departments. The remainder preferred virtual meetings or other video services to communicate. When communications for training was considered, watching a VoD was the clear preference. The results are mixed when considering executive communications, where several options were preferred, highlighting a need for executives to use various media to communicate their messages to employees. Figure 7-2 shows the survey responses that relate to how engineering teams prefer to receive different types of internal communications.

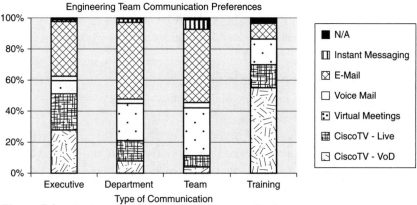

Figure 7-2   *Engineering Team Communication Preferences*

Further analysis of communication preference data identified anomalies based on a respondent's job role or the respondent's geographic location. One anomaly to note is the responses from executives; 70 percent preferred virtual meetings for interactions with their teams. This trend is consistent with the higher adoption of video by executives, who use it with their teams to build trust and enable more open communications (and to avoid travel). The adoption rate of videoconferencing by executives was double the average rate of all respondents. Other anomalies included different preferences based on geographic location, such as Canada, where there is also a higher preference for virtual team meetings, whereas European respondents prefer Cisco TV VoD for many communications.

Overall, the survey results indicate many delivery options are used when communicating, and employees have different preferences depending on the type communication they are receiving or their geographic location. Understanding your team's preferences will help ensure communications have the most impact.

Program Management and Videoconferencing

The Service Provider Group (SPG) within CDO has long been known as leaders and role models for their internal use of traditional videoconferencing (VC). For a group that spans 9 technical organizations, with more than 8000 employees in at least 10 engineering sites, effective collaboration and teamwork is critical to their success. The SPG requirement for VC services was so paramount more than six years ago, when the Information Technology department could not meet the SPG requirements, SPG invested in its own VC network (an investment that is now part of the Cisco IT VC infrastructure).

Al Navas, who oversees part of SPG operations, had this to say:

> Videoconferencing is a no-brainer; everybody gets programmed to use it. Then it becomes part of your DNA.

Within SPG, regular program review meetings are held between management, product managers, and program managers to ensure solutions requiring cross-functional effort are on schedule, with all issues under control. Each of these reviews is usually conducted using video, voice, and web conferencing between at least three engineering sites, with many participants joining by voice from other remote locations. The meeting requires use of the Cisco Videoconferencing Multipoint Control Unit (MCU) integrated with Cisco MeetingPlace.

These meetings are usually conducted monthly, with the communication tools easily scheduled as part of the Outlook meeting invitation. Meeting participants just need to follow the default instructions included in the meeting invitation. Video is truly part of their internal review processes. Al continued:

> Body language and facial expressions are really important just to get a sense that the audience is getting the message. You need to be able to see your audience and get energy from their reaction to what you are saying.

SPG is truly a role model for their use of VC within Cisco. It was the original routing technology departments who led the effort and deployed VC to their global locations. A key aspect of their initial service was its simplicity with a unified directory and easy way to bridge video and voice-only meeting participants. The result was a very high adoption rate. Videoconferencing became part of their culture for meetings, and that continued as the organization evolved and grew to the mammoth engineering organization it is today.

Note that the original departments involved in that early deployment still have a higher adoption rate than recent organization additions. A separate Baseline Communication Survey within one of these departments showed 90 percent of respondents used room-based VC, more than double the corporate average.

The SPG continues to invest in video capability for their employees by promoting the use of TelePresence, in addition to upgrading audio/video technologies originally deployed in conference rooms across their locations. The result of this investment is a distributed engineering and manufacturing team who truly values the face-to-face experience even though thousands of miles separate them.

Project Management and Desktop Video

From a project management perspective, the use of desktop video across CDO will surely evolve over time as internal availability of more integrated video-communication solutions expands. For example, the limited internal deployment of WebEx Meeting Center involves video use that is six times higher than use by other customers. The Cisco result confirms a trend of greater desktop video use with WebEx, a trend that will continue with the expanded deployment.

Oded Gal, manager, Product Management, and responsible for video at WebEx, offered this analysis:

> Video brings remote teams together. More and more organizations have working teams distributed across multiple locations or have part of the team telecommuting. Different than voice, video creates

"continuous presence" in the meeting and makes the remote participants feel less detached from their peers.

Gal further states that VC at WebEx is not a standalone application, but is part of an online meeting experience. He continued:

> One of the main benefits of video is that attendees of an online meeting can observe the body language and facial expressions of other participants.

Adding video to a WebEx meeting is easy and works from any Internet location, enabling all remote team members to more fully participate in project meetings. Figure 7-3 shows an example of Oded and team members participating in a virtual project team meeting and using video through WebEx Meeting Center. It is interesting to observe how organizations across CDO leverage the available video and rich media capabilities to manage their distributed project teams.

Figure 7-3 *Desktop Videoconferencing Through WebEx*

Best Practices for Multisite Product Development Using Video/Visual Tools

Engineers typically love to participate in technical debates, but are not always the most pragmatic when leading and documenting these technical discussions. Glenn Inn, senior member of technical staff for the office of the CTO, Voice Technology Group, has facilitated many technical teams during his career at Cisco. He recommends using the web-conferencing functionality of Cisco Unified MeetingPlace or Cisco WebEx to significantly improve communications during a meeting:

> Technical teams should notate the proceedings of their meetings, and focus on how to effectively summarize their status.

Inn recommends using a standard technical meeting template to record status during all phases of product development, including updates from required cross-functional teams. The meeting best practices used by Inn and his peers include the following:

- Sharing a meeting minutes document in a web conference to ensure accuracy and buy-in, while the minutes are being recorded.

- Using a standard well-structured meeting template to take technical minutes

- Including a calendar to help visualize dependencies and time pressure, and to establish more realistic deadlines

- Using tables whenever possible to summarize data

- Defining the team leader's role to separate transcribing the meeting from participating in detailed technical discussions

Glenn's latest work involves testing and integrating new technologies to better enable his dispersed technical team and thus contribute to innovative product development. Their use of video, Web 2.0 capabilities, and interactive whiteboards enhance their collaboration potential. Figure 7-4 shows Glenn Inn and his peers use of various video and web collaboration tools, including Cisco

Unified MeetingPlace, a 7980 IP Video Phone, Cisco Unified Video Advantage, and a SMART Technologies interactive whiteboard.

Figure 7-4   *Technical Collaboration*

The best practices mentioned earlier, and the use of more video and visual tools, realize several benefits, including the following:

- **Reduced language barriers**: When language and spoken dialects are a challenge, team communication is more effective when it is also written and shared in real time. Milutin Cvetkovic, a Belgrade-based software engineer within VTG, had this to say:

  I can read the meeting minutes as they are captured and shared during the meeting, and they make it clear what was said. When a new technical topic is discussed, the minutes make knowledge transfer much easier.

- **Time efficiency**: Team members can work effectively from home offices, especially when there are significant time zone differences requiring meeting participants to be online early in the morning or late at night. Participants can multitask, tracking the meeting agenda from their desktops and participating actively only when necessary.

- **Superior dynamics**: Team members like being able to "see" people join the conference through the participant list, and to know who is speaking or sharing information. The participant list is a powerful feature that associates team members' voices and names with their team roles, and thus greatly improves the information flow of a meeting.

Video and Behavior to Avoid Travel

The internal Baseline Communication Surveys from 2007 also captured communication tool use and travel-avoidance estimates from the use of these tools. Figure 7-5 shows travel-avoidance estimates, with 27 percent of respondents stating they avoided air travel at least one time in the past quarter through the use of video. Based on associated travel analysis, this reduced need to travel results in an average of $1800 in cost avoidance, plus time saved, for every business trip avoided.

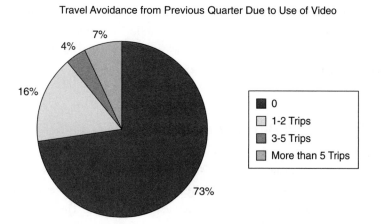

Figure 7-5   *Quarterly Travel-Avoidance Estimates from Video Use*

The results in Figure 7-5 were very different when analyzing just the executive responses, for whom travel-avoidance estimates were double, with 54 percent avoiding travel in the preceding quarter because of the use of video. The results from executives correlate with their higher adoption of video services in general.

Overall, the more that teams used video, the more they reduced their air travel. The strong correlation between video adoption and travel reduction helps to justify the business case to invest in the deployment of video services.

Current TelePresence survey metrics indicate an average of 31 percent of meetings are conducted via TelePresence to avoid travel. Today, an average of more than 1600 meetings occur per week using TelePresence, with an average utilization rate of 51 percent for the 185+ available rooms. Cisco estimates travel cost has been reduced more than $130 million since the internal TelePresence launch, with an estimated carbon reduction of more than 64,000 metric tons. TelePresence is definitely gaining widespread use by distributed project teams, particularly to avoid travel.

Product Testing and Support

Rich media tools are used effectively by some CDO teams to significantly improve the testing process with both their dispersed development team and their customers. The examples in the sections that follow describe the best practices used by members of the Cisco Unified MeetingPlace team in the testing and support of their own product.

Product Testing During Development

The engineering team responsible for the integration of Cisco MeetingPlace with Lotus Notes is distributed between Europe and the United States. Using their own product to collaborate, they effectively work as a team regardless of location, in large part because of their use of integrated conferencing. The simple process of scheduling, attending, and sharing information in a Cisco MeetingPlace meeting allows for planned team collaborations, but also quick ad hoc meetings to address an immediate issue.

Olga Volkova, the test engineer responsible for testing all changes and enhancements to their application code, stated:

> During the product test process, we have been able to significantly reduce the time required to fix bugs. Using Cisco Unified Meeting-Place is like being in the same room together, so we can all focus on the same problem at the same time. This makes it possible to resolve problems much more quickly than through email or phone conferencing alone.

Team members share applications or their entire desktop during a troubleshooting session to quickly understand the issue, and then collaborate to find a solution. They also share test results and, if required, actual lines of code, to assist in the collaborative process.

Troubleshooting with Customers

Heather Paunet, former senior software engineer and lead of the Cisco MeetingPlace for Lotus Notes team, explains her former group's requirements this way:

> We are a global team with members in San Jose and Belgrade. Frequent communication is critical to our success and to working effectively with the customers who use this product. Because of this, we need a technology approach that is much more effective than email.

When working on a customer support escalation with the Cisco Technical Assistance Center (TAC) or a customer, the team uses the reservationless feature of Cisco MeetingPlace for an immediate collaborative meeting. The engineers need to see what the customer is experiencing, and they always use integrated voice and web conferencing. They are better able to troubleshoot the problem with the TAC and customer by sharing each of their desktops. The engineers can even take control of a remote desktop to expedite the troubleshooting process, instead of walking another individual through a series of steps. With Cisco Unified MeetingPlace, participants can see who is speaking and sharing. This functionality enables an effective collaboration session, even when participants are in different locations and have not previously met.

Huy Quach, former senior software engineer and Lotus Notes expert, offered this insight:

> When there's a problem at a customer site, we don't have to travel to resolve it. We can work collaboratively with the customer just as though we were there in person. Cisco MeetingPlace saves us a tremendous amount of time. I have more quality time to spend with my family now that much less time is eaten up by travel.

Use of web conferencing provides the visual information necessary to process each identified bug, a significant advantage when the support teams are unable to replicate a problem.

Technical Training

Video is obviously an important medium to deliver training to a technical workforce. The examples in the sections that follow demonstrate how the Engineering Learning organization uses live video broadcasts, VoD, and other video services to increase awareness of technical subjects, transfer knowledge, and inspire employees.

The Engineering Learning Organization

Within CDO, Engineering Learning got its start as the Engineering Education department, which was focused on providing training for the Cisco IOS (Internet Operating System). It was renamed to Engineering Learning in August 1996, and the organization has continued to evolve ever since, responding to the growth in the internal engineering population and broadening the technology focus areas.

In the early days, the IOS function was small enough that they used mentors to teach required material. As the number of software engineers and the training demands increased, it was difficult to scale the training. As a result, the quality of the IOS code deteriorated because the newly hired engineers did not understand the complexities of the IOS code base. To address the issue, the Learning organization formalized a New Hire Program, predominately for IOS-focused employees, which leveraged the expertise of senior-level engineers to explain the code base, tools, and programming fundamentals; this solution resulted in significant improvements in IOS development.

Dave Cavanaugh, director of Engineering Learning, explained the evolution of the organization as follows:

> With 80 percent of engineering resources in San Jose and the remaining 20 percent outside, capturing and sharing the tribal knowledge using video was key. Scaling the expertise of senior level staff was accomplished using many approaches over the years. A few of the best folks were selected for sharing this tribal knowledge during "Chalk Talks" or "Nerd Lunches." We built the video infrastructure and tools to automate processes wherever possible so that anyone, in any location, could view learning events.

Today, Engineering Learning is focused on numerous learning opportunities for CDO staff. One interesting item is how Dave's organization uses humor in their videos to make learning fun and interesting, and more than just another talking head:

> Content must be visually interesting and balance the humor with the need to be technically credible.

Services provided by the Engineering Learning team include delivery of full-day or multiday video events around a major technology subject, with engineers spread across the globe. These technical seminars are broadcast live across the Cisco IP network, and recorded as VoDs for later viewing. Figure 7-6 shows how CDO staff can access information on the Engineering Learning website about available learning resources, including a learning calendar and catalog, events and workshops, learning roadmaps, a video library, documentation, and many other resources.

Figure 7-6   *Engineering Learning Website*

Using Live Broadcasts to Increase Awareness and Knowledge

Live video broadcasts are often used within CDO to increase awareness of technical development underway across CDO, and to transfer technical knowledge to a technical workforce. Engineering Learning received so many requests to conduct various types of workshops and events that they built their own facility to conduct and record these learning sessions. They offer a suite of standard and flexible services so that any organization can record their video content and make it available to the Cisco population. Events can vary in duration and forum, but one common denominator is that a live event can be viewed by any engineer, regardless of location, based on defined access controls for that event.

Since 1992, Engineering Learning has been conducting Nerd Lunches for the engineering community. Like many other services, they started as a homegrown video offering by a few engineers, and evolved into a standard service delivered by the Engineering Learning organization.

The Nerd Lunches are internal engineer-to-engineer technical communications, focused on providing exposure to the latest technological advances within the company. They are held in San Jose with a live video broadcast, and are recorded for permanent archive and later viewing via VoD. An average of 12 Nerd Lunches are scheduled per month, each with a typical length of 90 minutes. They are an effective way to increase technical awareness, and not only across CDO but across all of Cisco.

Another example of a video broadcast is TechViz, which was launched in 2007 and targets awareness of external advancements within an industry. TechViz in a combination of the words *technical* and *visionary*. The speakers are thought leaders in their industries, whose vision and insights are inspiring the future of networking. In some cases, these will be luminaries from high-tech companies, leaders in academic research, or cutting-edge customers who seek design solutions for new challenges that have the potential to influence and shape the future of networking.

Using Video on Demand for Technical Training

When it comes to training, VoD is always the clear preference for learning options, and this was confirmed in the Baseline Communication Surveys conducted within CDO. It is also validated through the Engineering Learning metrics, where 66 percent of engineers take online training versus in-person alternatives.

Engineering Learning, since their inception, has been using VoDs. Dave Cavanaugh recalled those early days:

> The first on-demand video capabilities were put out there around 1996. We captured videotapes, turned them in into VoDs, and added them to an online video library for the engineering community to access. Initially, there was only a Windows client, which was a challenge because it's not a "one size fits all" audience of engineers, and they are very vocal. We had to supply them with a set of services that enabled engineers to access the video content in many formats and from any location.

Within CDO, use of video for training purposes started as a grass-roots effort by a few keen engineers who toyed with some early technology. Engineering

Learning took those early requirements and built them into a world-class learning solution to scale quickly.

Dave explained the key benefit realized by his organization from their use of VoD as follows:

> To create a formal instructor-led course, there is a high degree of investment required for the course design, labs, etc. Content must be finalized early in the process. However, at times we needed to be more flexible because content was still undergoing modifications while the course was being structured. Video provides an alternative to formal course design that is very cost-effective, available to everyone, and changes can be made to the content right up to the point of filming. VoDs are a nice alternative to formal educational course design, when speed and transmission of information are more important.

Although a spectrum of learning solutions is required to mix and match as the business needs warrant, VoD overall is a very low-cost-per-person solution when compared to formal instructor-led learning. The broader audience reach through VoD use is also important. Engineering Learning found that for any live event, two to three times the original audience would later view the content online as a VoD. Replay is an important metric to consider when planning training.

Summary

Video and other visual networking solutions are used across all aspects of the Cisco Development Organization, from executive and employee communications, program and project management, testing, and training to a host of other examples. It truly has enabled various stakeholders to optimize their globally distributed engineering organizations. Key benefits of video highlighted in this chapter demonstrate improvements to executive communications, the acquisition process, program reviews, and technical training.

Video solutions enable scalable and consistent approaches to deliver consistent messages to employees from executives about product strategies and method of execution. They also improve knowledge transfer during the acquisition process. Employees can hear consistent messaging from their new executives, and they can quickly learn about required tools and processes that are essential to operate in the new organization.

When working with distributed teams, the most effective program reviews are conducted over videoconferencing. This continued use of video builds trust across the team and ensures that key participants understand messages. In addition, the higher the adoption of video, the higher the cost savings through travel avoidance. Desktop videoconferencing is an effective way to easily bring distributed project teams together.

For technical training, organizations can get very creative in their use of live or recorded video to increase technical awareness and to provide just-in-time training on the latest technical developments or processes. Video is also used to inspire the engineering community with thought-provoking industry information and challenges.

CHAPTER 8

MAXIMIZING YOUR HUMAN RESOURCES THROUGH IP VIDEO

Executive Summary

In this chapter, you will learn how video can improve the human resources functions of both medium- and large-size companies in relation to employee recruiting, orientation, training, and communication. Specifically

- Recruiting, ramping up new hires rapidly, knowledge transfer, and change management are the traditional areas where IP video can prove useful.

- IP video can also be beneficial in a company's childcare efforts.

- IP video can also help companies execute better during rough market fluctuations.

The benefits of IP video to the modern corporate human resources (HR) function are nothing short of revolutionary. In fact, we often see HR acting as a primary business sponsor for the deployment of IP video in the enterprise.

HR is chartered with creating a positive work environment for employees while simultaneously acting as a strategic partner to the lines of business. The HR function is so critical, in part, because a company's payroll is usually its single largest expense.

If you work at a major corporation, your annual payroll is in the hundreds of millions dollars annually, if not billions. A very small percentage increase in the return on the efficiency of the workforce, and therefore the payroll investment, can easily reach tens of millions of dollars.

The other chapters in this book look at how IP video can improve employee productivity. This chapter concentrates on the increased productivity that IP video can add to the employment process itself.

Recruiting in a "Flat" World

Your customer service team has an immediate need for a new manager based in New York. The executive in charge of the division is based in San Francisco. After an extensive search, it looks like the two best candidates are in London and Bangalore. They are both currently employed and are not able to devote the time to travel to both New York and San Francisco in the near term.

Unless the candidates were truly exceptional, many companies would give up at this point. In today's global talent competition, however, limiting yourself to a certain area, or even a particular hemisphere, can be dangerous.

Cisco has been able to leverage its IP video capabilities to take advantage of the global talent pool and greatly enhance its ability to close on a targeted candidate.

Video communication tools, such as TelePresence, make a candidate's physical location no longer a barrier to an effective interview. With more than 300 TelePresence units deployed within Cisco, candidates just go to the nearest Cisco office at the appropriate time to be interviewed by Cisco managers anywhere else in the world.

This capability to rapidly schedule "face-to-face" interviews is particularly valuable in a competitive job market.

In Bangalore, for instance, qualified candidates can easily receive multiple offers in a short period of time. Unfortunately, this "hot" job market makes it relatively easy for lower-performing candidates to mix in to the candidate pool. In today's global corporate environment, the Bangalore candidate might have to work closely with a team located on the other side of the world. Through no one's "fault," there can be personality mismatches just as in any corporate team.

Videoconferencing can help to mitigate the risk of a "bad hire" while still allowing a company to maintain the speed required in a competitive job market. When a candidate in Bangalore will be working with a team in California, we can easily include a "face-to-face" interview with the manager of the U.S.-based team to make sure the candidate is a fit in both skills and personality.

Combined with the ongoing collaborative benefits of video tools post-hire, this kind of capability can allow a global company to compete effectively for talent in today's environment.

New-Hire Orientation

The infamous new-hire videotape is a constant source of amusement in sitcoms and Hollywood movies. Americans with children might even remember that an entire episode of *SpongeBob SquarePants* was devoted to the Krusty Krab's new-hire videotape. Yet, for all the mockery around it, the format exists for good reason. It allows a consistent corporate image to be displayed and, hopefully, conveys the culture of the company.

Beyond the sometimes overly dramatic narration, however, there are real issues with the format. The two main issues are as follows:

- **Timeliness**: Because of the production and distribution expense, new-hire videos are often out of date shortly after they are made. In any industry, this can quickly kill the credibility of the message the video is trying to convey.

- **No follow-up**: Besides the work of the frontline manager, the new-hire video might be the only direct reinforcement of the corporate culture an employee receives. This is especially true for employees outside of corporate headquarters.

IP video can help with both of these issues.

The dramatically lower distribution costs of IP video allow new-hire materials to be refreshed at a more regular rate. There are no videotapes to ship out, and no reliance on a volunteer in the field office to properly receive the tape and file it in the back room. When new IP video material is produced, it is instantly available all around the world.

Like many large companies, Cisco has moved beyond the videotape to an e-learning curriculum for new hires. IP video is incorporated into our e-learning modules. When a particular chapter needs to be updated, just that section can be replaced. Figure 8-1 is a screen shot of Cisco new-hire training from 2008.

Michelle Marquard, director in the Cisco Human Resources Department, shared this with us:

> Our first attempts at an online New Hire curriculum were considered a success; however, we realized that it was still too focused on the U.S.-based employee. With that in mind, our latest build of the coursework is much more relevant to employees in our global offices.
>
> We created a customizable course that can be easily localized to a particular geography. Both the technical and instructional framework allow for a small section or an entire chapter to be replaced with country specific information.
>
> The use of IP video allows the curriculum to be flexible while retaining a human touch.

Figure 8-1 *New-Hire E-Learning*

The use of video at Cisco to maintain a global corporate culture just begins with new-hire orientation. There are repeated opportunities for video-based follow-up and reinforcement of the common goals of the company.

As discussed in Chapter 4, "Scaling the CxO," employees have regular access to the executives who help shape the company. Regardless of their physical location, all employees can watch the company meeting or any one of a number of events. Furthermore, the advantage of IP video is that it is not just a one-way communication of what the corporate culture is. As any HR executive knows, a company's corporate culture is a living thing. There might be consistent tenets that last through the years and need to be reinforced, but a company is constantly evolving. It is imperative to create a feedback loop between executives and employees so that they can share with each other their thoughts on what it means to work for the company.

Cisco is famous for the number of acquisitions it has done, and many of the "new hires" come from the acquired companies. The use of IP video helps to quickly bring the acquired employees up to speed and into the "mothership." For example, regardless of where they are physically located, they need only wait a few weeks before they will see each of the top executives at Cisco speak. On the receiving side, the sales force can be quickly trained on the new products and physically see the executives of the acquired company with whom they will soon be interacting.

Knowledge Transfer

As discussed in the other chapters, Cisco employees are continually presented with opportunities to improve their knowledge in a particular area. Whether it is the development of soft skills or delving in to a new technology, employees can easily access the information they are interested in on demand. As this book goes to press, Cisco has more than 5000 video on demand (VoD) offerings available to employees. So, if an optical engineer has a sudden interest in wireless technologies, the engineer can access informal or formal training materials on his own schedule.

From a HR perspective, this not only has the potential to improve employee satisfaction, but also improves the flexibility of the workforce. As the pace of one part of the business increases while another slows, the existing workforce is more able to adjust to shifts in the business climate.

Mandatory training is also made available both through live broadcasts and VoD. The ability to instantly scale globally, let employees access information on their own schedules, thoroughly track viewership, and simply save money makes the use of IP video for e-learning a no-brainer.

Within Cisco, there is one famous example that Tom Kelly and Nader Nanjaini captured in another Cisco Press book titled *The Business Case for E-Learning*:

> In 2000, Cisco needed recertification on International Organization for Standardization, commonly referred to as ISO 9001. The task meant preparing several thousand individuals in customer service, manufacturing, and engineering departments on ISO 9001 guidelines. Based on the events three years prior, the ISO readiness training program had budgeted $1.4 million in travel, classroom, content development, and materials expenses over a period of four months.

Transforming the ISO recertification training program to an Internet learning platform took a little more than three weeks. Voice, video, and data presentations were prepared along with accompanying tests. The program was delivered over the web. Not only did Cisco pass its inspections. But it also was rated second nationwide in ISO readiness that year. Compared to the $1.4 million of three years ago, the training program ended up costing Cisco less than $17,000 because of e-learning.

Tom and Nader's book contains several other examples of the benefits of e-learning, and we recommend it to any HR professional interested in the benefits of IP video for training.

Less-formal transfers of information for HR using IP video include providing employee benefits updates or communicating new compensation plans. For example, there are quarterly VoD updates from senior executives on progress toward the annual bonus payout. Because the bonus is paid based on progress toward companywide goals, it can vary from year to year, and employees are very interested in where they stand.

Onsite Daycare

Onsite daycare is a benefit that is growing in corporate America. Working parents enjoy being close to their children while at work. Companies appreciate the productivity benefits from employees being able to focus without worrying about their children's well-being.

Cisco partnered with a company that specializes in running onsite daycare facilities to provide a daycare facility for employees based at our headquarters in San Jose, California.

When the center opened in 2000, it provided parents with a feature that was fairly rare at the time: Each daycare room was outfitted with two cameras. These cameras fed Cisco IP/TV servers that allowed parents to see what their children were doing at any time during the day.

The streams are sent only on the Cisco San Jose Campus network and are not sent across the WAN. Because of this, the streams can be at a fairly high bit rate, and the quality is quite good.

Parents are provided with a secure account that lets them see their child's main daycare room. The streams are always on and can be accessed through the parents' work computers. Only people with children at the facility can access the streams, and even then, a parent can see only his or her own child's room.

Two of the authors of this book have had children at the facility, and we can both vouch for the peace of mind it brings to a parent during the workday.

The next phase in the use of IP video at the daycare center is the introduction of the Cisco Unified Video Advantage system to enable desktop video-conferencing. This two-way video link is being used by the facility to allow parents to interact with a child that might need special attention, such as when a child is ill or upset. Parents can then decide whether they need to leave work to take their children home.

Change Management

Without doubt, one of the most powerful uses of IP video is in change management. After all, communication in any form is critical during times of change.

Cisco is in an industry where change is constant, and the use of video technologies has enabled us to continue to adapt rapidly while growing both geographically and in absolute number of employees.

At the time of this writing, Cisco is enjoying a continued expansion of its business within this ever-changing environment. However, the most dramatic change that Cisco has ever seen was not a positive one. However, it remains one of the most powerful examples of the use of IP video.

During the dotcom expansion of the late 1990s, the biggest challenge for Cisco was managing the rapid growth. In fact, since it was founded in 1984, Cisco has always had rapid growth rates. Then in early 2001, the dotcom bubble burst. For the first time in its history, Cisco sales actually began to shrink.

The shift was a dramatic one. Cisco revenue in the quarter ending January 27, 2001, was just over $6 billion. By the next quarter ending on April 28, 2001, revenue dropped $2 billion to just over $4 billion. Having our total revenue drop by one-third in just three months after gearing the company for more than a decade of growth was staggering. The total dollar amount of the drop in itself was amazing: more than $2 billion! Many companies have foundered and fallen from such a dramatic shift in their businesses.

The management at Cisco, however, realized that rapid action was required to get the company competitive and profitable again as quickly as possible. Unfortunately, layoffs were needed to get the company down to the proper size for the new fiscal reality.

Layoffs were a totally new phenomenon at Cisco. Senior management was largely composed of experienced professionals who had guided companies through tough times before, but the average line manager at Cisco had never experienced a large layoff. It was critical that action be taken quickly. The company was losing money every day that it carried a workforce sized for $2 billion more a quarter than it had.

To prepare average line managers for their roles in the layoffs, Cisco turned to IP video. Literally thousands of people had to be trained on how to manage through a downsizing effort, most of whom had never been involved in a layoff. IP video was simply the only way to get so many people trained consistently in the short timeframe required.

Live IP video broadcasts were conducted every day for two weeks. Managers were given a password to log in to sessions based on their availability. Many managers watched multiple sessions to make sure they understood how to handle the situation with respect and accuracy. In the meantime, CEO John Chambers regularly appeared in both live and recorded sessions to explain to the entire employee base what was happening and why.

In the end, the layoffs went off as smoothly as could be hoped. The end business results speak for themselves. IP video ensured information was distributed to employees accurately. Instead of still recovering from that awesome blow of 2001, Cisco in 2007 has not only exceeded the revenue rates of the dotcom era, but is now stronger than ever before. The company employs more people than it did in 2001, and its revenues per quarter are now more than $8 billion.

One of the keys to this return to growth was undoubtedly the ability to rapidly execute a dramatic shift that was in part enabled by IP video.

Summary

Video comes closer than any other medium to replicating the way humans naturally communicate. Whether it is looking at their children in daycare, considering joining a new team, or hearing about a change in compensation, people prefer to see with whom they are communicating.

IP video allows the "human" communication that is part of any HR function to scale in a way that has never been possible before. It is one of those rare technologies that can actually make processes more efficient and more personal at the same time.

Any modern HR department should consider the implementation of IP video, both to increase functional efficiency and to create the "human" connection that drives incremental productivity and job satisfaction.

CHAPTER 9

SAVE MORE, MAKE MORE: INCREASING SALES PRODUCTIVITY WITH IP VIDEO

Executive Summary

In this chapter, you will learn how video can have a tremendous impact on cost savings and increased revenue, exponentially increasing the bottom line. Specifically

- Enterprises should look to revenue generation and not just cost avoidance when measuring the return on investment of IP video.

- That revenue ROI comes in part from making the sale force more efficient, conducting product launches faster, and making subject matter experts available sooner.

- As the forms of IP video continue to blend and become more available, IP video will become more and more ingrained into the sales process.

One of the top priorities for Cisco is to profitably grow revenue.

Whereas that alone is not surprising, what is surprising is how many companies approach the deployment of video as a cost-savings activity rather than an opportunity for revenue growth. This might simply be because it is easier to estimate cost savings or perhaps because the groups deploying the tools are usually considered an operating expense. However, cost savings alone greatly underestimates the value of the tools. In fact, in some companies the revenue opportunities outweigh cost savings by a factor of three to four times.

This chapter explores some of the benefits Cisco has experienced from the use of IP video to drive both cost savings and top-line growth.

Early Drivers

The first use of video-based "distance learning" within Cisco was in 1995, when Cisco was growing rapidly and needed to get the sales force trained in an effective manner.

These early broadcasts did not use the IP network at all. They were conventional business television broadcasts. We rented a television studio, satellite time, and viewing locations around the United States every quarter or so. Each broadcast was about four hours. VHS tapes were sent to offices after the broadcast for review.

Deena Delville, Cisco TV program manager, offered this reminiscence:

> Each time we did a broadcast, it would cost us around $200,000.
> However, it was still cheaper than flying everyone in to San Jose
> and renting a large auditorium for the session.

Lori Biesen, who originated the program, remembers those early days:

> The primary driver for putting on the broadcasts was not cost sav-
> ings, but time to market. Cisco was growing rapidly and constantly
> coming out with new products. However, we couldn't maximize the
> revenue opportunity on those new products until the sales force was
> up to speed on them. At the same time, we couldn't pull the sales
> force out of the field constantly for training. So, the broadcasts were
> seen as a good vehicle for getting information out quickly with
> minimal impact to a salesperson.

After we started using our IP network to broadcast, the cost began to drop
dramatically. For example, we no longer had to rent satellite time or downlink
facilities to put on a broadcast. By 1998, the fully burdened cost of the same high-
quality production had dropped to approximately $20,000 (a tenth of the price of
a conventional broadcast). Today, the fully burdened cost is approaching $8000
per broadcast.

Even though the cost has dropped dramatically over the years, the main driver
remains the same as it was in 1995: getting revenue-generating information out to
the sales force without impacting the sales process. What has changed is that the
IP network has proven to be a vastly superior and more cost-effective delivery
vehicle for this information.

In 1995, for example, salespeople had to drive as far as 50 miles (81 km) to a
local downlink location. Today, a salesperson can access a live broadcast
anywhere in the world with a network connection.

In 1995, if salespeople missed the live broadcast, they had to wait weeks for
the VHS tape. Today, a video on demand (VoD) is available within 24 hours for
review at each salespersons's convenience.

Product Launch

The pace of business in a global environment is driving the volume of video we produce. Cisco is coming out with new products almost daily and acquiring companies at the rate of one per month.

As of late 2007, Cisco was doing about 100 live broadcasts per month. This compares to about 1 per month 10 years earlier in 1997. The single largest topic in those broadcasts is new product information.

When we come out with a new product or complete a new acquisition, we cannot realize the revenue benefits from that new product until the sales force is trained. Traveling from location to location to train the sales force takes too much time in our competitive environment.

Saving on plane tickets and hotels is certainly beneficial, but these are but a fraction of the overall ROI when compared to speed-to-market revenue generation. Maximum revenue potential cannot be achieved until everyone is trained, but it takes a long time to get everyone up to speed through travel. With IP video, everyone can be brought up to speed almost instantly. So, your entire sales force can start intelligently positioning an offering right away.

Scaling the SME

At the start of a product launch, only a few people are familiar with the product. During a product launch, it is critical for these subject matter experts (SME) to rapidly scale themselves for the product to be successful. The last thing you want to do with these people is to kill their productivity by putting them on a long "road show" going from city to city.

The other option is to "train the trainer." In this scenario, a small group of people are trained directly by the SME. Once trained, those people are expected to go back to their home office and share their knowledge with the rest of the team. Beyond the expense of the travel this method incurs, a real danger is that the trainee might not have a full grasp of the product. Misinformation and a lack of direct access to the true SME can damage the ability to execute for everyone who learns about the new product secondhand.

Compare this "train the trainer" methodology with doing a live broadcast. When doing a live broadcast, the most knowledgeable people on a particular subject speak directly to hundreds of salespeople, take questions, gather feedback, and are then available to refocus on their current job rather than their travel arrangements.

The use of video to scale SMEs does not end with internal broadcasts. In conjunction with the internal sales broadcast, a product manager might be asked to produce a Video Data Sheet that will appear on Cisco's external website, such as that shown in Figure 9-1.

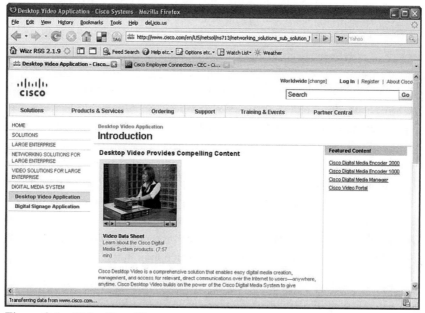

Figure 9-1 *Video Data Sheet*

These Video Data Sheets put the product managers directly in front of customers who are considering their products. Customers appreciate hearing the information directly from the product manager, and the product managers love knowing that their product is being represented the way they would do it themselves.

Michael Metz, the director in charge of Cisco.com, offered this insight:

> The new short-form Video Data Sheets have had a profound affect
> on Cisco.com visitor behavior. Those who view the 2 to 4 minute
> videos behave differently after viewing them than before, and dif-
> ferently than other visitors who haven't viewed them. They stay on
> the site substantially longer, view 3 to 4 times as many pages, and
> return to the site at 50 percent higher rates than those who don't see
> the videos. On the same day they watch the videos, their usage rates
> for Partner Locator and Click-to-Chat go up substantially also.
> We're living in the age of video, and we intend to push the envelope
> with video usage on Cisco.com. Our next step is to migrate these
> Video Data Sheets to our worldwide country sites.

After the "big bang" of the product launch, IP video continues to help scale the SME and reduce sales cycle times.

For example, Cisco TelePresence tools are rapidly becoming the preferred method of getting our SMEs in front of customers in a way that is convenient for everyone involved. Customers can speak directly with key individuals within Cisco rapidly instead of waiting for a travel opportunity; at the same time, Cisco benefits by the shortened sales cycle associated with these key conversations.

Gale Lightfoot, senior program manager within the Cisco Scientific Atlanta Division, recalls an instance where Cisco TelePresence was critical in getting a team of SMEs together quickly to respond to an opportunity:

> Last summer we had a major customer that issued an RFI with a
> very short turnaround. With the Atlanta-based Cisco team, we were
> able to quickly arrange a meeting via TelePresence with key Cisco
> and SA folks in Great Britain, Denver, and Atlanta, that would not
> have been able to travel on short notice. This enabled us to impress
> the customer with our response time, and actually even made possi-
> ble a follow-up meeting (again using TelePresence) with the very
> same team assembled previously, this time including the customer.
> Not only was this a convenience, but TelePresence enabled a conti-
> nuity of resources that would not have been possible previously,
> and personally connected the customer with those very resources.
> This would not have been possible without TelePresence.

Customers are also obtaining greater access to people who, because of travel restrictions, might not have been previously available. For example, directors of HR, IT, or supply chain management can now have "face-to-face" best practice sharing meetings with customers on the other side of the world. This kind of direct interaction between people outside of the sales process used to be rare or done over the phone, but it is now occurring regularly via TelePresence.

Brendon Hynes, a senior manager working on IP video within Cisco and outside of Cisco for several years prior, summarized the benefits as follows:

> In today's global business environment, the ability for enterprises of all sizes to apply timely subject matter expertise virtually to customer opportunities and internal business processes is becoming a game-changing strategy.
>
> Whether it be the strategic application of a CEO communicating with the employees driving organizational alignment and fostering a corporate culture or more tactically focused like inserting a business or technology expert into the customer process, video is the only communication tool that can replicate the personal experience required to create confidence through credibility and drive the collaborative relationships needed for business today and tomorrow. It closes the gaps of time and distance without removing the personal and interactive experience.
>
> Three years ago, having a video infrastructure was a "nice to have." Today, it is a requirement. Three years from now, it will be woven through every task, activity, and process within the enterprise.

Saving Time for Sales

Like many other companies, some of the most highly compensated people in the organization work in sales. The importance of making this function more effective is reflected by the billions of dollars in consulting, training, and research put toward the issue from both inside and outside of the corporate world.

IP video can play a huge role in increasing the productivity of the sales force. Instead of spending time traveling to regional meetings or product training, the sales force can use this time to be in front of customers and still attend the meetings via video. In addition, the ability to access timely information on demand means that the time spent with customers is often more productive.

Michael LaManna is the business operation manager within the Cisco Corporate Communications team. Part of his role is spending time with the sales function to help them maximize their benefits from the available IP video tools. He shared this story about the use of WebEx in commit calls, where sales teams have to "commit" to their sales targets:

> For example, leveraging IP video in Monday morning conference/ commit calls is saving time and money in the central regions of the United States. Instead of driving into the office every Monday, account teams now can leverage WebEx with IP video. It is like having everyone in the same room without driving. Account managers and system engineers now can leverage IP video tools just about anywhere they are. One estimate showed three and a half weeks in time back to account managers a year. Ask any account manager and they will tell you that "time is money."

Michael also mentioned that there is a feeling among the regional managers he spoke to that the commits are more accurate using IP video when compared to a straight audio conference call. It might be harder to either exaggerate or "sandbag" in front of a video camera than into your cell phone.

As mentioned in the opening paragraph of this chapter, it is beneficial to look at productivity savings from both a revenue-generation perspective and a cost-savings view. For example, if you could give your entire sales force 5 percent more sales time, it is reasonable to expect some increased revenue from that time savings.

"Scale the Power"

One of the most aggressive IP video programs at Cisco is coming out of the U.S. and Canadian sales theater led by Rob Lloyd, senior vice president for the United States, Canada, and Japan.

The initiative, called Scale the Power, looks at ways to use the latest in IP video to increase customer contacts and enhance the overall relationship with customers while simultaneously reducing costs.

Jere King is a long-time promoter of IP video and, along with Donna Rhode, is one of the vice presidents driving the initiative for Rob Lloyd. Jere mentioned three main challenges for the U.S. and Canadian theater that the initiative is addressing:

> 1. How do we effectively communicate to an increasingly larger customer and partner base without increasing travel [cost and time], while still maintaining a high quality of customer experience?
>
> 2. How do we ensure more "scale and reach" of our critical technology experts across a wider set of customers without hiring more personnel and requiring extensive travel?
>
> 3. How can we reduce travel costs overall, while also supporting the Clinton Global Initiative for a reduced carbon footprint?

One of the most interesting uses of IP video within the initiative is to invite customers into Cisco offices to participate in a live, two-way broadcast with key executives at the company. The broadcasts mix TelePresence with IP video streaming to create an interactive broadcast that can also scale to almost any network connection.

In a very open and direct way, customers can hear the questions and concerns of other customers while gauging the responses from the Cisco experts.

The broadcasts are programmed with a focus on one particular area so that customers know whether it is worth their time to participate.

On the Cisco end, we are able to have more executives hear the concerns of more customers while making efficient use of their time.

Jere King shared his experience:

> Using IP video broadcasts to customers and partners, a program we call Cisco Interaction Network, we're seeing a 5 to 10 times increase in customer interactions compared with more traditional events such as face-to-face seminars and trade shows.

The initiative is also focusing on increasing organizational efficiency within the sales team itself. Communication and training from senior staff on down are increasingly using IP video in new and exciting ways.

Next Generation

As IP video continues to evolve, so does its use within the sales function. In this section, we discuss two new uses of the tools that leverage Cisco technology. Note, however, that these implementations are not available as a packaged product at the time of this writing.

The first example is the blending of Cisco TelePresence with IP video broadcasting for senior staff communications.

Rob Lloyd and other Cisco executives have been holding senior staff meetings via TelePresence for quite some time. With an increasingly geographically dispersed leadership team, TelePresence has been a powerful tool in maintaining corporate productivity and direction.

However, what Rob has started to do differently is to take particular meetings and broadcast them live to the desktops of individuals in the sales team. Senior staff members are in an open, multipoint TelePresence session that maintains the intimacy that is a key part of the TelePresence experience. At the same time, the TelePresence session is viewed by the sales team on their desktops.

By broadcasting the executive TelePresence sessions, key initiatives can be shared throughout the region in an open manner while closing the knowledge gap between the executive and the individual member of the sales force.

Another innovative tool that is being used by all levels within the sales force is something called Cvision. Cvision is a video wiki with some of the same functionality as YouTube or Yahoo! Video.

Anyone within Cisco can now upload a video recorded using a Cisco Unified Video Advantage camera. This reduces the cost of production down to next to nothing. Within the sales function, we are seeing Cvision being used in three areas:

- Product managers can get information to the sales force even more rapidly.
- Salespeople are sharing best practices more often.
- Sales management at all levels are providing regular updates to their teams.

These two new capabilities, broadcasting TelePresence sessions to the desktop and easy creation of Cvision video blogs, reflects major shifts we are seeing in the evolution of IP video: All forms of video are starting to converge on the IP network (TelePresence and broadcasting, for example) as access to product information and best practices becomes readily available (Cvision).

Summary

While cost savings are always nice, the potential for top-line growth is truly one of the most compelling reasons to deploy IP video in the enterprise.

When properly aligned with your sales processes, IP video can increase customer intimacy, make your sales force more productive, and reduce the overall sales cycle.

Every tool in the IP video toolkit has a role to play in the sales process. The key is aligning the right tool for each phase. For example, basic VoD services can be used to provide information, but higher-end systems such a TelePresence may be better suited to promote true customer interaction.

PART III

SHOW ME THE MONEY

CHAPTER 10

TRANSFORMING EDUCATIONAL PARADIGMS WITH IP VIDEO

Executive Summary

In this chapter, you will learn the following:

*   Video adds a compelling dimension to e-learning efforts.

*   Use of e-learning in video is increasing in not just the education sector but also in the business sector.

*   Cisco commitment to video based e-learning has generated significant value on investment for the company.

*   Social networking and podcasting facilitate the adoption and increase the effectiveness of video content among learners.

Video has been used extensively over the years in distance learning when remote locations were connected using satellite TV or Instructional Television. Now with IP streaming media and on-demand content, the lines of traditional distance learning and online computer instruction have blurred to a point where audio, video, web, and collaboration tools blend to deliver not just formal curriculum, but also lifelong learning and networking opportunities to learners of all ages.

Beyond merely replicating classroom instruction over satellite, as the traditional models used to deliver, the current IP-driven model, commonly referred to as e-learning, has had a greater impact in not only reaching greater numbers of learners at lower cost but also transforming the learning process itself. The combination of IP video and Web 2.0 technologies has helped to finally deliver on the long-envisioned goal of delivering instruction that is learner centered, anytime-anyplace, self-paced, and collaborative. From being a mere travel-avoidance proposition, e-learning has matured into becoming an essential component in many learning environments.

Before we discuss the way e-learning is being currently deployed by various organizations globally, let's review the e-learning adoption process and its evolution at Cisco.

Evolution of Video-Based Learning at Cisco

E-learning took a significant turn at Cisco almost a decade ago when a strong need was felt across the organization to keep a growing field force trained and current on networking technologies. E-learning at Cisco evolved over the years as a cost-efficient way to share information with the Cisco sales team, and soon transformed into a competitive advantage in the marketplace as the capability was extended to employees of Cisco reseller organizations (see Appendix A, "How Cisco Uses Streaming Video for Worldwide Corporate Events and Training").

The Cisco Press title *The Business Case for E-Learning* discusses the cost-benefit analysis of e-learning for organizations. One statistic from the book that is worth reinforcing here is a value-on-investment study that was conducted for the e-learning portal used by members of the Cisco reseller ecosystem, Partner E-learning Connect (PEC). The study demonstrated that for every dollar Cisco spent on PEC, the project returned a value of $16 to Cisco.[1] The study helped crystallize in the minds of stakeholders, senior management, and employees at Cisco a concept that seemed intuitive all along: E-learning makes great business sense. It was important, because of the resource commitment involved in delivery of video-based content for e-learning, that senior management support the effort. Video broadcasts and video-on-demand (VoD) formats were favored at Cisco over other forms of e-learning in that they most readily replicated the one-to-many meeting presentations without extensive lead time for instructional design and development.

As with most innovative practices, intuition preceded proof in the adoption of IP video for e-learning at Cisco a decade ago.

Three factors continued to spur Cisco's success with video-driven e-learning projects:

- **Organizational commitment**: Originated from the demand to support the field force, and borne out of sheer necessity to keep up with the volume of content being delivered to the diverse global field force.

- **Economies of scale**: Because the organizational commitment was at the executive level, use of video-based e-learning was widely adopted, enabling economies of scale, which made sustained investment in the necessary infrastructure viable.

  Today that level of video e-learning infrastructure is probably available on demand to organizations starting afresh in the arena from various e-learning vendors at a mere fraction of what it cost Cisco back then.

- **Alignment with the sales process**: Stemmed from a willingness on part of the Cisco sales force to accept technology delivery of content as a credible alternative to having to travel to training locations.

  Meeting the skills gap at the time otherwise would have been near impossible. Staying ahead of competition by staying abreast of changes and developments was a primary consideration that made sense to pursue anytime-anyplace instruction. Economic rewards tied to engineering certifications and assessments created the learner motivation to tolerate any of the teething problems that e-learning might have presented over face-to-face instruction. Sales personnel across Cisco and its reseller ecosystem quickly calculated that the opportunity cost of staying out of action for a week to pursue training was much greater than putting up with any perceived dilution of the learning experience through video-based instruction on the Internet.

The e-learning adoption not only formalized for sales training but also enabled Cisco to launch a business around it. The Cisco Digital Media System enables organizations to create, manage, and access compelling digital media to easily connect customers, employees, partners, or students anywhere at anytime.

It is a flexible and comprehensive solution for publishing dynamic content to both networked, on-premise digital signage displays (Cisco Digital Signage) and the desktop (Cisco Desktop Video). The two businesses are as follows:

- Cisco Digital Signage for publishing of digital media to on-premise displays

- Cisco Desktop Video to create and manage digital media, VoD, and live webcasts on desktops

Video in Today's Diverse Education Settings

The examples in this chapter are meant to illustrate how organizations are globally deploying video technologies to transform learning and education management. The case studies explain how the current use of IP video has enabled innovation in four different spheres of education:

- **Learning for career advancement**: In the area of professional development, we discuss how social networking and video podcasts are creating a just-in-time learning offering for a community of shipping professionals in the United Kingdom.

- **Securing campuses with IP video**: In the discussion about campus physical security, we highlight the use of IP video surveillance to help foster safer learning environments in public schools.

- **Reaching dispersed learners**: When highlighting use of video for curriculum and instruction, we point out how U.C. Berkeley uses podcasting to deliver content to students on and off campus.

- **Enriching the classroom**: In covering education enrichment, we cite how IP video helps Cleveland Metroparks Zoo deliver virtual field trips to schools and how the Cisco 21st Century Schools Initiative brings interaction through technology into classrooms.

The sections that follow provide greater detail in each of these areas.

Collaborative Learning for Career Advancement

As the requirement for shipping certification grows in emerging markets, the ability to meet the learning needs of shipping professionals between the ages of 25 and 35 years has been enhanced through the deployment of an e-learning program.

Case Study: The Institute of Chartered Shipbrokers

The Institute of Chartered Shipbrokers (ICS) is an internationally recognized professional body representing shipbrokers, managers, and agents. The organization, formed in 1911, was awarded a Royal Charter in 1920 and a Supplemental Charter in 1984. Today, it is an examining body and holds exams annually at more than 80 locations around the world. With more than 3500 certified professionals worldwide and individuals continually preparing for the certification exams, the ICS provides opportunities not only for professional development and learning, but it also gives candidates career networking opportunities.

Shipping represents an international business responsible for the carriage of approximately 90 percent of all world trade. The estimated income from freight rates equates to around 5 percent of all world trade. There are approximately

50,000 ships worldwide registered to 150 countries. With an excess of a million seafarers and multiples of that number working in shore-based support jobs, an industry such as this is also a community. As the industry's recognized professional body, the ICS represents a significant stakeholder in that community. With freight and shipping contributing about 5 percent of the global GDP, there is an emphasis on the part of the industry to strengthen its professional credentials by encouraging learning and development within its constituents.

The e-learning solution from ICS is delivered by a U.K.-based start-up, Coracle Online Limited, and it includes a variety of video and nonvideo collaborative tools to facilitate learning. E-learning support facilitated by ICS consists of a host of tools, including the following:

- Online courses (see Figure 10-1)

- Podcasts for lectures and interviews

- Online instructional video clips

- Social networking site

- Test preparation tools

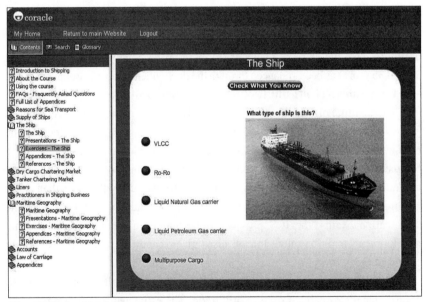

Figure 10-1   *Video-Based Assessment for Shipping Professionals*

For instance, with a social-networking site, the ICS intends to facilitate professional discussion and networking among shipping professionals. The site will also offer resources such as an interactive maritime glossary containing about 18,000 terms and definitions.

As part of the lifelong-learning materials available on the same portal, Coracle also records audio and video seminars and interviews with industry leaders for the ICS and makes those available as podcasts on iTunes.

These podcasts have proved to be tremendously popular with students and professionals alike. As another example of building e-learning collaboration between learners and potential employers using IP video, the institute has also undertaken an effort to have employers in the industry provide resources in video and audio form for use in supporting those courses.

With the membership of the ICS growing rapidly, in the first year of operations, exports accounted for 80 percent of Coracle's e-learning sales. The learners were largely new members from the quickly expanding economies (such as China and India) that rely so heavily on the maritime sector to satisfy their need for economic expansion. What used to be a $5000 to $6000 cost of preparing for the exams could now be achieved for a fraction of the cost. The reduction in cost and increase in distribution has helped keep up with a surging demand from learners worldwide.

Safeguarding Schools with IP Video Surveillance

Nonintrusive, yet effective security to ensure a student-friendly environment on educational campuses has long been a desire of administrators, communities, and students alike. Video offers the option to deliver surveillance capability to monitor antisocial behaviors such as bullying, altercations, or vandalism that might take place on an educational campus.

Case Study: Grant Joint Union High School District

Like many school districts, Sacramento's Grant Joint Union High School District has concerns about student safety and the financial impact of property destruction.[2] Video surveillance offered a unique solution to both concerns. Not only was video surveillance a known deterrent to property theft and destruction, it also significantly enhanced student and faculty safety by enabling faster response. This latter concern was the key priority for the district's chief of police, school administrators, and the district's IT group.

The district deployed video surveillance cameras throughout school campuses to address the problems of break-ins, vandalism, and the liability of students entering areas such as swimming pools after school hours. With the legacy analog video systems, it took longer to search for video on the disparate systems, and the video quality was not always adequate to identify perpetrators. Furthermore, the systems were unable to provide video access to mobile users, or to store recorded video in both local and remote locations. Under the U.S. Department of Justice Securing Our Schools program, Grant's Chief of Police, Bill Roberts, submitted a proposal and received a grant to upgrade the video system to support higher-quality IP video cameras.

Administrators at Grant Joint Union High School District recognized that the district's IP network, which had already improved and enhanced productivity, communications, and collaboration among faculty, school district police, and students, could be extended to support the district's video surveillance application. It was determined that easy-to-use web browser–based software would work best. In addition, the software would run on reliable Linux-based, IT-caliber network servers, not single-vendor-specific hardware. The team recognized that if authorized district personnel could access and manage live and recorded video from wherever they might be, it would not only permit additional cost savings, but would also enable faster event response and faster investigation / event resolution. Figure 10-2 demonstrates a network environment supporting video-based physical security.

During school hours, counselors and administrators use the video system to quickly resolve confrontations and other events. As a result, altercations between students have decreased, thereby creating an environment more conducive to learning. The solution has also helped maximize human resources, allowing campus buildings to be remotely monitored after school hours or during summer vacations. The cameras are directed to focus on certain locations automatically.

Grant District has greatly benefited from the investment, which enables administrators and law enforcement to respond more quickly to events and reduce theft or property damage. As a result of the deployment, Grant District personnel can view live video from cameras at different campuses simultaneously with high-quality images. Archived video can be quickly retrieved and used to provide evidence in disciplinary situations.

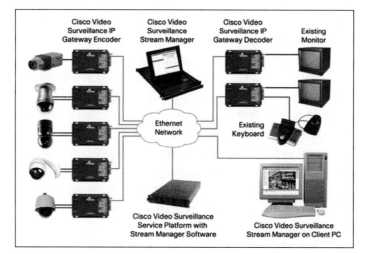

Figure 10-2   *Network-Centric Video Surveillance and Recording Deployment*

Reaching Dispersed Learners: Mobile and Video Ready

Today's learners respond favorably to content delivered over the media of their choice. Content delivered on a mobile and video platform naturally grabs the attention of a generation of learners who grew up on video and now communicate on the go. An initiative by the Educational Technology Service at the University of California at Berkeley exemplified this mobile learning approach when the university chose to work with Cisco to enable course delivery using podcasts to on- and off-campus students.

Case Study: University of California at Berkeley

For more than a decade, Berkeley has offered a variety of educational content to a worldwide audience on topics ranging from astronomy to psychology, through its locally managed website. The program, called the Berkeley Internet Broadcasting System, has delivered webcasts for 12 years. Although the concept was innovative when it began in the mid-1990s, it was labor-intensive and costly. Today, it no longer meets the needs of a new student body arriving on campus expecting to access and download podcasts of class lectures and other content.[3]

The university began reviewing a podcasting system that would meet the expectations of its student population and encourage faculty members to create podcasts by simplifying the process. The campus also wanted to enable wider content distribution to provide lifelong learners outside the school the opportunity to access class lectures that had been recorded and stored as podcasts.

Berkeley set a goal in 2007 to implement an iTunes U initiative to expand podcasting to more than 200 classrooms in conjunction with other multimedia applications that would run over the campus network.

They chose to provision a next-generation network system to allow audio and video files to be captured, reviewed, processed, published, and distributed through a wide array of distribution channels for use on portable devices. The process would depend on a stable IP network that was robust enough to handle the increased bandwidth demand.

Berkeley integrated Apple's Podcast Producer application, a comprehensive solution for producing and distributing high-quality podcasts. Podcast Producer was a key component of a next-generation podcast capture and delivery system, and provided the necessary framework for recording content, encoding, and publishing podcasts for playback on various devices. Podcast Producer is a natural extension of Berkeley's adoption of iTunes U as a distribution channel to students and to the world for audio and video content, such as presentations, performances, lectures, demonstrations, debates, tours, and archival footage. The marriage of Podcast Producer and Berkeley's next-generation system will allow the capture of high-quality audio and video from local and remote cameras and screencasting, and will enable the uploading of existing content into Podcast Producer for encoding and redistribution.

Berkeley easily met student and faculty expectations for a next-generation campus through a comprehensive network that enables the creation and delivery of podcasts, as shown in Figure 10-3. With a comprehensive campus network in place and a plan for how to expand as applications require, U.C. Berkeley was positioned to continue its mission as a public institution focused on providing a next-generation learning environment to students and making higher education available to a global community.

Figure 10-3 *University of California, Berkeley, Offers a Variety of Courses on iTunes U*

Berkeley's next-generation campus vision has resulted in the following achievements:

- Podcasting planned for 70 classrooms (one-third of U.C. Berkeley's course catalog) in the next one to two years.

- Two million iTunes U downloads occurred within the first year.

- More than 160 courses are available to the public for free.

- More than 200 special events, with prominent speakers such as Jane Goodall, are available.

- Faculty use increased because of easier podcast production.

Video Content Enriching the Classroom

Bringing a slice of real life into the classroom has always delivered value for learners in higher education. The extensive use of case studies in business schools offers proof of the popularity of the approach among students.

Now with the capability to share IP video content across locations, K–12 schools are also able to benefit from live and interactive content pulled in from outside of class.

The sections that follow review a few case studies where Cisco has enabled innovative applications for use in schools.

Cleveland Metroparks Zoo Distance Learning Program

With a goal to deliver free programs to school districts located across the state, Cleveland Metroparks Zoo came up with a unique approach to using wireless videoconferencing solutions to roam the zoo facility and share the video with remote public schools[4] (see Figure 10-4). The approach allows students to participate remotely from their classroom in a live electronic field trip where they would otherwise have limited opportunities to visit the zoo. Students can learn by seeing the animals in their zoo habitat and participate in live discussions over videoconferencing.

Figure 10-4   Mobile Video Recording Unit to Deliver Live Video to Schools

Deployment of Interactive Voice, Video, and Web Tools in Classrooms with the 21st Century Schools Initiative

After Hurricane Katrina struck the Gulf Coast region in August 2005, Cisco Chairman and CEO John Chambers unveiled a $80 million initiative to assist in community rebuilding efforts while simultaneously creating a blueprint for 21st century schools. In addition to improving the quality of education in Mississippi and Louisiana, the 21st Century Schools Initiative (21S) aims to provide a holistic approach to education that will transform learning opportunities throughout the United States and beyond.

Cisco has developed a unique partnership with Digital Opportunity Trust, a nonprofit organization that promotes socioeconomic development, to establish a 21S Internship Program. Interns receive leadership and IT training to assist teachers in developing projects that integrate technology to help engage students and improve learning outcomes. Cisco has also partnered with government agencies, nonprofits, businesses, and experts across multiple disciplines to support various components of 21S, such as community outreach, classroom technologies, and lesson plans. Figure 10-5 shows students using technology under a Cisco initiative.

Figure 10-5 *Cisco Education Initiative at Work*

Cisco advanced technologies such as voice, video, and mobility have helped create a 21st century learning environment. Teachers can now leverage a host of Unified Communications applications and interactive whiteboards to engage students, collaborate with parents, and exchange ideas with peers. Core infrastructure upgrades have dramatically improved network response times, reliability, and robustness at 21S schools. As of October 2007, nearly 3000 teachers have received leadership training, 18 fellows have supported the implementation of 21S components, and more than 30,000 students have participated in connected learning programs.

Summary

Although use of video in the education sector is not new, the arrival of IP video (with its collaboration potential) has enabled new models of how institutions deliver and manage education. This chapter demonstrated how some of the current use cases around video in education are generating increased value for students, administrators, and communities. With the adoption of video on mobility platforms on the increase, we can expect even greater innovation in meeting the need for anytime-anyplace instruction.

End Notes

1. Tom Kelly and Nader Nanjiani, *The Business Case for E-Learning*, Cisco Press, 2004, 52.

2. "High School District Enhances Campus Security," A Cisco Customer Case Study, 2007.

3. "Podcast-Ready Network Prepares UC Berkeley for Next-Generation Campus"—A Cisco Customer Case Study, 2007.

4. "Cleveland MetroParks Zoo Distance Learning Program," A Cisco Customer Case Study (video), 2007.

5. "Promethean and Cisco Bring Learning to Life for '21S' Schools," Jenny Carless, 20 February 2007.

CHAPTER 11

FINANCIAL SERVICES AND VIDEO: ACCELERATING REVENUE, RELATIONSHIPS, AND MUCH MORE

Executive Summary

This chapter examines four examples that illustrate how video can help financial services companies achieve the following:

- Accelerate revenue by improving product rollout and training

- Enable new business models

- Build and maintain relationships across distance, particularly during growth periods

- Extend expertise to employees and customers

- Boost productivity, collaboration, and work/life balance for employees

The financial services sector encompasses banks and credit unions, investment houses, and insurance companies. Like every industry, a number of market dynamics influence it. This chapter examines three that have a particular impact on the application of technology.

First, the financial services sector is a very fast-moving industry, highly competitive and acquisitive by nature. Consequently, financial institutions are always looking for ways to streamline costs, accelerate decision making and time to market with new services, and rapidly integrate acquired companies to ensure consistent execution of strategy across potentially large geographic footprints.

Second, despite the need to move quickly, financial services is also one of the most heavily regulated industries, requiring institutions to comply with constantly changing federal and state guidelines. To stay compliant, firms must find new ways to communicate policies quickly and consistently with employees in all locations, including topics such as transparency and documentation in financial reporting.

Third, myriad options, including purely online financial firms, provide consumers with greater choice and control than ever before, forcing firms to think very differently about customer service if they want to remain competitive. Given that customers are placing their livelihoods in the hands of these institutions, it is really no surprise that clear communications, quality customer service, and personal relationships, even across large distances, are keys to ongoing success.

This is where technology can help. Collaborative technologies such as video help financial services companies bridge time and distance, reduce travel, and improve productivity. Video also helps them scale expertise; improve communications, decision making, and training processes; and deliver new capabilities that give them a competitive advantage in the market.

Financial services institutions tend to take a more conservative approach toward technology adoption, needing to ensure its security and reliability before deployment. Nonetheless, these companies are forward looking at the potential of new technology to help them do business more effectively. It is no surprise, therefore, that the financial sector offers up some great examples with respect to the successful use of video. This chapter examines four specific examples that illustrate the benefits of video. These examples show how video makes a measurable impact on collaboration, training and relationship building, new product rollout, customer service, and regulatory compliance.

Improving the Product Rollout Process, and More, with Video

One of the largest U.S. banks used to have an inefficient, protracted new-product rollout process. As new products were introduced, the sales training team would go on a road show to visit all branches in an effort to get the local teams up to speed on new offerings. With all the branches that they needed to cover, the road show typically took up to three months to complete. In addition to being tough on the training team and costly, the branch employees received the information over the course of the quarter. This hindered the bank from serving all its customers equally regardless of location, and contributed to "leakage" (that is, missed opportunities) in product sales.

Looking for alternative ways to address this process, the bank deployed an IPTV solution that enabled its training team to deliver the content over video from a central broadcast studio to all employees simultaneously. Employees now tune into the broadcast on their PCs using a browser, and can submit questions to the presenters in real time. Using this method, the training team no longer has to spend significant amounts of time away from home, enduring the wear and tear of travel, and the company no longer has to cover the significant road-show expense. Because all bank employees receive the information at the same time, training is more consistent and of higher quality, leading to better customer service and reduced revenue leakage. Figure 11-1 illustrates the marked difference in the product rollout process before and after the implementation of the IPTV solution. Because of the use of the new solution, new revenue from these offerings is realized from day one at all sites.

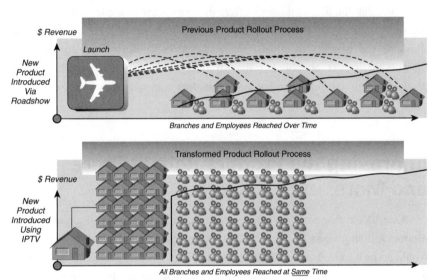

Figure 11-1   *New Product Rollout and Training Process, Before and After Implementing an IPTV Solution*

The bank has seen great response from employees based on the new training method, and more significantly, has seen that they can accelerate new-product revenues by nearly a quarter. This amounted to tens of millions of dollars in new-product revenue for them in the first quarter of use alone, against an initial investment of about $6 million.

The bank has also been able to use the IPTV solution for a variety of other applications, including corporate communications and sharing best practices among its sales associates on an ongoing basis. This enables them to elevate the performance of all salespeople, and prevents churn among associates. Being able to maintain a stable, knowledgeable sales staff is much easier on the bank that having to replace and retrain associates every few months. One of the other significant benefits is that they can accelerate new-hire training by four to five weeks, meaning that sales associates who normally take up to a quarter to become truly "effective" can now do this in approximately half the time. This drives additional revenue for the bank, further contributing to the return on investment (ROI) of the solution. Figure 11-2 summarizes the bank's key benefits from deploying video.

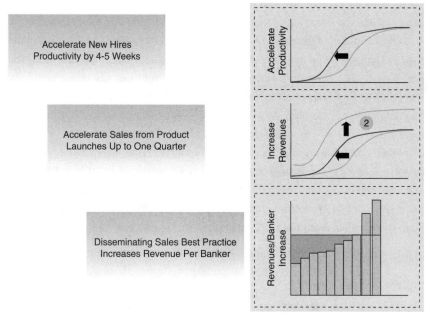

Figure 11-2   *Summary of the Business Impacts from Implementing Video*

This example provides interesting proof of how the use of video to improve one key process can actually benefit users and organizations in many other ways (for example, by providing greater returns than initially imagined). The next example describes how it can also enable businesses to operate and to build relationships across significant distances.

Bridging the Gap: Magnet Bank

Magnet Bank is a *de novo* bank based in Utah. A de novo bank is defined as a state member/commercial bank that has been in operation for fewer than five years. Magnet has a unique industrial loan charter that only a handful of states, principally Utah, offer. This charter creates a structure under which commercial companies such as retailers can get a financial services license to do specific things such as issue credit cards. As an industrial bank, Magnet raises capital for lending by selling jumbo certificates of deposit through independent brokers and online. With a streamlined staff and selected locations in major markets, Magnet has a low overhead and can consolidate some of the best offerings in the marketplace.

One condition of the charter requires all management staff to reside within the state of Utah; however, more than 90 percent of Magnet's operations are along the East Coast. The company's management realized very quickly that technology was going to play a large part in keeping them connected to their remote locations. Magnet deployed a secure LAN/WAN, Cisco Unified Communications, and both room and desktop videoconferencing. Videoconferencing enables Magnet's corporate staff to work closely with loan officers, relationship managers, and customers, even though they are thousands of miles away. If a relationship manager and client are meeting in another city, and want to include the senior management of the bank from Utah in the meeting, the client manager can just add them in via video. According to Christopher Worel, president and CO

> It makes the relationships with the bank much more tangible.
> There's that old saying about putting the face with the name.

This can be particularly important when dealing with high–net worth clients or with complicated higher-margin product offerings. Magnet makes optimal use of the system. In addition to customer meetings and daily business transactions, they use videoconferencing for staff training and meetings (see Figure 11-3). Instead of traveling to all offices individually, they save time and improve compliance by doing a single collaborative meeting. Meeting as a group using video gives staff a chance to hear everything at the same time, review new materials as a group, and ask questions of senior staff.

Figure 11-3 *Room-Based Videoconferencing Enables Staff Meetings, Training, and Customer Interactions Across Distance*

It is also a big productivity gain for management. Lindsay Jones, CFO, noted the following (see Figure 11-4):

> I can hook my laptop up to the videoconferencing system and share spreadsheets, for example, and I haven't had to fly across the country to all of my cities to do it. I can get everyone together at one time for one training, in one hour.

Because using video is both efficient and effective, the bank has also taken the opportunity to use the system to do "mini-trainings" more often, improving product rollouts, expanding sales opportunities, and improving customer service.

In this case, Magnet is making great use of video to enable a new business model and remain highly effective across long distances. Their success is clear: Magnet was ranked third on the list of Top 25 New Banks in the United States in 2006.

The next example provides insight into how video can support growth and a company's primary mission.

Figure 11-4 *Desktop Camera Linked to the Phone Allows Corporate Staff to Communicate Easily with Branch Staff. Dialing Is Tied to the User Extension, Making a Phone Call into a Video Call*

Supporting Growth While Maintaining Corporate Culture: Mountain America Credit Union

Mountain America Credit Union (MACU) is the second-largest credit union in the state of Utah, with 850 employees serving members at 48 branches in 4 states, and one of the Southwest's largest financial institutions. The credit union has grown rapidly in the space of just a few short years. When the company moved into new corporate offices a few years ago, they realized that they had a chance to examine how it could better serve current members and attract new business while reducing operational expense and maintaining the high quality of employee interactions. MACU realized that technology would play a vital role in meeting these objectives, and that video in particular would allow it to transform some existing processes and provide some completely new capabilities.

In its new location, MACU installed an end-to-end Cisco network, including routing, switching, wireless, security, Cisco Unified Communications, IP contact center applications, and a host of video applications (video surveillance, digital signage, room videoconferencing, and desktop video cameras). Video surveillance provides increased security to employees and members alike, and it gives MACU a chance to monitor and improve traffic flow at its branches. Meanwhile, digital signage provides marketing and product information to customers and allows MACU to differentiate themselves from other financial institutions.

On the videoconferencing front, Cisco Unified Video Advantage desktop cameras were rolled out to approximately 300 individuals across all 48 branches. The desktop cameras are linked to the extension of each user, allowing staff to turn phone calls into "video calls" whenever they feel like it (see Figure 11-5). Because Video Advantage is easy to use, employees immediately adopted the technology and were able to begin building collaborative relationships with employees at corporate and at other branch locations.

Figure 11-5 *Desktop Video Camera Linked to the Phone Allows Corporate Staff to Communicate Easily with Branch Staff Whenever They Want*

Desktop video also made it significantly easier to scale subject matter experts. For example, MACU has a small team of experts related to commercial real estate offerings. This team used to travel to each branch on a rotational basis. They can now be available to customers at all branches all day long via video without leaving headquarters. Figure 11-6 shows how a corporate expert can meet 1:1 with employees or customers in branch locations.

Figure 11-6 *Desktop Videophone Enables Point-to-Point and Multipoint Calls Between Corporate and Branch Locations*

From a technology standpoint, Ray Carsey, vice president of IT for Mountain America, says

Videoconferencing is one of the biggest wins our IT group has experienced at Mountain America. Cisco Unified Video Advantage was exceptionally easy to install and manage on the network, and from the users' perspective, videoconferencing is just like making a phone call; they don't need to learn anything new. Little to no training was required.

MACU's solution also includes Cisco Unified Videoconferencing for conference rooms, which enables them to conduct point-to-point and multipoint videoconferences for meetings, training, and for customer interactions, as shown in Figure 11-7. Because the credit union's main mission is high-quality customer service, video options are helping them to scale expertise and train remote employees to better serve customers. From an operations perspective, video helps them be faster and more efficient in how they train, ensuring consistent communications and timely information dissemination to all employees.

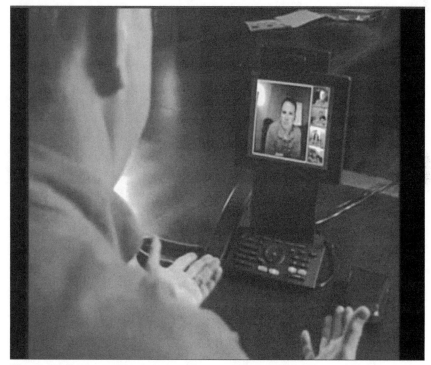

Figure 11-7   *Mountain America Holds Staff Meetings and Training Using Multipoint Videoconferencing and a Variety of Desktop Video Devices*

Cisco Unified Videoconferencing reduces travel costs by replacing many in-person meetings. According to Carsey

> Person-to-person and group video communication has had a
> dramatic impact. It's more personal than a telephone call, and
> allows us to address certain business functions, such as training,
> more immediately because we no longer have to wait for a critical
> mass of people to schedule classes. We are simply flying fewer
> people around, which saves significant cost.

Perhaps most important, employees have embraced videoconferencing as away to retain the "family" atmosphere that makes MACU an attractive place to work. Clair Buck, branch manager, says

> The visual connection I can make eliminates the "remoteness" of
> working with team members in outlying offices. Videoconferencing
> has made it easy for everyone to communicate in a personal way,
> making Mountain America still feel like a small company although
> we're now quite large.

Video has also helped create telecommuting options for employees who had to relocate to new branches as the credit union grew. This has helped MACU retain longstanding employees by making them still feel connected to corporate headquarters.

MACU has seen some great results from their implementation, including increased revenues, increased new membership, improved collaboration among employees, and significantly reduced travel costs (averaging $7 to $10K in savings per meeting). In addition, they have been able to maintain their corporate culture during this time of rapid growth.

Our last example shows how one bank is thinking differently about how video can help them not only enhance productivity and customer service, but also provide employees with new ways to collaborate and be better corporate citizens at the same time.

Thinking Differently About Collaboration: Wachovia

Wachovia Corporation is the parent company of the fourth-largest bank and the third-largest investment brokerage (Wachovia Securities) in the United States. Much of the growth in the company's operations has taken place over just the past five years, stretching Wachovia offices from the East Coast out to California. This rapid expansion has driven an increased focus on improving collaboration across these long distances, preferably without requiring travel. Although in-person meetings will always be an important part of the financial services business, travel significantly impacts employee productivity and drives up costs. Wachovia clearly needed options to address its ever-increasing geographic footprint, particularly between key regional locations.

Jim Ditmore, Wachovia's CTO, offered the following insight:

> You wouldn't think getting from Charlotte, North Carolina (corporate headquarters), to Richmond, Virginia (Wachovia Securities headquarters), would be a big deal; they're not that far apart. But because Richmond is not a hub airport, there are relatively few flights. We also have a major site in San Antonio, Texas, and we would like to be able to collaborate with the folks in that office without having to be there in person. Further, now that we have facilities out in California, it can take a whole day to execute a meeting for a group of our key executives and senior managers. So, we have been looking for an alternative to help drive our productivity, yet maintain the same level of collaboration that you get in a face-to-face meeting.

At the same time, Wachovia's mission is to be the best in customer service. Technology is helping them to achieve both goals.

Wachovia has tried various collaboration technologies, including traditional videoconferencing. However, they experienced very low usage on their systems because employees thought that they were difficult to use and did not provide the collaborative experience they sought.

Finally, Wachovia decided to try a pilot of Cisco TelePresence technology, connecting the Charlotte headquarters with the Richmond headquarters for Wachovia Securities. Figure 11-8 shows an example of a TelePresence meeting room.

Figure 11-8 *Cisco TelePresence (3000) Creates an "In-Person" Collaborative Experience for Teams at Wachovia*

Ditmore recently commented on how their TelePresence pilot is helping Wachovia employees:

> We are using Cisco TelePresence to help our people be more productive with their time. It comes down to effective collaboration. If people can get together, without having to get on a plane, that drives up their productivity and the quality of their collaboration dramatically. With TelePresence, you really do feel like you're in the room with everyone. To me, that means you can have those difficult discussions, those highly productive discussions that you just can't have over the phone or with a typical video or audio conference. The spontaneity and nonverbal communication that occur are valuable for any conversation, and that's really where TelePresence comes in. It

gives us all the advantages of face-to-face collaboration without many of the costs. So that's the driver. Our line-of-business leaders have all seen it and are really enthusiastic. And they're all signing up for time, which, to me, is really where the rubber meets the road.

When it comes to measuring its impact on their business, Ditmore continued:

We use a number of metrics. The first is the occupancy rate of the TelePresence room, because we know that will then drive how many folks didn't have to travel to be present at a meeting. We will also survey those individuals to determine how many trips they avoided as a result of using the conference room and what productivity they feel they gained. We'll use that to calculate the hard benefits in terms of saved time and cost from the travel avoidance. In addition, we'll look at what we get out of improved collaboration (because in some cases, people would not have bothered to travel); they might have just dialed in to a conference call. Then it would have been a less-effective meeting.

In early surveys, the top benefits seen by Wachovia users include the following:

- Improved sense of community/team
- Improved communications and collaboration
- Improved management
- Better work/life balance because of reduced travel
- More productive meetings

Being able to collaborate more effectively and to get to faster decisions while reducing expenses and increasing employee productivity all added up to a powerful combination for Wachovia. The reduced travel also helps them support their green initiatives. Jim Kittridge, senior IT leader adds, "[With TelePresence] we can support our goal of expense reduction while also furthering our corporate commitment to environmental responsibility."

Jim Ditmore concluded his comments with the following:

If the early pilot is as successful as we think, then I would say this will become part of our infrastructure. Wherever we have a significant corporate site, we'll probably put a TelePresence room in because that would help us handle things across distance. We do not invest lightly in new technology. The reason we've chosen Cisco TelePresence is that we've closely reviewed and evaluated all of the collaboration applications like this on the market, and we really feel this one is head and shoulders above what else is out there. It really delivers on that promise of collaboration.

Summary

As these examples show, video helps financial services firms improve internal processes and external customer relationships equally, with benefits including the following:

- Improved relationships, communications, collaboration, and training
- Accelerated revenue
- Extended expertise to customers and employees in remote locations
- Enhanced, high-touch customer service across distance
- Better work/life balance for employees
- Support of corporate green initiatives by reducing travel
- Improved profitability and the creation of sustainable competitive advantage

In these highlighted cases, the firms generally implemented video for one specific purpose and yet ended up realizing a much broader range of benefits, many of which they had never considered. They also realized significant returns in a short period of time, in some cases as little as one quarter. This has enabled them to expand and add new functionality in a self-funding model and to further expand the benefits to the business.

CHAPTER 12

THE DOCTOR WILL SEE YOU NOW: TRANSFORMING HEALTHCARE WITH VIDEO

Executive Summary

Today, video solutions are providing hospitals, medical groups, and even governments with improved access to support and expertise, and helping to ensure that patients receive timely, effective, and safe delivery of care.

In this chapter, you will see how healthcare organizations are using video to

- Build and extend medical expertise

- Improve staff communications and collaboration

- Transform patient care

- Lower the cost of care

- Improve patient experience with new, innovative services

While healthcare is as much a critical public service as police and fire departments, it is also very much a business. Considerations such as staff productivity, communications, efficiency, and cost controls play as strong a role in day-to-day operations as the quality of patient care. At the same time, shortages of healthcare practitioners and aging populations have put significant strains on health systems worldwide. To address these issues, healthcare needs to transcend geographic and resource boundaries, and video has a key role to play in making that happen.

The Technology Transforming Healthcare

Technology has always played a strong role in healthcare. From X-ray machines to pacemakers to MRIs, technology has helped to diagnose, treat, and heal. Its use has expanded from purely medical applications to supportive roles in staff communications, digitizing and storing of patient records, and the processing of pharmaceutical orders. A natural extension is for technology to be applied in ways that enable telemedicine treatment (sometimes called telehealth) and remote patient monitoring using audio and video capabilities, including videoconferencing, store-and-forward imaging, streaming video, and wireless video communications. From clinics to doctors' offices to hospital operating rooms (see Figure 12-1), video is becoming as much a part of medical care as stethoscopes. Let's take a look at how we got to this point.

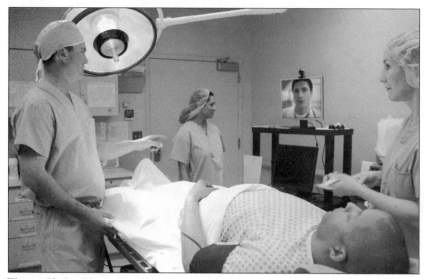

Figure 12-1 *Physician Using Video Consultation During a Surgical Procedure*

The earliest recorded use of telemedicine was a 1950s Nebraska project using closed-circuit television to provide mental health services from a university medical center to a state hospital 100 miles (160 km) away. Then, in the early 1960s, the NASA space flight telemedicine program began so that medical personnel on the ground could monitor astronauts' biomedical responses to space flight.

These elaborate deployments are, of course, unique. Because of the expense of equipment and lack of available high bandwidth for video, it is really only within the past 15 years that telemedicine has become more widely available. The most common method for remote clinical diagnosis uses desktop, room, and portable videoconferencing units. Video telemedicine has been practiced most often in underserved rural areas or in situations where patient transport poses a hazard. In the case of the former, a rural doctor or nurse typically consults with a specialist physician based at a metropolitan or university hospital. Using videoconferencing technology and specially adapted medical tools, the remote doctor can see the patient, talk with the local healthcare practitioner, hear a heartbeat through a remote stethoscope, see images from ear/nose/throat exams, or examine skin conditions. Although enormously beneficial, this application has typically required leased T1 telephone or ISDN lines, which can be prohibitively expensive. In addition, telemedicine services were not always covered by patient insurance plans, further limiting early adoption. However, the Balanced Budget Act of 1997 and Benefits Improvement Act of 2000 finally made telemedicine eligible for coverage by Medicare payments, enabling many citizens in rural areas to receive video medical treatments of all types.

Because of a number of issues (legal, cost, patient/physician acceptance of the technology, payment issues), the most common use of video telemedicine has actually been to provide healthcare to prison populations. Prisoners have a legal right to medical treatment, but the cost and danger of transporting them to a medical facility is extremely high, because at least two guards and possibly an ambulance are required for transport. However, the high risk factor more than cost-justified using telemedicine in many states and paved the way for its use by other organizations.

Now that we have a better appreciation for video's past role in healthcare, let's take a look at how it is being used today. The first step toward the use of video in many medical environments has been to accommodate for digital video imaging (sometimes known as picture archiving and communications system, or PACS) and record storage. This typically requires a network and bandwidth upgrade to support the volume of information being transferred and stored. The offshoot for organizations who have done this is that they can now support full motion video for telemedicine and related applications. These new capabilities have a significant impact on the quality of patient care, allow staff to collaborate and communicate differently, help organizations to build and extend expertise, offer new services to patients and their families, and lower the cost of care. The ten case studies that follow provide real-world examples of the many innovative uses for video in healthcare today. Let's start with two that impact the medical staff directly.

Building Expertise and Boosting Communication: Alabama Department of Rehabilitation Services

The Alabama Department of Rehabilitation Services is a state agency that offers medical, educational, vocational, and independent-living services to children and adults with disabilities. The department has two dozen locations throughout Alabama, and rehabilitation professionals need to attend meetings, conferences, and training sessions to maintain certifications and stay up-to-date on best practices. However, limited time and budget made it difficult for staff to attend every mandatory meeting in person. They had looked to the state's existing ISDN-based videoconferencing system as an option for certain meetings, but at a cost of $80,000 per year to run, it was too expensive to be a practical alternative. They needed a more cost-effective way to enhance the team's collaboration and educational access. In the end, they decided to migrate the state's existing ISDN-based system to one that was IP based. The department was pleasantly surprised to find that the new solution cost 90 percent less than maintaining the existing one, which allowed for the addition of new sites. Director Buck Jordan addressed their experience:

> We're spending approximately $58,000 total during this first year and already have more than 10 of our sites running. With Cisco technology, we can run data and video across the same circuit, so we are saving a lot of money.

Their solution features both desktop and room videoconferencing systems and accommodates both point-to-point and multipoint calls. Weekly staff meetings are now conducted via videoconferencing, saving numerous hours of travel time and thousands of dollars in phone-conference call charges. The staff is also able to meet federal mandates to achieve the highest degree and certification possible by participating from their offices in e-learning courses from colleges and universities instead of having to travel.

Improving Employee Communications and Collaboration: Niagara Health

The Niagara Health System (NHS) is Ontario, Canada's largest multisite hospital group, consisting of 6 hospitals and an ambulatory care center serving 434,000 residents across 12 municipalities. The NHS has approximately 4200 employees, including 1800 nurses and 650 physicians. Care provided is wide ranging, and includes approximately 186,000 patient visits annually at the emergency departments and urgent care centers, and more than 184,000 ambulatory clinic and community program visits.

A recognized leader in the healthcare industry, NHS needed a way to enhance employee communications across its seven, geographically dispersed sites. The NHS is also dedicated to the continuous improvement of its patient services and was looking for innovative technology solutions that would enable the organization to meet this goal while achieving operational cost savings. After deploying a converged voice, video, data, and wireless network, they were able to connect in-house and remote staff to one another, strengthening communication and enabling higher-quality patient care. Clinical staff are now taking advantage of new videoconferencing capabilities to collaborate about patient case loads, share their expertise, and participate in certification training without having to travel.

These two examples clearly illustrate how video can help healthcare practitioners build and maintain certifications, communicate more efficiently, collaborate more effectively, and enhance many other day-to-day activities.

Extending Expertise While Providing Improved Patient Care

As noted previously, there is a shortage of physicians of all types in many parts of the world, particularly in rural and remote areas. The next six examples demonstrate how video, and now TelePresence, is being used to extend medical expertise and services across town, across countries, and around the globe (everything from rounds to regular checkups to lifesaving to critical care).

Robots Enable Physicians to Be in Two Places at One Time

UCLA and Johns Hopkins are world-renowned medical facilities; they stay that way in part because they focus on using innovative approaches to treatment. In the past few years, both organizations have begun to use remote presence robots to improve patient care. With systems from a company called InTouch Technologies, doctors can now project themselves to another location via remote-controlled mobile robots, which enable them to move, see, hear, and talk as though they were actually there (see Figure 12-2).

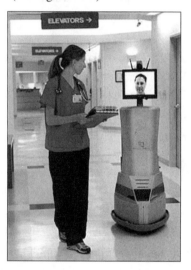

Figure 12-2   *InTouch Remote Presence Robot Enables Doctor and Nurse to Discuss Patient Case*

The 5-foot, 4-inch robots feature a flat-screen computer monitor and a two-way audio/video feed. They are guided by a physician using a joystick from a computer console in another location, such as an office, clinic, another hospital, or even home. The robot enables physicians to "beam in" to the hospital, visit with patients, and consult with colleagues and staff; the physicians can move, see, hear, and talk as though they were actually there. The screen rotates 340 degrees and pivots up and down, enabling the physician to see and hear everything going on around the robot, and to check injuries and monitor equipment readouts. The robot is not meant to replace important daily interaction between patients and physicians, but it does serve as an extension to traditional patient-physician interaction, improving communication and increasing patient (and family) satisfaction. The robots provide the organizations with a wide range of benefits, including the following:

- **Providing consistent, high-quality services more effectively to a greater number of both patients and staff**: When travel time is reduced between all the locations they serve, physicians can be more available for consultations.

- **Extending healthcare professionals' presence to anywhere they might be needed at the right times**: For example, a specialist might not always be available onsite when a patient needs a procedure, dressing change, or emergency surgery, but a specialist can be available via video.

- **Making expert consultation available during off hours**: Many specialists are generally available on an on-call basis during overnight shifts. Hospital staff can typically access them only by phone for consultations, requiring the specialist to rely on verbal descriptions to make a diagnosis. The robots allow specialists to go into the patient room directly as if they were there and examine the patient for themselves.

- **Increasing the frequency of patient contact**: Today, specialists are onsite only about 40 percent of the time. However, the efficiency of the robots enables physicians to conduct "telerounds," adding another round of patient visits per day. When specialists are "available," particularly in wards such as the ICU, the rates of morbidity and mortality, length of stay, and cost of care all decrease.

- **Extending expertise for training and supervisory purposes**: Physicians can conduct training and supervise medical student procedures even from remote locations.

Survey results from physicians who have used the robots indicate that

- 96 percent said the technology allows them to advance or improve patient care and learn more about their patient's condition.

- 88 percent said the robots save time, increasing physicians' overall efficiency.

- Three out of four said the systems allow them to accelerate the time of patient discharge.

Bringing Life-Saving, Specialty Care to Rural Regions: Ontario Telemedicine Network

The Ontario Telemedicine Network (OTN) in Ontario, Canada is another excellent example of both extending medical expertise. In this case, OTN extends medical care to an underserved rural population using video, and the technology helps to improve the speed of care in critical, life-or-death situations.

The northern part of the province is physically the size of Texas and California combined, but its population numbers just a few million. Consequently, there is a shortage of specialists throughout most of the province. In response, public and private sector partners joined together in 1998 to establish what is now known as the Ontario Telemedicine Network, an extensive telehealth service designed to provide remote consultations, medical education, and patient support to remote hospitals and clinics. Two other telemedicine networks also came about during this same period, but all three were challenged by technology incompatibility issues. In 2006, the three merged into a single secure platform known as Ontario Telemedicine Network. OTN uses a private IP network (dedicated to healthcare applications) to link nearly 400 sites in the north to large urban teaching hospitals. They currently facilitate more than 32,000 video consultations per year (see Figure 12-3), and run an extensive number of educational broadcasts using the same technology. A government grant allows them to directly pay consulting physicians, bypassing the typical billing problems for remote telehealth consultations.

Figure 12-3 *Dr. Soucie Uses the OTN to Consult with a Nurse and Patient from His Office (courtesy of Ontario Telemedicine Network)*

Although patients can access more than 30 specialties, perhaps the most dramatic application of the power of the application is within the neurology and cardiology practices. Because winter in Canada features lots of snow and ice, a trip from more rural areas to see a specialist in Toronto can be not only a long trip, but a potentially dangerous one. The treacherous roads also mean that a patient who needs rapid treatment, such as in the case of a heart attack or stroke, might not be able to reach a specialist in time before the damage becomes irreparable. The telemedicine application enables patients to go instead to their local hospital, connect via video to a specialist in a major city, and be diagnosed at the earliest onset of symptoms when life-saving treatment can still be administered. Some of the physicians affiliated with OTN are also equipped with virtual private networked laptops, enabling them to do consulting from their personal office or even from home (see Figure 12-4). Of patients who have used OTN's capabilities, 96 percent reported that they were satisfied or very satisfied, and would use it again if appropriate. It has significantly reduced the cost of delivering service and transporting patients by $8 million, and has reduced hospitalizations among people in the region.

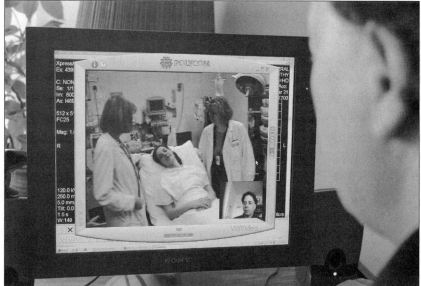

Figure 12-4   *Doctor Frank Silver Uses a Networked Laptop and the OTN to Conduct a Video Consultation from His Home Office (courtesy OTN)*

Video Brings Critical Care to the Littlest Patients: Adena Health System

Adena Health System, a healthcare organization that serves the residents of a 10-county region in southern Ohio, deployed a Cisco networked video solution that included high-definition videoconferencing and clinical imaging. With this solution in place, Adena Health System can now link its main facility, Adena Regional Medical Center, to Nationwide Children's Hospital in Columbus as part of an ongoing initiative to provide a higher level of care for patients, particularly expert neonatal care.

Adena Health System's telemedicine initiative began in 2006 when it connected its neonatal department with Nationwide Children's Hospital's neonatal ICU via video. Adena Regional Medical Center provides outstanding care for mothers and newborns, but it has limited access neonatal critical-care specialists. For that reason, Adena doctors typically had little choice but to transfer any newborn that might need critical care to Nationwide Children's Hospital, located 70 miles (113 km) north. Adena typically transferred more newborns to Children's Hospital than any other provider outside Columbus. These transfers placed significant emotional and financial strain on families and newborn patients, and often separated newborns from still-recovering mothers.

Using video, specialists at Nationwide Children's Hospital can evaluate newborns with their own eyes. Therefore, they can make more accurate diagnoses, share test results and imaging films, and fully participate in treatment as if they were standing in the same room. For families, it means advanced care close to home and fewer newborns that need to be transferred. In just its first year of operation, the project helped cut the number of patients transferred in half. For those who are transferred, the medical staff at the receiving end are much better prepared to provide treatment; they have truly "seen" the child before he or she arrives at their door (see Figure 12-5). Families of transferred children can also use the videoconferencing system to see their little ones and keep up-to-date on their care without having to make a trip to do so.

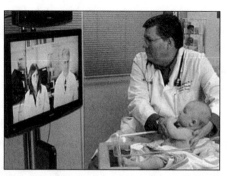

Figure 12-5   *Doctors in Adena Health System Use High-Definition Video to*
Provide Neonatal Care

As Adena Health System focuses on enhancing patient care, delivering cost savings, and increasing productivity, they are exploring other advanced uses of video. One area being explored is virtual classrooms in the campus near the medical center. The campus will comprise a four-year nursing school in collaboration with Wright State University in Dayton, Ohio University in Athens, and other Adena educational partners. In these virtual classrooms, physicians from anywhere in the world will use a telemedicine application to teach remote students. The new facility will also support video recording and broadcasting.

The impact of Adena's success with this project is already being felt on a broader scale. The Federal Communications Commission recently awarded a $14 million grant to build a fiber-optic network connecting healthcare providers across 15 counties in southern Ohio. Based on their own success, Adena was chosen as one of the organizations that will oversee the new project.

Beyond Videoconferencing: TelePresence Becomes the Next Step in Telemedicine in Scotland and New Zealand

In 2008, the Scottish Centre for Telehealth (SCT) and the National Health Service began the world's first trial of Cisco HealthPresence, a new patient-care delivery concept based on Cisco TelePresence technology. SCT develops and disseminates best practices, standards, protocols, and processes that support telehealth solutions. It supports a range of projects that contribute toward preventive care, improved standards, and speed of care.

Cisco HealthPresence combines life-size high-definition video, rich audio, and call-center technology to create a virtual face-to-face experience for patients and caregivers who are remote from each other (see Figure 12-6). The HealthPresence platform also interfaces with medical diagnostic equipment, such as stethoscopes and otoscopes, and monitors that can measure weight, blood pressure, temperature, pulse rate, and lung function to capture the physiological condition of the patient. An attendant is available to operate the medical devices on behalf of the caregiver/patient and to maintain the technology.

Figure 12-6   *Cisco HealthPresence Enables Patients and Medical Staff to Meet Virtually "Face to Face"*

The trial is designed to test the effectiveness of HealthPresence and patient and caregiver satisfaction. The goal is to improve the quality of what had previously been telephone-only advice and triage. It also brings healthcare services to remote and rural areas, where recruitment and retention of medical personnel is proving increasingly difficult, and helps extend healthcare beyond traditional doctors' office hours. Clinicians believe that being able to see patients and have all of their physiological parameters at the same time will improve patient care. Early reaction has been very positive, with physicians citing its ease of use and simple setup.

Gordon Peterkin, director of the Scottish Centre for Telehealth, spoke of his experience:

> In our efforts to provide better patient care and utilize our medical
> staff to the full, solutions such as HealthPresence enable us to offer
> convenience for patients and service efficiency for our doctors. We

look forward to drawing upon the results from this trial to optimize our regional and national healthcare delivery resources.

Building upon the trial in Scotland, New Zealand's West Coast District Health Board (DHB) announced in July 2008 that it would begin the first global trial of Cisco HealthPresence between two different organizations: Buller Health, in the town of Westport; and Grey Base Hospital, about 60 miles (97 km) away. This trial will help enable medical providers in two remote locations to better scale resources, collaborate on cases, and provide patients with more convenient access to the medical expertise of a multispecialty team.

DHB provides patient care to more than 32,000 people throughout some of the most remote areas of New Zealand. Cisco HealthPresence enables medical professionals to break down the distance barrier and provide direct support to these areas. Some patients can now be assessed by specialists without travel, reducing patient transfers and related costs. Specialists also benefit. Using the technology allows them to see more patients than they previously could, because they do not need to spend much time traveling to and from remote locations. It will also make medical services more sustainable and resilient to fluctuations in workforce availability and patient demand.

Improving Healthcare and Quality of Life: Afghanistan's Telemedicine Project

In 2007, Roshan, the leading telecom operator in Afghanistan, launched a first-of-its-kind telemedicine solution to expand healthcare access and delivery across the country. Using broadband technology, wireless video consultation, and digital image transfer, the telemedicine project is providing hospitals with real-time access to specialist diagnosis, treatment, and training expertise from abroad. Broadband technology provides high-speed access for the transfer of medical imaging, video, data, and voice. Applications include the capability to send X-rays, ultrasound and CT scans for evaluation in real time, and the technology enables e-learning and training through video consultation.

Even though the service is new, the expectation is that there will be an average of 10 to 15 videoconferences between hospitals per month, with the numbers increasing over time. Capabilities will be gradually expanded to address different services and procedures, including evaluation of tissue samples and the online performance of medical and surgical procedures.

Amirzai Sangin, the minister of communications and information technology, offered the following:

> Our government is striving to improve the quality of life of our people, and providing quality healthcare is one of our top priorities. Telemedicine is the perfect marriage of the speed, convenience, and cost-effectiveness of wireless and broadband technology. This innovative use of technology and telecommunications to enhance healthcare delivery will help underpin our efforts to meet the nation's other development challenges.

These case studies provide great examples of how video extends medical expertise whenever and to wherever it is needed, and in a wide range of applications. In every case, it benefits the medical staff and patients alike; it improves the speed, depth, and quality of care while lowering costs, travel times and stress involved. Patient acceptance and satisfaction is quite high, and with high-speed bandwidth becoming more and more ubiquitous, it becomes hard to imagine a place where video could not be used to provide medical care in a similar way.

The last two examples in this chapter address innovative uses of video in healthcare environments, where organizations chose to think differently about their basic operating processes and chose to invest in video in ways that would help them scale, improve existing patient services or provide new ones, and in both cases, improve their own image with the local area that they serve.

Connecting Clinicians and Patients with Innovative Services: California's Healthcare Interpretive Network

Language barriers are of particular concern in healthcare, where life-and-death decisions are made and medical regimens are agreed on through discussions between healthcare professionals and patients. Without good communication, patients' knowledge of their disease, treatment advice, and complications are compromised, while doctors struggle to understand symptoms or recommend treatment. This is why interpretive services are so critical.

In California, 40 percent of its residents now speak a language other than English. In response to this growing dynamic within the state, the Health Care Interpreter Network (HCIN) of Northern California was created in 2006. The HCIN is a system of shared remote interpreter services operated by seven Northern California public hospitals. Using an IP-based call center to provide access to trained interpreter services, participating providers use interpreters at their own hospitals or at other hospitals through videoconferencing and other telecommunications technologies. Figure 12-7 shows an example of the type of portable equipment that is brought into the patient's room to connect the healthcare provider with an interpreter. Calls are routed by several criteria including the hospital that initiated the call, special interpreter skills requested (such as particular language), special medical expertise required, or by male or female interpreter. These technologies enable member hospitals to eliminate time, distance, and language as barriers to effective communication between clinicians and patients. This program offers hospital staff rapid access to trained interpreters among all participating providers, and interpreters no longer have to travel between the facilities they support. Manual searches for an interpreter used to take up to an hour, but responses to a call now average just 22 seconds, and no response takes longer than 3 minutes. The service is also available 24 hours a day, and emergency calls can be "bumped" to the head of the call queue if necessary.

Figure 12-7   *Patients and Physicians Can Talk with One of Many Skilled Interpreters Using Portable, Rollabout Video Carts*

The interpreter network currently handles approximately 3500 video-conference and phone calls per month. Before this solution was available, 42 percent of hospital staff said that difficulties getting an interpreter posed a serious problem in the provision of care, and 79 percent of physicians said patients lacked understanding of medications, preventive care, and self-care instructions because of a language barrier. Since implementation, fewer than 20 percent of providers reported that they perceive confusion over procedures as the result of a language barrier. Every staff member surveyed found that HCIN was convenient, made them more productive, simplified patient communications, and improved the quality of patient care. There are now plans to expand the service to other languages, including American sign language.

HCIN hospitals are not alone in this success. Alameda County Medical Center and San Francisco General Hospital have implemented a similar video medical interpretation project of their own. Despite having a large in-house staff, wait times for an in-person interpreter used to be as long as two hours. Using the video-based solution, a clinician instead rolls a portable video station into the room and places a video call to the call center, which transfers incoming requests to the appropriately skilled interpreter. With the solution in place, wait times have been drastically reduced, and patients are very happy. Post-visit surveys indicate that patients feel like they are seen faster. When patients were asked to rank video services on a scale of 1 to 3, with 3 being "completely satisfied," the average score was 2.9. Both Alameda and San Francisco General found that they could make better use of their interpreters, too. Because they no longer need to travel to see each patient in person, less time is spent on each request. In fact, the average request time has been reduced from 37 minutes to just 17 minutes. Further analysis showed that the solution saves approximately 14,500 hours per year, or the equivalent of 7 full-time interpreters at a cost of more than $400,000. With these savings, language services can also be provided to departments that did not have professional interpreters before.

In both of these examples, the cost savings from not having to rely on commercial interpreter services or hiring additional staff simply to keep up with demand is a significant benefit. Instead, the organizations in these examples have chosen to think differently about how they can use their resources more effectively *and* improve the quality of the patient experience at the same time. These results are particularly important to public hospitals because they have to demonstrate commitment to patient services, good use of taxpayer dollars, and compliance with regulatory requirements such as equal access laws. Figure 12-8 shows video interpretation being conducted using sign language.

Figure 12-8   *Sign Language Interpretation Being Provided over Video*

Innovation Improves Image and Patient Care: Arras Hospital

Arras Hospital in northern France has 1200 beds and 2000 staff, treating more than 100,000 patients each year. Back in 2001, however, its extreme difficulties in providing care and maintaining financial viability prompted its leadership team to undertake an ambitious project to renovate many of its facilities. As part of this renovation, Arras conducted a complete upgrade of its network infrastructure, moving to a converged network for data, voice, and video. Its primary video application was to support digital imaging (PACS), but expanded bandwidth and video capability enabled Arras to add three other important applications.

First, they added videoconferencing capability with neighboring hospitals in France to expand the pool of medical experts who could contribute to patient care on difficult cases (see Figure 12-9). They made their own systems and records available to these remote physicians to encourage collaboration.

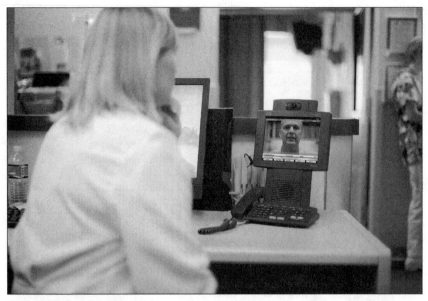

Figure 12-9 *Doctors Discuss a Patient's Case Using a Desktop Video Phone*

Second, they were able to add video surveillance to the hospital complex, with the goal of maintaining safety in certain patient wards, such as clinical psychiatry.

Third, in 2004, Arras began a pilot program in which mothers could monitor their babies in the neonatal ICU via video. The pilot was so successful that the hospital has begun expanding this capability to other patient units to enable those undergoing longer stays to maintain links to family, school, and work. Arras is also reaching beyond hospital boundaries to begin remote telemedicine projects with the regional jail system and with regional patients engaging in ongoing rehabilitation and chronic-care services from home.

Reaction to the new capabilities from patients, physicians, and the public has been overwhelmingly positive. Arras's innovative approach has even garnered them two unique endorsements from the French National Health Authority. They have also been asked to report their results in improved quality of patient care, improved physician access, and cost optimization in an upcoming parliamentary session.

Summary

In nearly every part of the world today, telemedicine and telehealth initiatives are viable in terms of technology, bandwidth availability, cost, and patient/physician acceptance. Organizations that use video telemedicine applications are experiencing a number of significant benefits, including the following:

- Improved patient care, including better quality, greater speed, access to more medical expertise, and frequency of patient/physician contact

- Shorter hospital stays and reduced rates of hospitalization for patients

- Improved staff communications, collaboration, and productivity

- Improved training and certification opportunities

- Reduced cost of care

- Competitive advantage and improved organizational public image in a unique marketplace that has both public and governmental pressures

The success of these deployments in clinics and hospitals leads to the next logical step: their availability in a home setting. Doctors tend to try to send patients home as soon as possible because they tend to feel better and heal faster in an environment where they are most comfortable. Because consumers have HDTVs and broadband at home in ever-greater numbers, it is not much of a leap to adding a camera and being able to contact your medical provider from your living room. When it is as simple as turning on your TV, it gives a whole new meaning to "the doctor will see you...*now*."

CHAPTER 13

THE INFLUENCE OF IP VIDEO ON OTHER INDUSTRIES

Executive Summary

This chapter discusses the use of video in several industries, including high tech, real estate and hospitality, sports and entertainment, and a cross-industry effort to give back to the community. Specifically, the chapter covers the following:

- **High tech**: TelePresence enables high-tech companies to increase agility, improve internal communication, and reduce travel. It also enables some types of firms to provide new service offerings that create competitive advantages for themselves and their customers. IP video is also used by firms to help clarify partnerships and to announce new alliances.

- **Real estate and hospitality**: The Cisco Connected Real Estate (CCRE) solution enables property managers and developers to build a foundation network in a facility, which can be leveraged by operators and tenants to reduce cost, to enable growth and new revenue opportunities, and to gain competitive advantages.

- **Sports and entertainment**: The Cisco Connected Sports solution enables traditional stadiums and sports facilities to transform the guest experience, to reduce operational cost, and to generate new revenue streams.

- **Multi-industry goodwill**: IP video offers many possibilities for companies to collaborate and give back to their communities. Operation Military Connect is one shining example of such an effort.

Besides the successful applications of video within the documented verticals for education, financial services, and healthcare, there are many other notable use cases. Through video, competitive advantages are developed, partnerships are both created and clarified, security is improved, new revenue streams are created, and entertainment experiences are enhanced.

This chapter provides selected examples of how video either has or will produce positive results within the high-tech, real estate, hospitality, sports, and entertainment industries. It also demonstrates how several different industries can collaborate to offer nontraditional video services by connecting families and by giving back to the community.

Video Use in High-Tech Organizations

High-tech companies, including service providers, are using video to improve their business, increase operational efficiencies, and gain competitive advantage. They are also using video to clarify partnerships and announce new strategic alliances. High-tech firms are one of the early adopters of TelePresence technology, primarily because of their technical knowledge and supply of network bandwidth. Companies such as Applied Materials, EMC, SAP, Yahoo!, and many service providers have all implemented TelePresence solutions for use with employees and customers.

The following sections provide an overview of how some of these firms are using video and the benefits they are achieving.

Software Developer Uses IP Video to Increase Agility and Reduce Travel

As a technology leader, SAP provides business software that includes enterprise resource planning and management solutions to address product development, supply chain management, and customer relationships. SAP products and services meet the needs of more than 75,000 customers that span small businesses to large multinational organizations. Ultimately, an SAP objective is to help customers accelerate their business innovation.

SAP employs more than 51,000 people from more than 50 countries worldwide. In April 2007, SAP announced its intent to deploy Cisco TelePresence to foster global collaboration, improve operational efficiencies, reduce travel, and become more agile. The first rooms were deployed in SAP headquarter offices in Walldorf, Germany; Palo Alto, California; and Newtown Square, Pennsylvania. After this initial deployment, SAP planned to deploy TelePresence to offices around the globe. Uwe Herold, CIO, SAP AG described the company's expectation for use of TelePresence as follows:

> By implementing the Cisco TelePresence system, we will take col-
> laboration to the next level by overcoming geographical barriers
> and enabling employees, customers, and partners to work together
> more effectively. We anticipate that TelePresence will substantially

enhance SAP's operational efficiency, particularly in the areas of new product development and customer engagement.

TelePresence usage at SAP was initially prioritized for executives to enable collaboration and improve customer interactions. It is now available to all employees to drive down travel costs and increase operational efficiency. Since SAP's initial deployment of CTS 3000 rooms, the company has expanded its Cisco TelePresence service offering to include the new larger CTS 3200 rooms, particularly to scale its training services and to handle larger meetings. Dietmar Bruder, vice president, SAP IT Infrastructure Services, offered the following:

> We are constantly rethinking success and what it takes to be agile, integrated, and flexible to respond to change and complex pressures, to do more, and deliver more effectively to our customers. With Cisco TelePresence, we can work faster without sacrificing any of the face-to-face interaction that is so crucial to gaining consensus across teams.

SAP is a thought leader for driving business process agility beyond the enterprise, enabling collaborative business transformation and creating innovative business models. Future plans for SAP involve a corporate objective to seamlessly integrate collaborative tools to provide customers with access to business information needed to perform critical business operations. By combining video solutions with SAP solutions, SAP will enable even more opportunities and compelling business transformation for their customers, and thus create a unique advantage over its competitors.[1, 2]

Executives Use Video to Clarify Partnerships

Many technology companies are involved in "co-opetition," wherein they can be viewed as competitors from one perspective but partners from another. This relationship is more common now than ever before as enterprises integrate their products and align roadmaps to improve their position in the global marketplace. Individual messages from each company can often be confusing to customers who would not expect traditional competitors to become trustworthy business partners. To reduce customer doubt and to increase the effectiveness of the message, announcements about new products and services are now often accompanied by a video. The video often consists of the top executives providing their corporate messaging and portraying a view that the partnership is strong between both companies.

Although this practice is not restricted to only high-tech organizations, the following examples show how Cisco, Microsoft, and Wipro have used video to clarify their intentions. It also shows the difference between taking a formal studio approach versus creating a quick, convenient video from your desktop.

Cisco and Microsoft Partnership

Microsoft is a global software company that competes and partners with Cisco. A Cisco/Microsoft alliance has been in place for more than ten years and spans multiple market segments and technology types. Through the combination of networking and software, both companies empower businesses and consumers with the tools and technologies to achieve success.

Cisco and Microsoft are two very competitive companies, and a lot of media attention is paid to how they are competing now or will compete in the future. What is often missing in the press is the amount of work that both do to promote interoperability of their products to improve the customer experience. Both companies have a key goal of making it clear to their customers that despite competition in some areas, minimizing interoperability challenges for customers remains an overall focus. Several videos have been released to confirm this messaging and each company's direction.[3]

Figure 13-1 shows Cisco Chairman and CEO, John Chambers, and Microsoft CEO, Steve Ballmer, in a formal recording studio in New York City making a joint video in August 2007. The video explains the direction on interoperability of products from the two companies, confirms the strength of the partnership, and confirms where they will continue to compete. Videos were accessible from both Cisco and Microsoft company websites and via other news services, providing additional avenues to deliver accurate messaging directly from the CEOs. All videos available through the Cisco News video portal are powered by the Cisco

Digital Media Solution, which provides a complete set of products to encode and manage video content for distribution to internal and external audiences.

Figure 13-1   *Cisco and Microsoft Clarify Their Partnership Using Video*

Cisco and Wipro Technologies

Another partnership example taking a less-formal approach in the use of video is the statement from Cisco and Wipro Technologies in October 2007, announcing a strategic alliance to jointly develop and deliver technology service solutions. Wipro is known as the world's largest independent provider of research and development services, and a provider of many other services. As a global services provider, Wipro Technologies delivers technology-driven business solutions to meet strategic objectives of their customers. The company is headquartered in Bangalore, India, and has 40+ Centers of Excellence that create industry-specific solutions. The alliance between Cisco and Wipro is designed to help both companies meet customer requirements, particularly in fast-growing global markets.

As part of the press release, Steve Steinhilber, vice president of Strategic Alliances at Cisco, created an informal video from his office to post on YouTube. The video addressed a number of questions that were expected from customers and press about why these two technology companies were forming an alliance and its potential impact.

Figure 13-2 shows the video recording of Steve that was posted on YouTube by the Cisco Public Relations department. Although YouTube started as a purely consumer video-sharing portal, it is now a common way for companies to reach a broader audience with their message. Executives can quickly create and upload video messages from their desktops, without going through the time and expense required to create a more formal studio recording.

Figure 13-2   *Cisco and Wipro Announce New Alliance*

Service Providers Use TelePresence to Improve Internal Communications and Provide New Service Offerings

Cisco TelePresence is an integral component within the Cisco Service-Oriented Network Architecture (SONA), which is an architectural framework that helps enterprises evolve their existing communications infrastructure into an intelligent information network. Working within the SONA framework, Cisco offers real-time collaborative applications such as voice and video that feature quality of service (QoS), security, and high availability on a single integrated network. All these components are of particular interest to the service provider industry.

Numerous telecommunication companies from across the globe are beginning to offer TelePresence services to their customers to enable business-to-business, next-generation communications. Many of these services were announced in 2007 by providers such as AT&T, British Telecom, and Rogers Communications, with deployments already well in progress. Most of these companies made internal deployments for employees their first phase of production, while planning for externally facing services.

To date, 43 service providers from across the globe have implemented Cisco TelePresence. It is increasing network traffic, and service providers have a great opportunity to grow their business. Randy Harrell, director of marketing for TelePresence Systems Business Unit, describes these deployments as not just for internal use, but to create inter- and intracompany network services. Randy also described a new trend:

> For the first time in a long time, applications like Cisco TelePresence
> are creating new packets of usage in service provider networks.

This trend is a major opportunity for the service provider industry, particularly for those early adopters.

AT&T TelePresence Initiative

By early 2008, AT&T had 11 Cisco TelePresence rooms deployed for internal use in their offices across the United States, and plans are in place to expand globally. Ronald E. Spears, AT&T group president of Global Business Services, described the result of their deployment:

> We're already seeing tremendous value from the ability to bring our
> management team together for face-to-face meetings on a regular
> basis, even though they are scattered across the country. Not only
> are we saving time and expense associated with travel, but we are
> much more productive.

In April 2008, AT&T announced a global plan to deliver the industry's first, fully managed Cisco TelePresence solution enabling companies to connect via TelePresence with their customers, suppliers, and partners worldwide. It includes a "meet-me" feature that enables intercompany connectivity to more than 750 Cisco TelePresence rooms worldwide, a feature that distinguished the AT&T solution from other TelePresence offerings at that time.

The fully managed solution covers end-to-end components such as AT&T-owned Cisco TelePresence equipment, installation, full monitoring and management of the application, network provisioning, virtual private network (VPN) transport, remote help desk service, and onsite equipment maintenance and repair. The solution is expected to be available in the second half of 2008 in 23 countries, with additional countries planned for 2009.

Trials between key U.S.-based multinational customers and selected companies headquartered outside the United States have already begun. Spears added the following:

> When we implement the intercompany TelePresence capability, we expect to quickly start using it to build closer relationships with our key customers throughout the world.

Much like the SAP integration example, Spears expects AT&T's TelePresence offering to help customers become more agile:

> The AT&T Telepresence Solution is the latest example of how we're helping enterprises to improve "business velocity" by enabling them to move quicker and make better business decisions.

AT&T is also focusing on industry-specific TelePresence applications for development across a range of industries that include health care, high-tech, retail, and government. These applications are expected to generate new revenue and growth possibilities for businesses while helping them reduce costs and improve productivity. An example is the retail industry, where supply chain efficiencies will help speed time to market. The expected solution will enable timely global collaboration among key stakeholders to discuss product-development activities, creating time-to-market advantages and improving competitive positions.[4]

British Telecom TelePresence Initiative

British Telecom (BT) has helped customers deploy internal TelePresence services from the time Cisco TelePresence was first announced. However, fast on the heels of AT&T, BT formally announced its launch of a fully managed TelePresence solution with business-to-business interoperability in June 2008. Known as BT One Source, it combines Cisco TelePresence technology with BT Conferencing's comprehensive management services to provide customers with a simple, reliable, and cost-effective immersive videoconferencing solution. A differentiator is that customers can tailor services based on their individual requirements. Combined with BT's support services and a global IP network presence in 170 countries, the BT One Source offering ensures QoS for every conference.

Jeff Prestel, general manager of BT Conferencing's Video Business Unit, highlighted another benefit of TelePresence for building relationships:

> In today's business environment connecting the right people at the right time is the key to building successful relationships. Video and TelePresence are taking conferencing to the next level, and One Source simplifies this solution for customers.[5]

BT One Source for Cisco TelePresence was initially launched in the United States, with plans for commercial availability in Europe and Asia-Pacific in September 2008. A demonstration of the solution was shown in April 2008 during the Cisco Expo in Berlin. It involved Media-Saturn, a consumer electronics retail giant based in Germany, which is one of BT's early customers for internal TelePresence. Figure 13-3 shows the demonstration at Cisco Expo of Media-Saturn conducting a meeting using the BT One Source service with Cisco TelePresence.

Wolfgang Lux, managing director Media-Saturn-Holding GmbH, described his experience using BT's service for Cisco TelePresence:

> We have been using this technology for more than a year now. The innovative character of TelePresence has enhanced our internal cross-border communications and shortened the distance between the countries. Furthermore, it helps us saving costs, and it will allow us now to include our external business partners in our videoconferences. BT

and Cisco are our dedicated partners in this area. Media-Saturn is cutting edge in the electronic retail business in Europe, and we always strive for excellence in everything we do. This is what we expect from our international partners as well.[6]

Figure 13-3   Demonstration of BT One Source During Cisco Expo 2008

Rogers Communications TelePresence Initiative

In Canada, the leading diversified service provider, Rogers Communications, selected Cisco TelePresence to improve productivity and collaboration between its offices across Canada. Besides improving internal collaboration, Edward S. Rogers, president and CEO of Rogers Communications, also expected other benefits:

> Rogers has always been an innovator in the deployment of leading-edge technology. We are particularly excited about the opportunities TelePresence presents to improve the way we communicate and collaborate internally and with our customers, partners, and shareholders. Using TelePresence will enable us to increase productivity while reducing travel.[7]

Numerous service providers are creating TelePresence services for their employees and their customer base. By choosing to deploy TelePresence solutions, these operators are using their IP network investments to improve their internal communications, to promote their technology leadership with new service offerings, and to grow their business.

IP Video Enables New Business Models in the Real Estate and Hospitality Sectors

Within the real estate development and hospitality industries, the IP network is transforming traditional property construction and management functions to create new business models and service offerings. Cisco Connected Real Estate and Public TelePresence are two models described in this section that are transforming these sectors.

Cisco Connected Real Estate (CCRE) is a solution that converges key building functions, such as communications, security, and building control systems, onto an IP network to create a digital foundation for the building. It enables improvements in workforce effectiveness, building performance, and physical security, resulting in reduced operating costs and streamlined management. The CCRE solution provides services such as wired and wireless high-speed network access; Cisco Unified Communications for IP voice, video, and data; TelePresence; IP video surveillance; and mobility solutions. Core building control functions such as lights, security, heating, ventilation, air conditioning, and elevators can be centrally managed to enable a more energy-efficient, safe, flexible, and customized building space.

CCRE offers competitive advantages not only to the real estate, construction, and property management industries, but also to related industries such as hotel operators, multiplexed retail outlets, and any business tenants where guests, shoppers, or occupants can also take advantage of new services. Many property developers, particularly in the Middle East, are adopting this strategy to enable a building foundation that will ultimately support next-generation services using video.

Public TelePresence is another new business model created from partnerships between Cisco and third-party partners such as hotels, convention centers, and commercial real estate owners. It incorporates a pay-per-use model to enable executives to leverage TelePresence-equipped suites across the globe, while avoiding the network and service investment to deploy TelePresence in their own organizations. It also enables a company to "try before you buy" to determine whether the results from the use of TelePresence will justify the investment for internal deployment.

The examples in the sections that follow demonstrate how IP video is used in Public TelePresence and as a component of CCRE to create competitive advantage and enable growth.

Luxury Hotels Create Competitive Advantage Through TelePresence

Taj Hotels Resorts and Palaces was established in 1903, and is considered one of Asia's largest and finest luxury hotel groups, with 61 hotels across India and 16 international locations. The company is part of the Tata Group, one of India's largest business conglomerates.

In July 2008, Taj Hotels Resorts and Palaces introduced publicly available, pay-per-use TelePresence services with lifelike high-definition video. The first five locations are focused on major business centers (Mumbai, Bangalore, London, Boston, and New York). Use of these high-tech rooms is billed at an hourly average cost of $500 per room. This is a cost-effective way to hold a virtual face-to-face meeting when travel is not an option.[8]

As a company that places high value on providing new innovations to corporate customers, Taj Hotels Resorts and Palaces has already introduced other leading technology systems such as WiFi, IP telephony, radio-frequency identification (RFID), and integrated entertainment systems to its hotels in India. The introduction of TelePresence is another example of this company objective. Raymond Bickson, managing director of Taj, stated the following:

> It is our constant endeavor to provide state-of-the-art, value-added services to our customers. With the TelePresence facility, we will be one of the first hospitality companies worldwide to offer this kind of cutting-edge technology.

These first five locations are the initial phase of the Taj deployment, and more locations are expected to be announced. Tata Communications, a service provider that is also owned by Tata Group, launched the service with Taj, and they plan to enable an ecosystem of TelePresence partners, further expanding availability options.

The key benefits of using such a service include the time and expense saved by not traveling, and it is a more cost-effective pay-as-you-use model versus making major corporate infrastructure investments. In addition, companies will use TelePresence to reduce their carbon footprints and demonstrate their commitment to the environment. For Taj Hotels Resorts and Palaces, offering TelePresence Meeting facilities gives it a competitive advantage over other global, luxury hotels.

Casinos Use IP Video to Enable Growth

The gaming industry is heavily regulated and requires the capture and retention of video to record activities within the casino. This video is used to ensure fair play and to monitor employees' procedural compliance. Casinos have traditionally relied on analog video to comply with regulations, but it is manually intense and does not scale well. IP video offers an opportunity for gaming operators to migrate to a more scalable solution with significant advantages.

The Pechanga Resort and Casino is one successful example of how a casino can migrate from analog video to IP video to enable future growth without impacting daily operations. Pechanga is a high-class resort located in Southern California, and offers a casino experience much like those in Las Vegas. Based on its expectations for significant growth, Pechanga's security and gaming surveillance groups decided to migrate their surveillance operations from an analog to a digital video solution that would easily scale to support that growth. Because they could not impact current operations, migrating to this solution during regular business hours was a challenge for the team.

The new IP video system had to meet many requirements, including the following:

- Compliance with gaming regulations for live and recorded video quality
- Ease of use for operators, including access to live and recorded video from the same keyboard
- Support redundancy and failover situations
- Support for safety and security applications in nongaming/nonresort operations (such as monitoring financial transactions, protecting property, and supporting loss prevention for retail and restaurant/bar operations)
- Support for safety and security services for people attending large events at the resort

Pechanga selected the Cisco Video Surveillance solution, which met all these requirements and was compatible with existing analog systems, to enable a smooth migration from analog to digital recorded video. The IP gateway decoders and the Cisco software enabled new capabilities for ease of use when investigating suspicious activity. The system also provided flexible options for managing the archive of video, which optimized storage. Figure 13-4 provides an overview of the Cisco Video Surveillance Manager that enables a customized, integrated video-surveillance network, meeting Pechanga's exact security requirements, while maintaining ease of use and scalability.

Figure 13-4   *Cisco Video Surveillance Manager*

The benefits to Pechanga from migrating to IP video were very positive from many perspectives. The surveillance and security groups can now spend more time protecting people and assets and less time on maintenance and searching for video. Investigations can now be done in minutes versus the hours it used to take, thus improving the overall player and guest experience. Pechanga was able to reuse several analog components in the solution, particularly the cameras, which avoided additional investments. For investigation staff, the hybrid solution minimized the training required because changes to user functions were limited. Finally, the interoperability functions of the Cisco IP gateways and Cisco Integrated Services Platforms allowed multiple vendor products to be integrated into the overall system. Pechanga was able to deploy a custom surveillance system that met requirements for every location of the property, including casino, hotel, restaurants, bars, parking lots, and more.

As Pechanga prepares for expansion as one of the largest U.S. casinos, it can now leverage a surveillance architecture that will enable it to scale and offer new services to guests. Through the use of video-analysis applications, a future operational benefit is the ability to reduce customer wait lines, leading to increased revenue opportunities and higher guest satisfaction. Overall, migrating to IP video has proven to be a wise investment for Pechanga.[9]

IP Video Takes Sports and Entertainment to the Next Level

Cisco Connected Sports solutions include innovative offerings to enable new revenue opportunities, enhance the fan experience, and streamline operations to make venues more efficient, flexible, and secure. It provides the following benefits to sports executives and venue operators:

- Create personalized experiences that increase fan loyalty, differentiate the venue, and extend their brand

- Create new, revenue-generating applications for advertising, ticketing, merchandising, and concessions

- Gain flexibility to support new types of events

- Streamline operations, improving staff productivity and responsiveness to fans

- Create more secure, efficient, and cost-effective facilities

Six custom modules are provided through Cisco Connected Sports, which can be implemented independently and allow operators to add or change services over time:

- StadiumVision Video

- Interactive Luxury Suites

- Safety and Security

- Interactive Fan Experiences

- Connected Fan Community

- Connected Stadium

Within a traditional stadium environment, these modules offer many video use cases. At the time of this writing, Cisco Field is under construction and will be home to the Oakland Athletics baseball team. This next-generation stadium will be equipped with the modules in the preceding list. A few of the unique use cases follow.

Digital signs can be customized to display advertising or other tailored messages based on where the sign is located, or based on the user preferences of the person viewing the sign. Examples of displays with this capability include those located in family sections at a stadium that can show child-appropriate content, and those deployed in luxury boxes that can display the latest sports scores of the viewers' favorite teams. These targeted communications increase the capability for increasing sales and user satisfaction.

Another use case of targeted advertising is at a concession stand. Toward the end of a game, concession operators can change their displays to announce discounted specials for surplus product. Figure 13-5 is an example of a concession display during a football game, with sodas on sale toward the end of a game.[10]

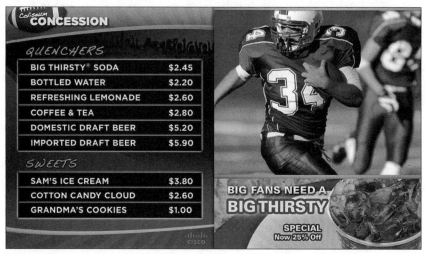

Figure 13-5   *Concession Stand with Tailored Messages*

With so much sports coverage available from other sources, stadium and team management need to find new ways to draw fans to the stadium to watch a game live. A use case that improves the fan experience is enabling fans to speak with players using TelePresence after a game. Fans can walk up to a kiosk and talk to their favorite players via high-definition video (almost as real as walking into the locker room after the game). The fan experience is also enhanced during a game by enabling anyone in the stadium to connect any video-enabled device wirelessly to any source of video that is being recorded. For instance, at Cisco Field, if a fan is sitting out in right field, that fan can use a smart phone or laptop to watch the live video that is being captured from behind home plate. Figure 13-6 is an example of this use case. Fans now have the control to see the game from any vantage point in the stadium. These experiences cannot be achieved at home and give fans an additional reason to pay for tickets to attend the live game.

Figure 13-6   *Fans Watch Video from Any Vantage Point in the Stadium*

Following are two case studies of how a sports stadium and a sports-focused museum can take advantage of video using modules from the Cisco Connected Sports solution to enable new customer experiences. Also, while writing the final content for this book, the 2008 Olympic Games were in progress in Beijing, China, and it provided an opportunity to share some of the latest benefits of using IP video, demonstrating how video has evolved to expand coverage and access to world sports news via television, computers, and smart phones.

Sports Stadiums Are Transformed Using IP Video

Watford Football Club was founded in 1881 and competes in professional leagues within England and Wales. The club spent the past 83 years based at the Vicarage Road stadium in London. In 2007, it started to upgrade the stadium with components of the Cisco Connected Sports and Connected Real Estate solutions. The video solutions to be deployed include a Unified Communications system, streaming video, and video surveillance, making it one of the most technologically advanced European stadiums. In addition to the network and communication system upgrades, Watford FC is also making physical improvements to access, seating, and corporate hospitality, which will enable it to take advantage of additional capabilities in the future.

Results of these upgrades are expected to transform the experience for fans and corporate guests, to significantly reduce costs, and to deliver efficiencies in stadium operations. Fans can already use smart cards to quickly go through turnstiles and to make purchases at the stadium. In the future, the smart cards will provide club management with valuable fan information to further enhance services and offer rewards. Corporate guests will enjoy new services such as video on demand in corporate boxes and access to team and match information. Stewards will use wireless devices to enhance crowd management and control.

During the off-season, the club will lease the building for corporate events, providing various business services, including videoconferencing and wireless networking, and thus create a new revenue stream for the facility. Plans are also in place to integrate and migrate the building management systems to IP so that services such as lighting, heating, closed-circuit television security, and digital signage can be managed centrally and more cost-effectively.

Through these upgrades, Watford FC will be able to improve customer service, control building management costs, offer new services to fans, and increase revenue opportunities. Katie Wareham, Watford FC's head of new projects, summarized their financial benefits as follows:

> Watford FC doesn't have the financial clout of the top U.K. and
> international football clubs, and yet we have deployed what we
> believe is the most powerful and fastest communications network of
> any sports venue in Europe. The Cisco solution means we can give
> fans a host of innovative services that transform their experience
> when visiting Vicarage Road and increase revenue potential outside

the football season. And we have an infrastructure that is more than capable of supporting additional services and applications for at least the next 10 years.[11]

Museums Enable New Experiences with IP Video

The Sports Museum of America (SmA) opened in New York City in May 2008, and is the first and only U.S. all-sports experience focused on the history, grandeur, and significance of sports in American culture. It is home to the Heisman Trophy and the Billie Jean King International Women's Sports Center. Visitors to the museum are able to interact with exhibits, memorabilia, and artifacts donated by individual athletes, over 50 partner sports organizations, and private collectors. SmA also provides a view of how future stadiums will enhance the fan experience through technology and new fan services.

The SmA is a state-of-the-art facility that selected Cisco to be the technology solution provider. John Urban, president of the Sports Museum of America, summarized his primary goals:

> We chose Cisco for the Sports Museum of America because of its superior technology solutions and industry leadership. Cisco has demonstrated a strong commitment to sports and is helping us create a unique experience for our visitors. We've designed SmA for sports fans first and foremost, and ensuring that they enjoy every moment of their visit and want to come back again is our primary goal.

Several of the implemented Cisco video technologies are part of the Cisco Connected Sports solutions and are used to help improve the fan experience. These technologies include the following:

- High-definition digital signage displays show a variety of content, including live sports video, ticketing information, special offers, sports facts, and real-time museum updates. These displays can also show custom exhibit messaging.

- Cisco TelePresence enables visitors to meet face to face with well-known athletes and sports celebrities and to participate in roundtable discussions. SmA can also use TelePresence to host events with experts, coaches, and sports leaders from around the world.

- Multiple kiosks are available throughout the Fan Culture Gallery,
  providing access to exciting interactive content, such as trivia, statistics,
  and game video on demand.

Other solutions include a sneak peek into the "Stadium of the Future" that will
make sporting events more interactive for fans and provide teams with new
revenue opportunities. It also includes the latest social-networking capabilities, to
virtually bring together communities of fans via the Internet.[12]

Figure 13-7 shows an interactive kiosk in use at the SmA displaying baseball
sports trivia and entertaining and educating baseball fans.

Figure 13-7   *Sports Museum of America Interactive Baseball Kiosk*

2008 Olympic Games Has Greater Coverage Through IP Video

Coverage of the 2008 Summer Olympics was taken to new levels as NBC
provided access to more video from all competitions and enabled the video to
be viewed from more types of devices. NBC chose Cisco to provide the

foundation network and video-encoding solutions, primarily to reduce complexity and risk.

NBC Universal presented a historic 3600 hours of coverage from China over 17 days. The digital video was captured in Beijing, edited in Los Angeles and New York, and delivered to three different device types: TVs, PCs, and smart phones. Craig Lau, vice president of IT, NBC Olympics, had this to say:

> The 2008 Olympic Games has the most ambitious media plan in history, with 3600 broadcast hours, 212 hours a day. It surpasses the combined total of all previous Summer Olympics.

The audience experience was significantly improved as viewers were able to use their PCs and laptops to access 2200 hours of video on demand and 3000 hours of highlights and encores. Mobility solutions enabled people to watch the video and view results on their smart phones. These new services offered more content to more devices and were expected to generate significantly more revenue for NBC through their advertising sales.

NBC solved many technical challenges to achieve its objective, delivering the following results:

- A high-bandwidth, high-performance network was created between Beijing and NBC studios in the United States to prioritize real-time video and to make recorded content and edits available as soon as possible.

- The number of employees required on location in Beijing was reduced by 400 people, avoiding the cost of travel and minimizing the environmental impact.

- The video from Olympic venues for broadband viewing was encoded and transmitted low resolution, enabling NBC to expand Internet coverage of more sports that were never previously available on the web.

In addition to the preceding results, several new capabilities were provided as part of the IP video solution. The ability to perform shot selections and extract high-resolution material from files as they were being recorded was a first-time achievement. NBC was able to provide more localized content to its affiliate stations than in past Olympics. For example, viewers in a particular town could see video clips of their local athletes. Figure 13-8 shows the NBC Olympics website and the options to view recorded or live video from the event.

Figure 13-8   *Video Options from the NBC 2008 Olympics Website*

In summary, when describing the requirements of the networking components to support the Olympic Games, Lau added the following:

> We probably have the most demanding network environments in the world because we're moving gigabyte-sized files, where most administrative offices are moving megabyte-sized files. The Cisco network solution accelerates our ability to make good decisions in terms of content and quality. Cisco is a trusted partner, and in the demanding IT environment for the Olympic Games, we depend on trusted relationships. We have absolute deadlines for when Olympics coverage begins and ends. Cisco technologies help us exceed expectations and meet our timetables in an unforgiving environment.[13]

Cross-Industry Effort Uses TelePresence to Connect Families

The final example of this chapter demonstrates how multiple industries can partner together for a more philanthropic cause to connect distributed families and give back to the community. Cisco, Verizon Business, Wal-Mart, SkyPort Global Communications, and the United Service Organizations (USO) are helping to provide virtual family reunions via Cisco TelePresence for U.S. troops serving in Iraq.

It all began with a conversation between Cisco Chairman and CEO John Chambers, and Wal-Mart CEO Lee Scott at the World Economic Forum in Davos, Switzerland, in 2007. They discussed new ways to use TelePresence technology, including recognizing and thanking U.S. military troops and families for enduring the hardships and making the sacrifice of living apart for the duration of their tours of duty. A short while later, Operation Military Connect was created.

Four major companies participated in the effort with the U.S. military to create the opportunity for virtual family visits. Cisco provided the TelePresence units and satellite systems, Verizon contributed network bandwidth to connect the locations, Wal-Mart hosted the systems at stores close to each home base, and SkyPort provided satellite services and installed the satellite ground links at the two bases. Wal-Mart employees built and decorated special rooms in its stores to allow the families privacy and comfort. The sponsorship of the USO and U.S. military helped the project progress smoothly.

John Chambers, chairman and CEO of Cisco, said this:

> Our companies are very proud to join together to honor and recognize our troops and their loved ones. We hope military families will take advantage of this technology and connect with our service men and women overseas during the upcoming holidays.

The effort enabled troops based in Iraq to connect with friends and family members back home. The free connections were available 24 hours a day, 7 days a week, from April 2 to July 6, 2008, covering many special family holidays. The service linked two remote bases in Iraq to two Wal-Mart stores located near Camp

Pendleton in California and Fort Drum in New York. John Killian, president of Verizon Business, stated the following:

> Verizon Business is proud of the technology we deploy to help members of the U.S. armed forces stay in touch with their families at home. The women and men serving overseas make sacrifices every day, and we hope this effort will help them feel closer to their loved ones by being able to sit across from each other and talk, even though they are located at opposite ends of the world.

Traditional videoconferencing has been intermittently available, but the Cisco TelePresence deployment is the first lifelike communications between these particular troops and their families back home. The families are using the technology to reconnect with loved ones, see children, and even hold virtual birthday parties. Figure 13-9 shows Major Doug Thornton, his wife, Julie, and their children, Matthew and Sydney, during one of many TelePresence visits. Doug was based at a forward operating base in Iraq, and his family was back in New York. Nate Mayfield, the Cisco project manager for the Wal-Mart account, was there during their first visit and described the happy event:

> Doug called his wife in the early morning and told her to go to Wal-Mart and that he would see her when she got there. That was the first time they had seen each other since he had deployed about six months earlier. I think that Doug will be the first to admit that he really didn't think that TelePresence would be much more different than the traditional video teleconference - VTC solutions they had used before. By the end of the project, he was one of our biggest champions for extending the program.

Doug described his experience as follows:

> Cisco TelePresence is a phenomenal piece of equipment. It brought me and my family together, although literally we were half a world apart. Hundreds of soldiers in my unit experienced the capabilities of TelePresence, and were overjoyed to have the ability to see and speak with their families and loved ones so clearly and quickly. It is a great piece of kit.

Figure 13-9 *Thornton Family Visit as Part of Operation Military Connect*

Rollin Ford, executive vice president and chief information officer of Wal-Mart, added this:

> Wal-Mart is committed to supporting not only our troops but the entire military family, and we are proud to join with Verizon and Cisco to help connect military families with their loved ones serving in Iraq. Through TelePresence, our customers have the unique opportunity to support and connect with our men and women in uniform through a virtual face-to-face interaction.

Overall, the effort was a huge success, and the smiles on the faces of adults and children who could see and talk to loved ones as if they were in the same room was well worth the effort. What a wonderful example of how these companies were able to give back to their communities.[14]

Summary

The application of IP video provides benefits and opportunities across many industries. In this chapter, we observed some interesting examples of how video is used within the high-tech, real estate and hospitality, and the sports and entertainment sectors.

The high-tech industry is an early adopter of TelePresence. It enables companies to increase agility, improve internal communication, and reduce travel. It also enables service providers to expand service offerings that create competitive advantages for themselves and their customers. IP video is also used by firms to help clarify partnerships and to announce new alliances.

In the real estate and hospitality sectors, the CCRE solution enables property managers and developers to build a foundation network in a facility, which can be leveraged by operators and tenants to reduce cost, improve security, enable growth and new revenue opportunities, and gain competitive advantages. A hotel and a casino example were used to demonstrate the use case.

The Cisco Connected Sports solution provides next-generation experiences for the sports and entertainment industries to ensure fans keep coming to the stadiums. It enables traditional stadiums and sports facilities to transform the guest experience, to reduce operational cost, and to generate new revenue streams. Use cases were shared from a traditional soccer stadium and a relatively new sports museum. In addition to video applications, other Cisco network and encoding technologies can be used to expand the viewing options for sports fans, as demonstrated by NBC and Cisco during the 2008 Summer Olympics.

Finally, the application of IP video offers many possibilities for companies to collaborate and give back to their communities. Operation Military Connect is one shining example of such an effort.

End Notes

1. "SAP Selects Cisco TelePresence System for Virtual Meeting Experience," Cisco.com, April 2007.

2. "Cisco Introduces Personal TelePresence," Cisco.com, May 2008.

3. "Cisco and Microsoft CEOs Share Vision for Future of the Industry," cisco.com, August 2007.

4. "AT&T First Service Provider to Deliver Intercompany Cisco TelePresence for Businesses Around the World," Cisco.com, April 2008.

5. "BT Conferencing Launches BT One Source for Cisco TelePresence," BTplc.com, June 2008.

6. "BT Demonstrates Inter-company TelePresence Service at Cisco Expo," BTplc.com, April 2008.

7. "Cisco Announces First Canadian TelePresence Sale," Cisco.com, June 2007.

8. http://www.tajhotels.com/press_room/press_releases/ Corporate%20News/3_0_4_July2008.htm

9. "Resort Casino Readies for Growth with Cisco Video Surveillance," Customer Case Study, Cisco, October 2007.

10. "Cisco Connected Sports: Reinventing the Sports Experience in Stadium and Beyond," Cisco, October 2007.

11. "Cisco Helps Watford Football Club Transform Vicarage Road Stadium with One of Europe's Most Advanced Information Networks," Cisco.com, June 2007.

12. "Cisco Technology Powers the New Sports Museum of America," Cisco.com, February 2008.

13. "NBC Provides Unprecedented Coverage of 2008 Olympic Games," Customer Case Study, Cisco, May 2008.

14. "U.S. Troops in Iraq Connect With Family and Friends via TelePresence," Cisco.com, May 2008.

PART IV

NO MORE WALLS

CHAPTER 14

OPPORTUNITIES IN THE ERA OF VISUAL NETWORKING

Executive Summary

In this chapter, you will learn the following:

- Visual networking refers to combining Web 2.0 capabilities with video.

- The opportunities and applications of visual networking in businesses for e-commerce, advertising business-process improvements, and collaboration are extensive and varied.

- Besides businesses, other segments such as entertainment, education, and public communications also stand to benefit from visual networking applications.

This chapter discusses how organizations will benefit when all things Web 2.0 are embedded into video to unleash the era of visual networking. By *Web 2.0*, most experts refer to the interactive nature of how content is delivered and generated on websites. Unlike in the days of Web 1.0 when websites reflected the site author's viewpoint, Web 2.0 enables the authors to deliver content with greater interactivity (through customized programs that combine functionality of multiple applications, also known as mash-ups). Moreover, users of the website in a Web 2.0 environment can also contribute content by posting their blogs, videos, commentary, ratings, and feedback to make the content more engaging.

The Internet of today is often referred to as Web 2.0 to distinguish its current evolution from that of the 1990s.

The distinction is largely based on the emergence of empowered users connecting with each other in ways and at speeds vastly enhanced from years past. With blogs, social networking, video sharing, immersive games, and personalized portals, our societies have experienced a global connectedness among all people that was barely imaginable several years ago. Compared to prior years of the Internet, the current form of the web enables unparalleled levels of peer engagement, collaboration, and personal involvement for individual users.

Despite its strength and widespread acceptance, critics of Web 2.0 remain vociferous. Many in the industry often wonder whether socially engaging applications such as LinkedIn, Facebook, YouTube, wikis, and Twitter (the stalwarts in the Web 2.0 world) have the potential to deliver productivity, business transformation, cost savings, or revenue streams that the Internet has delivered in the past to economic entities. The tough business question remains: How will Web 2.0 transform the core value of people connecting with people for organizations and economies to where they might experience significant productivity gains over a five-year period? The following passages illustrate scenarios of what visual networking might look like in a few short years.

Beyond Web 2.0: To Visual Networking

For Web 2.0 to live up to its promise, productivity gains will result from practices that extend beyond the mere scaling of the past tried-and-true processes to encompass fundamental innovation in how individuals connect, collaborate, and interact with each other. The answer lies in first transcending the appeal of Web 2.0 beyond the core social audience into more of the economically sensitive segments of web audiences (including businesses, organizations, government, individuals, and markets). And second, the answer lies in transforming the social-networking practices of social audiences into collaboration best practices at work.

The notion of embedding all things Web 2.0 into video is what we refer to as *visual networking*. Because video remains a familiar medium in its appeal and convenience to users, embedding Web 2.0 practices in IP video is an intuitive way to not only empower new segments of the population with unified communications capabilities but also to deliver a compelling experience through those capabilities to influence faster adoption. Simply put, visual networking delivers the potent payload of instant collaboration over the user-friendly medium of video (see Figure 14-1).

Figure 14-1 *Real-Time Living Room Communication over TV*

Visual Networking at Work

Straightforward as the concept might sound, combining streaming or on-demand IP video with Web 2.0 capabilities stands to increase engagement and productivity for users by order of magnitudes. But how might that experience impact the way individuals, organizations, and society benefit from the web? What might be some of the specific manifestations of visual networking in products or services? The sections that follow review some examples from diverse spheres of commerce and economics to highlight potential business value of visual networking.

Enabling E-Commerce Through Visual Networking

What if video content that interests and inspires us were to also act as an e-commerce portal with which to interact? Many of us would value viewing videos where we can purchase what the actors are wearing right from within the scenes of our favorite TV shows or movies. Clips from movies, TV shows, documentaries, or talk shows with products and services featured in them will be available for sale on our TV sets, mobile phones, or over the Internet, with an easy point-and-click using your remote, mouse, or cursor. You view the video and just click a hyperlink within the video to be dropped into an e-commerce site to purchase the merchandize for sale.

In an age where IPTV, Internet video, and mobile video offer greater interactivity, the opportunity to purchase products placed within entertainment content will influence the shopping behavior of many consumers. The model delivers an online shopping experience that captures the interest piqued in a product from its placement in entertainment content and almost instantaneously transforms that interest into a purchase decision (see Figure 14-2).

Figure 14-2　*Click to Buy What the Stars Wear*

Connecting Live Through Visual Networking

Being able to initiate a live conversation right from within a video will reduce the chances of viewers delaying their desire to interact with the message owners. Using an auto manufacturer as an example, visualize a car commercial streaming over the Internet, playing on your TV, or running on your mobile phone. For those in the market for a new automobile and seeking to learn more about the featured automobile in the commercial, one point and click on any scene right from within the video commercial places them into a live conversation with a contact center representative. The representative at the other end can assist the prospect with more information about pricing, features, availability, and scheduling a test drive. Using the communications capabilities of Session Initiation Protocol (SIP) embedded within video, such instant conversations or live chat sessions will be convenient to set up.

For the prospect, the benefit lies in the timely information readily available on demand. It eliminates the need for the prospect to visit the website, look up the car details, and send in a request for a representative to contact during normal business hours. For the automaker, the benefit is establishing contact with a potential customer as the desire for the product is piqued through the advertising. A relationship between the prospect and the provider is established right when the interest on the part of the prospect is high (without delay, reducing the risk of the potential sales lead growing cold over time).

Media Conferencing (Sharing) Through Visual Networking

Sharing exciting shows, sporting events, or news items with friends and family has always been desirable but difficult because of distance, schedules, and the inability for others to see what you see. What if, for instance, you are watching exciting live sports coverage and choose to share the excitement with a friend. You reach out to connect with him to share your play-by-play stream with him. When you try to connect, you receive presence information indicating he is available, but because he is on a train back from work in a different time zone, he prefers that only his mobile phone be used to contact him. You choose to conference him in to share the live video stream from your TV set right on his mobile phone. Along the way, you converse, comment, exchange, taunt, or trash-talk your way through the viewing experience. The excitement is shared across locations, time zones, and devices while preserving the nostalgia of enjoying a scintillating sporting event with an old friend (see Figure 14-3).

Figure 14-3   *Conferencing Video Content Across Devices*

E-Learning Through Visual Networking

Visual networking will have a tremendous impact on how we learn. Consider a how-to video clip on troubleshooting a technical problem (see Figure 14-4). In a learning environment, the video clip could present a pop-up midstream containing a quiz page that enables you to test your knowledge gathered thus far from the video. Based on your performance on the quiz, the video either repeats the recently played content to reinforce the learning objectives or proceeds to the next sequence. The content displayed on the video stream is determined by your quiz performance, creating conditional viewing based on your competence. In situations where you excel at such pop-up quizzes, the video stream has the capability to skip to advanced levels to engage with you at your personalized readiness level.

Figure 14-4 *Troubleshooting at Work Using Visual Networking*

Business Process Integration Through Visual Networking

The potential of visual networking can be unleashed in an enterprise environment as business processes are integrated with real-time user video. Consider the case of a small business applying for a loan for the first time. After meeting with a loan representative either in person or over a videoconference, the applicant receives a video link to an online guide about the loan process. The entire process is embedded through links within a three-minute video clip. As the speaker in the video describes the loan process, the speaker prompts the loan applicant to complete the loan application by clicking the embedded links within the video. Should questions arise, one of the embedded links will enable live chat or conversation with a loan specialist from the bank.

By integrating on-demand videos with live support and business-process steps, the entire loan application completion process is simplified. The reduction in time taken to complete the loan application process not only allows greater productivity for the loan applicant but also helps the bank by speeding up decision inputs and reducing the risk of losing a potential client to another financial institution.

We can extend the illustration to other business-process integration examples such as filing vendor approval forms, completing purchase orders, tracking program compliance, managing costs or payables, and signing up for human resources benefits. In any of these examples, video could potentially assist the respondent through the process, cutting down on errors and speeding up decisions.

Video Wikis

Just as Wikipedia enables us to jump from one page to another simply by following a link to a reference site in a hypertext environment, visual networking will allow us to jump from one video to another reference video just by clicking the elements presented within the video. We can build on the example of troubleshooting tips. If there is a concept in the troubleshooting video that you need more background information about, you can just click an embedded link within a video to jump over to another video that provides the introductory content you seek. By embedding secondary video links within the primary video, content creators can save a user the time it takes to go searching for it elsewhere and can avoid not knowing whether the video the user might come across will do justice to the topic.

Advertising Through Visual Networking

One of the largest opportunities of visual networking is presented in the advertising arena. Advertisers who deliver rich media content in the form of video clips, video episodes, or teaser ads with embedded links are likely to prompt greater click-through rates than the current banner ads or search-generated ads do. Viewers seeking more information about a particular problem or a reference within a video could click a pop-up or a hotlink to learn more. Even search ads running as videos are likely to garner greater attention from visitors than a simple text rendition.

These visually stimulating advertisements delivered as teasers or stories will be delivered via TV, the Internet, and mobile devices and offer users the option to click and sign up for offers, download coupons, or initiate live contact over a SIP connection. For specific customer groups based on geography, demography, or personal tastes, the online advertisements could be triggered to a back-end database to run customized versions of ads when users fill out online forms for more information about a product (see Figure 14-5).

Figure 14-5   *Visual Networking Makes for Efficient Advertising*

Public Affairs and Government Relations Through Visual Networking

Whether at the local, state, or federal level, governments have an obligation to publish and make available information from all proceedings to the public. With visual networking, this information can be in the form of video feeds, which can be made available on line for all citizens to access. Within those videos could also be embedded content-specific links to legislation drafts, proposal designs and blueprints, maps, polling, constituent discussion forums, and instant feedback to the representative speaking in the video. Such real-time access and transparency could make it easier for citizens, staff, and other constituents to participate and engage in the democratic process and hold their representatives to a higher standard of accountability.

Games, Sports, and Virtual Environments

We are regularly seeing successful television shows, sporting events, and movies being adapted into online games and virtual environments. Links embedded into the video and the direction of which way the video proceeds based on user input could enable an array of quiz contests, games, and simulations. Video proceeding one way or another based on user choices and input could create unique forms of storytelling with alternative endings based on user preference for a particular adventure or outcome from a choice of various storylines.

Deploying video modules for audience engagement into immersive game environments will continue to grow. Such elements ensure more realistic renditions of virtual environments and blur the lines between games, movies, and web entertainment even further (see Figure 14-6).

Figure 14-6   Embedding Social Networking into Video

Live Feedback Through Visual Networking

Visual networking also enables capturing live comments, polling, and posts through pop-ups embedded in the video assets. As a presidential debate or speech is streamed live, visual networking will enable ongoing audience polling embedded within the live video. The poll queries viewers about their favorability ratings on what is being said in the ongoing debate or speech by the candidate. Instead of limiting response meters to a few select individuals, audience anxiety, emotion, interest, and response to the content could be captured across the board in the midst of the live streams over IPTV, mobile video, or Internet video. The feedback stream from the viewers would empower content providers with the ability to make instant and future decisions about the choice, nature, and tenor of the ensuing content.

Knowing which characters, dialogs, or settings resonate more with the audience can be incredibly cost-effective and useful for producers of pilot shows in development. Similarly, sports show producers can learn more from which plays, camera angles, and comments from the broadcasters the viewers are responding to more favorably. On the other side of the spectrum, news coverage and the types of questions or comments being posted by the viewers about particular breaking news can clue news producers in to which direction to proceed with further reporting.

Summary

The illustrations in the chapter offer only a brief glimpse into how video may be used in the future. However, as the technology becomes available, all these applications will be manifested in one form or another using video, in what we refer to as the era of visual networking. The era of visual networking will be device independent, spanning a host of devices using technologies such as IPTV and Internet video to be pervasive and accessible to users. If we build collaboration, social networking, and audience participation into video streams and on-demand video clips, users will have the interactive capability to influence content creation. And there are worse things that can happen in business than for content developers to become more responsive to the desires of their users.

CHAPTER 15

COLLABORATION LIKE NEVER BEFORE: TO MAKE A DIFFERENCE

Executive Summary

In this chapter, you will learn

- IP video when combined with other collaboration tools, such as audio, web, and conferencing empowers organizations to address environmental challenges stemming from climate change.

- By using these technology tools for remote collaboration and productivity, organizations can not only collaborate effectively for improved productivity, but also do right by the environment.

On the morning of March 18, 2008, former U.S. Vice President Al Gore and Cisco CEO and Chairman John Chambers shared the podium at the VoiceCon 2008 conference event in Orlando, Florida, to discuss how video and collaboration technologies enable organizations to reduce carbon emissions. As if to make a point about cutting travel costs and reducing carbon emissions, the two chose to appear at the event over TelePresence instead of flying in person to Orlando.

The forum took place at the VoiceCon 2008 event and involved four locations joining in real-time with lifelike presence using Cisco TelePresence technologies. Chambers participated from San Jose, California; Gore joined from Nashville, Tennessee; Sue Bostrom, Cisco chief marketing officer, participated with the audience from the conference in Orlando, Florida; and the panel moderator joined from London, England (see Figure 15-1).

Figure 15-1   *VoiceCon 2008 Event in Florida with John Chambers, Al Gore, and Sue Bostrom*

John Chambers emphasized a priority to involve global, political, and business leaders to address global warming concerns by working together, but without necessarily adding to carbon emissions with flights across the globe. In bringing diverse groups to collaborate in their technology and policy initiatives against climate change, Chambers emphasized that the tipping point will be unified communications, Internet, video, and Web 2.0 applications. Referring to the Internet and its current wave of applications, Chambers said the following:

It can address all of these issues.

The passion of the speakers around the topic and the audience interest in the panel discussion were historical for the VoiceCon event. Both in terms of what was said and how it was said, the proof point was the message. According to Al Gore, decision makers in businesses were beginning to see the value in launching green initiatives and reducing travel through the use of video. Referring to TelePresence, Gore said this:

I think this is really the most realistic effort I've seen so far.

The discussion got beyond technology and turned to policy. Al Gore, a Nobel Laureate for his work on climate change and an Academy Award winner for his documentary *An Inconvenient Truth* on the same topic, offered policy suggestions to spur progress in environmental technologies:

The single best thing we can do is reduce taxes on business and employees and replace that with CO^2 taxes. If we put a price on carbon, that would unleash the innovations.

Al Gore commented that policies should be aimed at not stifling, but rewarding those with creative solutions to preserve the environment. Where companies are still promoting outdated "polluting" technologies, appropriate regulation is the answer.

So, let's explore in the next few sections a little about the economics of carbon emissions.

Business Benefits and Carbon Benefits

It is easier to measure the financial impact of changes in technology and business processes than to gauge the environmental impact of those changes with any precision. Calculating financial return on investment (ROI) is familiar territory. The same is not true for calculating a carbon-reduction ROI. That situation is changing.

As we move to a carbon-constrained world, businesses may well need to track their emissions exactly. Europe is ahead of the rest of the world in developing regulatory frameworks to reduce greenhouse gas emissions, but in the United States, too, several states are moving toward regulating greenhouse gas emissions. And in its 2008 budget, the Canadian province of British Columbia announced the first carbon tax in North America.

Such developments are matched by evidence of mounting public scrutiny. In the 2007 Cone Consumer Environmental Survey, 93 percent of Americans agreed that companies should take responsibility for helping to preserve the environment, and 85 percent would consider switching to another company's products if their usual supplier turned out to have a negative social-responsibility record.

How Cisco Is Cutting Emissions

By cutting unnecessary travel in two short years, Cisco was not only able to save millions of dollars, but also able to cut emissions by 10 percent per employee. Sue Bostrom, chief marketing officer for Cisco, reported during the VoiceCon panel discussion in March 2008 that Cisco had launched an eco-board and several green initiatives to reduce the company's carbon footprint:

> Climate change definitely has everyone's attention, but it doesn't have everyone's participation.

So how is Cisco responding to the need for combating climate change? Cisco is developing a set of coherent, companywide environmental policies so that sustainable business practices can be cost-effectively combined with growth and profitability. This entails a twofold approach to IT energy policy, concentrating on rapid emissions reduction in current IT operations and on the adoption of solutions to modify business practices in pursuit of sustainability goals.

Today, Cisco is reducing its energy consumption through more environmentally focused practices in its internal operations and by promoting energy-saving practices in its travel policies and buildings management. The company is sourcing more "green" energy. The green efforts at Cisco involve both the programmatic initiatives and product-development endeavors. Cisco is working to ensure that growth and profitability targets can be fully harmonized with the mounting importance of cutting carbon emissions:

- Cisco TelePresence reduces travel and saves $80 million.

- By January 2008, Cisco had installed more than 170 TelePresence units in company offices in more than 20 countries and almost 60 cities worldwide. Average utilization of all units had increased to almost half of the total time when they are available, based on a 10-hour workday. More than 62,415 meetings (amounting to 78,137 meeting hours) were conducted over TelePresence, and 10,316 of those TelePresence meetings involved participants who were able to collaborate freely while avoiding travel. This saved nearly $80 million in travel costs alone (see Figure 15-2).

Figure 15-2 *Avoiding Travel and Staying Productive with TelePresence Meetings*

- Cisco Unified MeetingPlace and WebEx are used for thousands of meetings daily.

- In 2007, Cisco conducted nearly 2 million virtual meetings using Cisco Unified MeetingPlace and WebEx, bringing together its employees, partners, and customers. Although not all these meetings used video, the capabilities were made available. Cisco does not yet track how many of these virtual meetings displace long-haul and regional travel, but the travel saving is certainly in the tens of thousands of miles, if not hundreds of thousands, with a corresponding impact on the company's carbon emissions profile (see Figure 15-3).

Figure 15-3 *Virtual Meetings Using Voice, Video, and Web Collaboration*

- Cisco Connected Workplace trial shows improved energy efficiency.

- Cisco has run tests at its San Jose campus to verify that properly designed working environments save space, become more energy efficient, and reduce greenhouse gas emissions. Comparing a traditional to a redesigned building, Cisco found an estimated 44 percent improvement in energy efficiency within the redesigned building, a 40 percent cut in its employee space requirements, and a 22 percent drop in per-capita consumption of materials and equipment.

Besides the commitment to improving the environment, these efforts also drive the need for individuals across organizations, governments, publics, and cultures to work together. All the previously mentioned efforts mean a major shift in individual and organizational behavior, with an integrated set of communications tools to build trust and efficiency quickly between dispersed and multicultural teams.

Strategies for Making Organizations Emissions Savvy

Based on its experiences and research, a team of experts developed best practices for other organizations and practitioners to review and consider. A Cisco-sponsored report from the Economist Intelligence Unit[1] emphasizes the potential of increased success for those who collaborate well. Cisco-sponsored research by independent experts also shows that 60 percent of human communication is nonverbal,[2] underscoring its value in collaboration. The guidance offers some practical steps that any organization with a green initiative can pursue.

Make Fewer Business Journeys

Business travel is responsible for a major part of company greenhouse gas emissions. This includes national and international trips for high-level meetings, sales conferences, group training, or live exchanges. Here, too, technology offers ways to cut down on the need for physical presence, without losing the human contact that remains an essential part of doing business effectively.

There is a significant reduction in greenhouse gas emissions when TelePresence and Unified Communications virtual meeting tools are used as opposed to airline, automobile, or rail travel to a attend a meeting. Considering that a commercial flight from Chicago to New York results in an estimated

633 pounds of greenhouse gas emissions,[3] the environmental benefits can be substantial. Ongoing analyses are being performed to further quantify the environmental benefits of Cisco virtual meeting tools.

Decrease Commuting

A study of people working from home at least 1 day a week, by the U.S. Consumer Electronics Association, suggested that telecommuting saves 840 million gallons of gasoline a year and 14 million tons a year of greenhouse gas emissions. The report calculated that the total saving in electricity amounted to 9 to 14 billion kilowatt hours a year. approximately equivalent to the energy used by 1 million U.S. households.

Telecommuting has grown rapidly since the 1990s. In 2006, there were an estimated 29 million U.S. teleworkers working from home[4] at least 1 day a month, including the employed and self-employed (about twice as many as their European counterparts during that year). The European figure is on track to double by 2010, whereas the U.S. total could hit 100 million by that date. Governments have long anticipated better air quality and improvements in the transport system from the easing of congestion and emissions.

Case in Point: Sun Microsystems

Cisco WebEx helped the Open Work Services Group at Sun Microsystems deliver on its initiative to enable employees to work from anywhere at any time (reducing costs, increasing productivity, and opening up new opportunities). Chris Saleh, program manager for the Open Work Services Group, said this:

> Today, more than half of Sun employees no longer have permanent offices. WebEx provided the collaboration tool we needed to bridge distances and geographies, and effectively boost productivity.

Smarter Home Working Means Smart Travel-Reduction Policies

The equation between reduced commuting and reduced greenhouse gas emissions is not necessarily straightforward. The environmental impacts of home working depend on specific conditions of climate; on organizational needs and characteristics; on geography, population distribution, travel patterns, public transport, and government policies. Video and collaboration technologies therefore need to be combined with smart travel-reduction policies to ensure they genuinely help reduce carbon emissions, and that the emissions saved by reduced commuting are not outweighed by factors such as higher energy use for home heating and lighting.

As we have already discussed in previous chapters, direct business benefits of telecommuting include improved performance and staff retention, higher productivity, and less absenteeism. Most employees report positive effects, such as reduced stress, and home workers generally use part or all the commuting time saved for working. The potentially beneficial environmental effects should now be added to that list, and be considered as a key business benefit on its own.

Better Use of Office Space

Buildings are estimated to account for no less than half the world's energy consumption, and property operating costs represent the second largest business expense for a typical organization after human resources. The potential to cut both costs and greenhouse gas emissions by reducing office space is substantial.

Both aims can be facilitated partly through building design and management, and partly by new working practices such as home working, hot-desking, and "hoteling." In a pilot project, Cisco has achieved space savings amounting to 40 percent, while producing greater employee comfort, satisfaction, and productivity.

Embedded Costs

The economic benefits of using less office space include lower rental costs and a lower bill for heat, light, and power. In the medium to longer term, a further potential gain is the avoided environmental side effects of new office construction. On the embedded environmental cost of a new building of 100,000 square feet, a 40 percent space saving translates into 1500 tons of concrete, 280 tons of steel,[5] and 2850 tons of CO_2 emissions, an amount equivalent to taking 560 cars off the road for a year, according to Cisco estimates.

Leveraging the Mobility Trend

Reduction of office space often implies a greater mobility among workers, whether they are working at client premises, on the road, or moving from one location to another on a large campus. Provision of workforce mobility can be approached with the same energy-saving objectives as the policy for enhanced collaboration, enabling organizations to combine voice, video, and web technologies in a way that achieves better performance against their environmental aims.

A recent study by International Data Corporation (IDC) suggests that by 2011, more than a billion workers worldwide will be mobile (approximately 30 percent of the global workforce). In the United States, 70 percent of all workers are expected to be mobile by then.[6]

Although mobility is variously defined, the projected increase in these numbers requires careful integration of mobility policies with wider green aims to ensure that more physical movement in the workforce does not push up emissions again.[7]

Case in Point: Renault

In France, automaker Renault is working with Cisco to create a new way of working with greater flexibility and mobility among its workforce, enabling home working and transforming traditional office environments into shared work spaces. The plan will allow Renault to close several office buildings in Paris, saving $130 million a year and reducing its carbon footprint.

Carbon Conscious with Clinton Global Initiative

As mentioned earlier, Cisco manages an internal program that reduced the overall carbon footprint of Cisco employees by 10 percent in 2008. The program originated from Cisco's participation in the Clinton Global Initiative, an endeavor of the William J. Clinton Foundation to develop innovative solutions for some of the world's most pressing challenges. Under the internal program, Cisco encourages its employees to replace air travel with communications tools that enable meetings to be conducted in a virtual collaboration space over the network.

In 2006, Cisco launched Connected Urban Development (CUD), as part of another effort under the Clinton Global Initiative that was focused on cities. CUD is a five-year program, in which Cisco has invested $15 million in people, research, and equipment to help create a global community of cities committed to addressing environmental sustainability. Changing the way cities operate has a positive impact on the ways in which citizens work, live, and play.

Beneficiaries of Connected Urban Development

CUD is a partnership between Cisco and cities around the world to create urban communications infrastructures that demonstrate how network connectivity can reduce carbon emissions in urban environments. By using network connectivity for communication, collaboration, urban planning, and other activities, CUD will help change the way in which cities do the following:

- Deliver services to residents
- Manage the flow of traffic
- Operate public transportation
- Use and manage real estate resources

How CUD Works

Measures for reducing CO^2 by cutting energy consumption measures have been difficult to implement and impossible to enforce. Developing a new way to approach the problem is critical, given the urgency posed by rapid climate change. Cisco relies on its networking expertise of bringing voice-, video-, and web-enriched information to users instead of bringing users to the sources of information to provide a viable and sustainable solution to help cities reduce their levels of CO^2.

The CUD program draws on expertise from Cisco's global, strategic consulting arm and from researchers from the Massachusetts Institute of Technology (MIT). CUD demonstrates how to reduce carbon emissions by introducing fundamental improvements in the efficiency of the urban infrastructure using information and communications technology.

Progress So Far

The CUD program initially involves three pilot cities: San Francisco, California; Amsterdam, The Netherlands; and Seoul, South Korea. These cities were selected because each had implemented or planned to implement a next-generation broadband (fiber/wireless) infrastructure, each suffers from significant traffic-congestion issues, and each is led by a visionary mayor already involved in green initiatives. Cisco's global business consulting arm manages the CUD program, supporting each city's efforts to create a more sustainable future through ICT. CUD helped to support the cities' innovative use of technology in reducing carbon emissions, while fostering economic growth at the same time.

Learnings from the CUD partnership will serve as a blueprint of best practices and methodologies that other cities can use as a reference. The scope of the program will transcend the environmental dimension, delivering innovative, sustainable models for urban planning and economic development.

Now in its second phase, CUD has added four additional cities to this collaborative community: Madrid, Spain; Lisbon, Portugal; Hamburg, Germany; and Birmingham, England. Each will focus on developing information and communications technology solutions to meet their own, specific environmental and transportation challenges.

Summary

At the forum in Orlando, former Vice President Al Gore identified that both policies and technologies are needed to bring about change. Speaking of efforts needed to stem climate change, he chose an African proverb to describe the need for collaboration:

> If you want to go quickly, go alone; if you want to go far, go together. We want to go far quickly.

According to Gore, the latest voice, video, and web collaboration technologies will form the necessary components in helping to create a global plan of action against climate change. He summed up with the following:

> If we make up our minds to act, there's no doubt we can do this; we have the sustainable technologies.

End Notes

1. Collaboration: Transforming The Way Business Works, *Economist Intelligence Unit,* April 2007.

2. Human Productivity Lab 2006 Pearn-Kandola: The Psychology of Effective Business Communications in Geographically Dispersed Teams, 2006.

3. Estimated using the TRX Airline Carbon Emissions Calculator.

4. WorldatWork Telework Trendlines for 2006.

5. Davis Langdon City of London Commercial Sector Cost Estimation, December 2004.

6. Worldwide Mobile Worker Population 2007–2011 Forecast, IDC, December 2007.

7. Ibid.

PART V

Appendixes

How Cisco Uses Streaming Video for Worldwide Corporate Events and Training

Streaming video lowers costs and improves timeliness and availability of corporate communications.

Cisco IT Case Study / IT Services Expense Management / Streaming Video Solutions: This case study describes the history and current use of streaming video applications within the Cisco corporate infrastructure. With constant priority on minimizing travel budgets and an increasing need for fast, effective training and real-time companywide communications, Cisco IT has deployed streaming video solutions that serve a broad base of internal users. Customers can draw on Cisco IT's real-world experience in this area to help address similar enterprise needs.

Every executive must ask sooner or later, "Can my employees keep up with the pace of change?"
John Chambers, president and CEO, Cisco Systems

Background

Cisco Systems experienced high growth in the mid-1990s. As a result, every Cisco team had to explore creative ways to rapidly and affordably manage the following:

- Increased demands for training and cross-team communications (with training and travel budgets that did not keep pace)
- Growing skill requirements
- A global shortage of skilled IT workers
- Rapid technological development
- Globalization pressures
- Hundreds of training content sources

The rapid change paralleled an increasing need to disseminate information and knowledge throughout the enterprise. Traditional classroom training and communications channels could not scale to accommodate the required demand; concurrently, Cisco management recognized the need for a solution that would strengthen the company's competitive edge. Cisco's IT group was charged with gathering the company's communications-related business requirements, planning and deploying a solution, and driving adoption within the geographically dispersed employee base. The goal included enhancing productivity, which entailed the following:

- Timely and direct executive communications
- Access to and completion of regulatory and standards compliance training
- Keeping the sales force (direct and distribution partners) current on new products and technologies
- Enabling frequent product announcements, updates, and training

Cisco's global stakeholders (employees, partners, and customers) understood the advantages and power of communications technology for meeting these goals. The result was a strong enterprisewide demand for multimedia business communications solutions.

Challenge

The Cisco media network was developed in response to an immediate need for wide-scale learning. In just one instance, the company required the ability to deliver technical training to 5000 sales account managers and 7000 systems engineers. In addition, Cisco had to provide much of the same training to approximately 35,000 employees, and to 25,000 channel distribution channel partners with more than 400,000 employees located around the world. A large, increasingly complex product portfolio and aggressive schedules further complicated the scope of the training. It was clear that traditional classroom-based training, requiring thousands of students to travel, was not only cost prohibitive but also impossible with the current resources and time allotted.

Solution

To meet these challenges, a rich media solution capable of delivering a wide variety of content, including graphics, animations, audio, video, and virtual lab access, was provisioned, and content access web portals were developed. The focus on multimedia reflected broadly accepted patterns for learning: People typically retain 10 percent of what they read, 20 percent of what they hear, and 50 percent of what they see and hear. The new media solution provided content authors and subject matter experts with a platform for creating multimedia content and making it available for easy, secure, anywhere-in-the world access by Cisco employees and channel partners.

A central part of the initial multimedia strategy involved streaming video for live events and on-demand content. Coupled with Cisco's content networking products, the video strategy provided unparalleled scalability for deploying training to global audiences.

As the IT team continued to gather business requirements, the project broadened beyond the scope of e-learning to embrace the entire spectrum of business communications. The company's evolution to a converged data, voice, and video IP network was vital to enabling the streaming video solutions designed to address the complete, expanded set of business communications requirements. The eventual solution was defined in terms of several critical elements:

- **Network delivery**: The Cisco Application and Content Networking System (ACNS) infrastructure, to enable network-efficient delivery of live and on-demand content

- **Content authoring and management**: An integrated platform for creating, managing, and deploying live and video-on-demand (VoD) content

- **Audio/video capture**: Design, implementation, and deployment guidelines for facilities

- **Web portal**: Integrated capability, including the tools, integration guides, and process information for viewing, creating, and producing live events and VoDs

- **Cisco Unified MeetingPlace solution**: An integrated rich media conferencing solution, including voice and web-conferencing capabilities
- **Cisco IP/TV solution**: A network video streaming system that delivers TV-quality, live video programming to desktop PCs, classrooms, and meeting rooms
- **Cisco IP/VC IP telephony solution:** A reliable, easy-to-manage, cost-effective network infrastructure for telephony and videoconferencing applications deployment

Within the multimedia environment, Cisco IT deployed several rich media solutions. These solutions started out primarily as off-network services; today, these deployments are transitioning to on-network solutions. Video streaming continues to play a vital role, as evidenced in videoconferencing, video telephony, web conferencing, and live and on-demand video broadcasts solutions used throughout Cisco.

Videoconferencing

Since 2003, the number of virtual meetings has exceeded the number of in-person meetings at Cisco. Currently, videoconferences exceed 9000 hours per year (2200 meetings). Users cite saved time, efficiency, reduced travel expenses, and increased productivity as the benefits derived from videoconferencing and the reasons for its widespread use.

Videoconferencing over a converged IP network gives Cisco users added benefits (see Figure A-1). Smooth integration of voice, video, and web components provides an enriched conference environment and simplifies integration of the conferencing systems with complementary collaborative applications such as instant messaging and calendaring systems.

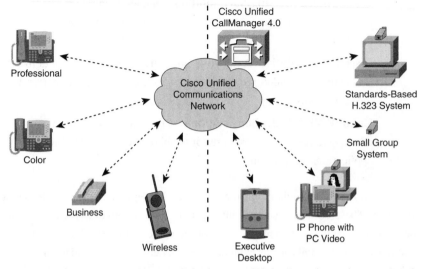

Figure A-1 *Enterprise-Class IP Telephony and Video Is Delivered over a Single Cisco Unified Communications Infrastructure*

IP Video Telephony

The Cisco IP telephony deployment supports video-enhanced communications. The converged infrastructure results in video service comparable to voice in terms of ease of use, ease of deployment, ease of management, and cost-effectiveness.

Web Conferencing

Cisco Unified MeetingPlace software provides universal access to web conferencing from standards-based platforms. Users can control voice, video, and web-conference functions from a single interface. Being able to see who is in the meeting, see the person talking, record and play back meetings, use a "whiteboard," and conduct polls helps enhance user productivity. Conference users can control their own interfaces (for example, mute their audio if necessary), and the conference host can control individual attendee sessions (for example, if one user has a noisy connection). The convergence of voice, video, and web foundations allows web-conference attendees to take advantage of common email and scheduling applications and directory services.

Within all of Cisco, web conferences exceed 16,000 hours per year (12,000 meetings).

Live Broadcasting and Video on Demand

Today, an increasing amount of all Cisco communications is done using streaming video. The Cisco media network can support both unicast and multicast streaming for efficient use of bandwidth (see Figure A-2).

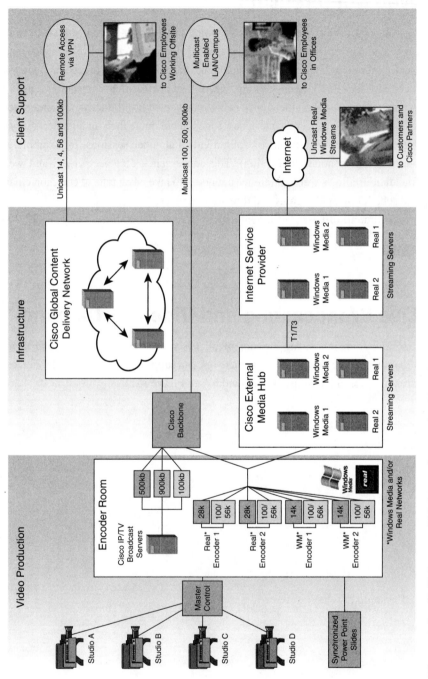

Figure A-2   *IP Unicast and Multicast for Bandwidth-Efficient Broadcasts*

Unicast streams provide point-to-point content transmission from a single source to a single PC. Multiple unicast streams can be established from a single streaming server to allow numerous individuals the ability to see the same event. This method serves remote Cisco employees accessing the Cisco intranet using virtual private networks (VPN), and external partners and customers accessing content on the Cisco.com public website.

In contrast to unicast, a multicast transmission involves a single high-quality stream to many users. Multicast provides the ability to reach a large audience without overloading the network. Multicast transmissions are used to broadcast over the Cisco intranet to Cisco employees located on numerous campuses worldwide. Cisco IPTV software is used for multicast broadcasts. For each live event broadcast, the Cisco broadcast solution provides a choice of standard encoded streams (see Figure A-3):

- 900 kb/s for satellite distribution to areas where the terrestrial WAN has insufficient bandwidth.
- 500 and 100 kb/s are accessible via terrestrial WAN.
- Unicast streams serve remote employees, partners, and customers.

For partners and customers connecting over the Internet, Cisco optionally serves other streams, including the following:

- 14-kb/s Windows audio streams
- 56-, 100-, and 300-kb/s Windows video streams
- 28-kb/s RealAudio 8 streams
- 56, 100, and 300-kb/s RealVideo 8 streams

These encoded streams are delivered to global Internet service providers that provide nearest-proximity streaming to partners and customers.

To serve remote VPN employees, Cisco uses its VoD content delivery network to split unicast streams in a cascading daisy-chain manner.

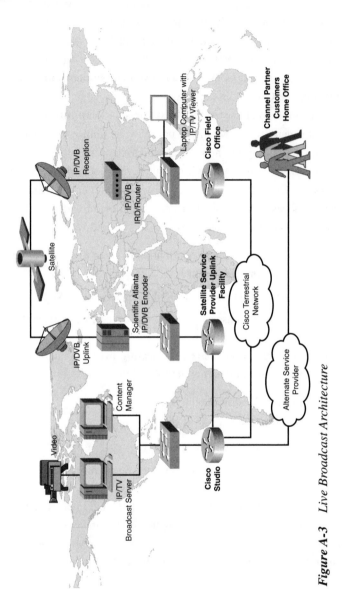

Figure A-3 Live Broadcast Architecture

The content delivery network supports 14-kb/s audio and 56-kb/s or 100-kb/s video streams. Cisco VoD content comes from many sources. Live events, offsite events, studio-created content, or any other video content created at any location can be stored and made available over the content-delivery network for viewing by Cisco employees, partners, and customers. Once created, every Cisco VoD is uploaded, meta-tagged, and pushed to production over the Cisco ACNS. The content is prepositioned on content engines. Viewer requests are served from the closest logical VoD server.

Production Studios and Broadcast Volume

Each month, 40 to 50 live video broadcasts are produced, with approximately 250 viewers per broadcast. In addition, 400 to 500 VoD modules are created either from these broadcasts or separately, with an average audience of 70,000 internal Cisco viewers and 50,000 partner viewers per month.

Multiple video studios deliver video-based content over the Cisco IP network from locations in San Jose, California; Raleigh, North Carolina; and London, England. Numerous ubiquitous, self-serve VoD authoring systems are used throughout the world for additional content development that does not require a studio.

Results

Industry analysts and experts consider video an extremely cost-effective tool for clarifying and improving business communications:

- **Increased learning**: A University of Wisconsin study determined that attendees learn 200 percent more in video classes and meetings, compared to audio-only experiences.

- **Improved rate of absorption**: According to a Wharton School of Business study, attendees absorb video information up to 40 percent faster than audio.

- **Augmented content retention**: Harvard University and Columbia University found that attendees in face-to-face meetings retain 38 percent more information than attendees in audio-only meetings.

- **Enhanced persuasiveness**: A study done by 3M found that face-to-face meetings are 43 percent more persuasive than audio-only meetings.

- **Improved impact of communications**: UCLA determined that 55 percent of the impact of communications comes from facial expressions and body language, versus 38 percent from vocal inflection.

Within Cisco, the IT streaming video projects have been evaluated and found to deliver benefits in terms of the following:

- **Productivity enhancements**: Cisco streaming video solutions enable the company to deliver information faster than the competition.

- **Increased information availability and convenient access**: Content can be provided to all Cisco employees, partners, and customers, as appropriate, and is more conveniently accessed when made available online.

- **Cost avoidance**: Delivering information over the Cisco IP network is inexpensive and results in multimillion-dollar savings per year.

Table A-1 highlights the savings in travel and time from virtualizing meetings through the adoption of various video and conferencing capabilities.

Table A-1 *Initial Cost Savings Related to Video Communications (FY2003)*

Video Event or Content	Savings (in $ Millions)
Live video events	$18.1
On-demand video	$25.0
Online meetings	$6.4
Collaborative workspace	$13.2
Instant message	$9.0
Total	$71.7

Live and on-demand broadcasts, in particular, have resulted in several significant benefits (see Table A-2).

Table A-2   *Seven Benefits of Video Streaming*

Abilities Enabled by Video Events	Business Benefits
Faster product launches	Accelerate time to market through rapid dissemination of products at the front line
Rapid dissemination of best practices	Enable peer-to-peer dissemination of best practices (for example, sales role plays and tips)
High-impact knowledge delivery	Quickly deliver mission-critical knowledge on business rules, regulations, and policies
High-impact corporate communications	Enable senior leaders to communicate strategy, results, and directions in real time
External collaboration	
Enable collaborative on/offshore outsourcing partnerships	
Enhanced store experiences	Differentiate store experiences with digital signage; virtualize subject matter experts

Business Benefit for Cisco: Cisco ISO Company Audit

Annually, Cisco must renew its ISO 9001 (process) and 14001 (environmental) certifications. The recertification process involves training approximately 20,000 employees at 9 sites. For 2005, recertification costs using traditional training methods were estimated at $1.4 million over nine months. Instead, Cisco created video- and audio-on-demand classes (with associated white papers), and accomplished the employee and auditor training in only three months for a total cost of just $32,000. The video training was so effective that Cisco not only passed the audit and identified areas for improvement of processes, but was rated number 2 out of 500 companies recertified that year, with only 7 minor infractions identified.

The video approach provided an additional unexpected benefit. The resulting library of VoD content has proven to be helpful for other initiatives involving the improvement of ongoing processes.

Benefit for Cisco: Emergency Process Implementation

Cisco's technical support organization must provide rapid response to discovered software bugs. Disseminating bug information and directions for software fixes often requires training the network of 430 support engineers worldwide. In one particular case, a 25-minute VoD was created to detail the directions for an emergency bug fix. The effects were dramatic; the support team was trained within 48 hours after the corporate team developed the fix. The cost of developing the VoD (done locally) was minimal.

Lessons Learned

Video communications make teams and extended teams more successful in their jobs, which translates into a more productive and competitive organization. Other high-level lesson Cisco learned include the following:

- Business problems drive communications solutions.
- Most forms of communications can be effectively converged on an IP-based network (IP telephony, video streaming, web conferencing, audio conferencing).
- Results must be measured in terms of time to competence and productivity gains.
- Access is the key to success.

Reference Documents

- "Streaming Video for High-Impact Business Communications: A Process-Centric Overview," a Cisco Systems white paper, April 2003.

  http://www.cisco.com/web/about/ciscoitatwork/white_papers/ cisco_streaming_video_white_paper.html

  Cisco customers and prospects often ask, "How did you do it?" or perhaps more importantly, "How can we do it?" This white paper answers these questions and assists anyone interested in integrating IP video as a network-based communications solution. It describes the processes that Cisco has in place to effectively use its internal media network architecture to create live and on-demand video content, publish and manage media assets, and globally deliver video-based content for multiple business communications and learning needs over the Cisco intranet. This white paper also outlines existing Cisco business and technical support systems that help ensure the successful creation and broad use of video content across the enterprise. It concludes with a look at what is next in this rapidly evolving medium.

- Cisco Business Communications Solutions: Live and On-Demand Streaming Video Guide.

  http://www.cisco.com/en/US/products/ps6902/products_ implementation_design_guides_list.html

  This document consists of four main sections. Section I provides a high-level overview of the Cisco Business Communications Solution. Section II provides details necessary for business managers who will implement a Cisco Business Communications Solution for streaming video within their organization. Section III contains essential information for operations managers and members of the audio/visual team who will support operations and planning for the streaming solution. Section IV provides facilities managers and staff with essential information, detailed equipment lists, and staffing requirements for a variety of usage scenarios. Appendixes offer essential information on the following topics:

Equipment vendors and service providers

VoD video vendor instructions

Using production vendors

Live broadcast and VoD slide-creation guidelines

Documentation and support

Cisco.com Resources

- Cisco Unified Communications

  http://www.cisco.com/en/US/products/sw/voicesw/

- Cisco Unified Video Advantage

  http://www.cisco.com/en/US/products/sw/voicesw/ps5662/index.html

- Cisco Unified MeetingPlace Web/Audio conferencing

  http://www.cisco.com/en/US/products/sw/ps5664/ps5669/index.html

- Video Solutions for Large Enterprises

  http://www.cisco.com/en/US/netsol/ns340/ns394/ns158/
  networking_solutions_packages_list.html

- Cisco IP/VC Videoconferencing

  http://www.cisco.com/en/US/netsol/ns340/ns394/ns158/ns280/
  netbr09186a00800f9218.html

- Cisco IPTV Solutions

  http://www.cisco.com/en/US/products/hw/contnetw/ps1863/

For More Information

To read the entire case study or for additional Cisco IT case studies on a variety of business solutions, visit Cisco on Cisco: Inside Cisco IT, at http://www.cisco.com/go/ciscoit.

NOTE   This publication describes how Cisco has benefited from the deployment of its own products. Many factors may have contributed to the results and benefits described; Cisco does not guarantee comparable results elsewhere.

CISCO PROVIDES THIS PUBLICATION AS IS WITHOUT WARRANTY OF ANY KIND, EITHER EXPRESS OR IMPLIED, INCLUDING THE IMPLIED WARRANTIES OF MERCHANTABILITY OR FITNESS FOR A PARTICULAR PURPOSE.

Some jurisdictions do not allow disclaimer of express or implied warranties, therefore this disclaimer may not apply to you.

CISCO VISUAL NETWORKING INDEX: FORECAST AND METHODOLOGY, 2007–2012

This forecast is part of the Cisco Visual Networking Index, an ongoing initiative to track and forecast the impact of visual networking applications. The purpose of this paper is to lay out the details of Cisco's global IP traffic forecast and the methodology behind it. For a more analytical look at the implications of the data presented below, see the companion article to this paper titled "Approaching the Zettabyte Era" at Cisco.com.

—June 16, 2008

Executive Summary

In 2012, the total annual volume of IP traffic will reach half a zettabyte (ZB). At 44 exabytes (EB) per month, the annual run rate of traffic will be 522 EB per year. A zettabyte, or 1000 EB, will be the new milestone to look for beyond 2012.

IP traffic will nearly double every two years through 2012. Total IP traffic will increase by a factor of six from 2007 to 2012. Driven by high-definition video and high-speed broadband penetration, consumer IP traffic will bolster the overall IP growth rate so that it sustains a steady growth rate through 2012, growing at a compound annual growth rate (CAGR) of 46 percent.

Last year was a year of phenomenal growth in IP and Internet traffic. Total IP traffic grew 55 percent during 2007, and is estimated to grow by 63 percent in 2008. Internet traffic grew 46 percent in 2007, and is estimated to increase 51 percent in 2008.

Traffic from all applications grew in volume in 2007, but the traffic mix shifted considerably. Peer-to-peer (P2P) file-sharing networks are now carrying 600 petabytes (PB) per month more than they did this time last year, which means there is the equivalent of an additional 150 million DVDs crossing the network each month, for a total monthly volume of over 500 million DVD equivalents, or 2 EB. Despite this growth, P2P as a percentage of consumer Internet traffic dropped to 51 percent at the end of 2007, down from 60 percent the year before. The decline in traffic share is due primarily to the increasing share of video traffic. A secondary factor in the decline is a trend toward web-based file sharing in place of P2P file sharing in some regions.

Video is now approximately one-quarter of all consumer Internet traffic, not including the amount of video exchanged through P2P file sharing. Internet video grew from 12 percent in 2006 to 22 percent in 2007, and will reach 32 percent by the end of this year.

Internet video will account for 50 percent of all consumer Internet traffic in 2012. Internet video to PC will make up the majority of Internet video at 40 percent of total Internet traffic, but Internet video to TV will grow rapidly to 10 percent of the total in 2012.

Non-Internet IP video will increase more rapidly than consumer Internet. The twin trends of on-demand viewing and high-definition video are generating very rapid growth in cable video and IPTV traffic transported over IP in the metro. Consumer IPTV and CATV traffic will grow at a 68 percent compound annual growth rate (CAGR) between 2007 and 2012, compared to a CAGR of 43 percent for consumer Internet traffic.

Mobile data traffic will double each year from now through 2012. Mobile broadband-enabled laptops are creating sharp increases in mobile traffic. In some parts of the world, mobile broadband is becoming a substitute for fixed broadband.

Japan's mobile data and Internet traffic was still twice as high as that of any other region in 2007. However, by 2009, North America will surpass Japan in mobile traffic, as will the rest of the Asia-Pacific region.

Internet traffic is growing fastest in Latin America, followed by Western Europe and Asia-Pacific. The rapidly increasing Internet penetration and the advent of high-speed connections to a greater number of universities and businesses will result in Latin America having the highest growth rate through 2012.

Business IP traffic will grow at a CAGR of 35 percent from 2007 to 2012. Increased broadband penetration in the small business segment and the increased adoption of advanced video communications in the enterprise segment will result in a CAGR of 35 percent for business IP traffic from 2007 to 2012.

Business Internet traffic will grow fastest in developing markets and Asia-Pacific. North America, Western Europe, and Japan will have slower growth rates. In volume, North America will continue to have the most business IP traffic through 2011, followed by Western Europe and Asia-Pacific.

Global IP Traffic Growth 2006–2011

Table B-1 shows the top-line forecast. According to this forecast, global IP traffic in 2008 stands at more than 10 EB per month, more than quadrupling to reach 44 EB per month in 2012. Consumer IP traffic will exceed 32 EB per month, business IP traffic will approach 10 EB per month, and mobility traffic will exceed 1.6 EB per month.

Table B-1   *Global IP Traffic 2006–2012*

	2006	2007	2008	2009	2010	2011	2012	CAGR 2007–2012
By Type (PB per Month)								
Internet	3339	4884	7394	10,666	14,984	20,662	28,339	42%
Non-Internet IP	895	1693	3353	5630	9244	12,321	15,179	55%
By Segment (PB per Month)								
Consumer	2641	4359	7674	12,003	18,261	24,760	32,183	49%
Business	1586	2193	3008	4140	5622	7479	9839	35%
Mobility	7	26	65	153	345	744	1496	125%
By Geography (PB per Month)								
North America	1471	2419	3997	5912	8542	10,694	14,309	43%
Western Europe	886	1354	2267	3591	5504	7646	10,882	52%
Asia-Pacific	1307	1963	3151	4740	7071	10,152	12,319	44%
Japan	267	373	571	843	1217	1637	2021	40%
Latin America	118	189	332	554	891	1390	2020	61%
Central Eastern Europe	116	172	264	414	656	983	1307	50%

Table B-1   *Global IP Traffic 2006–2012 (Continued)*

	2006	2007	2008	2009	2010	2011	2012	CAGR 2007– 2012
Middle East and Africa	69	107	164	243	347	481	659	44%
Total (PB per Month)								
Total IP traffic	4234	6577	10,747	16,296	24,228	32,983	43,518	46%

Source: Cisco, 2008

Consumer includes fixed IP traffic generated by households, university populations, and Internet cafes.

Business includes fixed IP WAN or Internet traffic, excluding backup traffic, generated by businesses and governments.

Mobility includes mobile data and Internet traffic generated by handsets, notebook cards, WiMAX.

Internet denotes all IP traffic that crosses an Internet backbone.

Non-Internet IP includes corporate IP WAN traffic, IP transport of TV/VoD, and mobile "walled-garden" traffic.

Generally, this forecast relies on analyst projections for Internet users, broadband connections, video subscribers, mobile connections, and Internet application adoption. Our trusted analyst forecasts come from Kagan, Ovum, Informa, IDC, Gartner, ABI, AMI, Screendigest, and Parks Associates. Additional splits of the forecast and details of the methodology for each segment and type can be found in the sections that follow.

Consumer IP Traffic 2006–2012

As shown in Table B-2, global consumer IP traffic is expected to surpass 32 EB per month in 2012. The majority of today's consumer IP traffic is Internet traffic, but consumer IPTV and VoD traffic will grow more rapidly at a CAGR of more than 68 percent.

Table B-2   *Global Consumer IP Traffic 2006–2012*

Consumer IP Traffic 2006–2012	2006	2007	2008	2009	2010	2011	2012	CAGR 2007–2012
By Type (PB per Month)								
Internet	2280	3397	5315	7735	10,884	14,950	20,331	43%
Non-Internet IP	361	962	2359	4268	7378	9810	11,852	65%
By Geography (PB per Month)								
North America	848	1571	2862	4371	6446	7866	10,522	46%
Western Europe	589	947	1704	2816	4438	6191	8884	56%
Asia-Pacific	917	1406	2356	3604	5472	7959	9323	46%
Japan	131	190	321	499	743	989	1151	43%
Latin America	68	114	217	366	596	899	1182	60%
Central Eastern Europe	68	98	156	259	437	679	889	55%
Middle East and Africa	20	34	57	89	129	176	233	47%
Total (PB per Month)								
Consumer IP traffic	2641	4359	7674	12,003	18,261	24,760	32,183	49%

Source: Cisco, 2008

Consumer Internet Traffic 2006–2012

This category encompasses any IP traffic that crosses the Internet and is not confined to a single service provider's network. P2P traffic, still the largest share of Internet traffic today, will decrease as a percentage of overall Internet traffic.

Internet video streaming and downloads are beginning to take a larger share of bandwidth, and will grow to nearly 50 percent of all consumer Internet traffic in 2012. Table B-3 shows the current and predicted consumer Internet traffic.

Table B-3 *Global Consumer Internet Traffic 2006–2012*

Consumer Internet Traffic 2006–2012	2006	2007	2008	2009	2010	2011	2012	CAGR 2007–2012
By Subsegment (PB per Month)								
Web, email, data	509	710	999	1336	1785	2337	3087	34%
P2P	1358	1747	2361	3075	3981	5161	6740	31%
Gaming	91	131	187	252	324	399	490	30%
Video communications	16	25	37	49	70	103	154	44%
VoIP	23	39	56	72	87	101	114	24%
Internet video to PC	269	647	1346	2196	3215	4501	6216	57%
Internet video to TV	14	99	330	756	1422	2348	3529	104%
By Geography (PB per Month)								
North America	605	862	1251	1705	2219	2818	3452	32%
Western Europe	530	821	1395	2203	3308	4812	6791	53%
Asia-Pacific	890	1342	2113	3035	4255	5818	8101	43%
Japan	114	158	226	308	406	526	644	32%

continues

Table B-3   *Global Consumer Internet Traffic 2006–2012 (Continued)*

Consumer Internet Traffic 2006–2012	2006	2007	2008	2009	2010	2011	2012	CAGR 2007– 2012
Latin America	60	98	163	246	363	516	721	49%
Central Eastern Europe	65	91	127	178	247	341	463	38%
Middle East and Africa	15	26	41	60	86	118	159	43%
Total (PB per Month)								
Consumer Internet traffic	2280	3397	5315	7735	10,884	14,950	20,331	43%

Source: Cisco, 2008

Web, Email, and Data includes web, email, instant messaging, newsgroups, and file transfer (excluding P2P and commercial file transfer such as iTunes).

P2P includes peer-to-peer traffic from all recognized P2P systems such as BitTorrent, eDonkey, and so on.

Gaming includes casual online gaming, networked console gaming, and multiplayer virtual world gaming.

Video Communications includes PC-based video calling, webcam viewing, and web-based video monitoring.

VoIP includes traffic from retail VoIP services and PC-based VoIP, but excludes wholesale VoIP transport.

Internet Video to PC includes free or pay TV or VoD viewed on a PC, excludes P2P video file downloads.

Internet Video to TV includes free or pay TV or VoD delivered via Internet but viewed on a TV screen using a STB or media gateway.

Cross-check: Japan's Ministry of Internal Affairs and Communications estimates that broadband Internet traffic averaged 636.6 Gb/s, or 206 PB per month, as of November 2006, and 235 PB per month at the end of 2007. Andrew Odlyzko publishes the most recent data on Japan and other countries on his website at the University of Minnesota. The ministry's traffic figures most likely include business broadband connections in addition to consumer, because service providers often do not distinguish between residences and small offices. Cisco's estimate for total Internet traffic in Japan in 2006 is 200 PB per month for 2006, and 270 PB per month in 2007. Consumer traffic is estimated by Cisco to have been 114 PB per month in 2006 and 150 PB per month in 2007.

Web, Email, and Data

This general category encompasses web browsing, email, instant messaging, data (which includes file transfer using HTTP, FTP, and so on) and other Internet applications. Note that "data" may include the download of video files that are not captured by the Internet Video to PC forecast. It includes traffic generated by all individual Internet users. An Internet user is here defined as someone who accesses the Internet through a desktop or laptop at home, school, Internet cafe, or other location outside the context of a business. Table B-4 shows the current and predicted consumer web, email, and data traffic.

Table B-4   *Global Consumer Web, Email, and Data Traffic 2006–2012*

Consumer Web, Email, and Data Traffic 2006–2012	2006	2007	2008	2009	2010	2011	2012	CAGR 2007–2012
By Geography (PB per Month)								
North America	152	209	280	365	478	620	799	31%
Western Europe	113	153	205	274	364	469	604	32%
Asia-Pacific	168	244	369	507	692	925	1266	39%
Japan	34	42	54	67	82	97	116	23%
Latin America	12	19	31	44	65	91	128	46%
Central Eastern Europe	23	31	42	55	70	89	112	29%
Middle East and Africa	7	12	17	24	34	46	62	40%
Total (PB per Month)								
Consumer web, data	509	710	999	1336	1785	2337	3087	34%

Source: Cisco, 2008

Figure B-1 shows the methodology behind the web, email, and data traffic forecast.

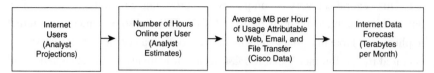

Figure B-1 *Methodology for Consumer Web, Email, and Data Traffic Forecast*

Analyst projections used in this portion were from IDC, Ovum, and Gartner.

P2P

This category includes traffic from P2P applications such as BitTorrent and eDonkey. Note that a large portion of P2P traffic is due to the exchange of video files, so a total view of the impact of video on the network should count P2P video traffic (estimated to be approximately 60 percent to 70 percent of P2P) in addition to the traffic counted in the Internet Video to PC and Internet Video to TV categories. Table B-5 shows the forecast for consumer P2P traffic from 2006 to 2012.

Table B-5 *Global Consumer P2P Traffic 2006–2012*

Consumer P2P 2006–2012	2006	2007	2008	2009	2010	2011	2012	CAGR 2007–2012
By Geography (PB per Month)								
North America	370	416	493	570	632	736	842	15%
Western Europe	304	378	484	620	801	1014	1299	28%
Asia-Pacific	556	773	1125	1534	2074	2774	3754	37%

Table B-5 *Global Consumer P2P Traffic 2006–2012 (Continued)*

Consumer P2P 2006–2012	2006	2007	2008	2009	2010	2011	2012	CAGR 2007–2012
Japan	49	63	88	112	140	181	220	29%
Latin America	38	61	97	140	203	284	397	45%
Central Eastern Europe	37	47	62	82	107	137	179	30%
Middle East and Africa	5	7	11	17	24	34	49	46%
Total (PB per Month)								
Consumer P2P	1358	1747	2361	3075	3981	5161	6740	31%

Source: Cisco, 2008

Figure B-2 shows the methodology behind the P2P forecast.

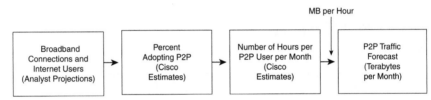

Figure B-2 *Methodology for Consumer P2P Traffic Forecast*

Internet Gaming

The Internet Gaming category includes only the traffic generated from gameplay. The download of the game is included in Web, Email, and Data. Table B-6 shows the forecast for Internet gaming from 2006 to 2012.

Table B-6   *Global Consumer Internet Gaming Traffic 2006–2012*

Consumer Gaming 2006–2012	2006	2007	2008	2009	2010	2011	2012	CAGR 2007–2012
By Geography (PB per Month)								
North America	14	17	21	26	32	38	45	22%
Western Europe	16	30	48	67	84	94	105	28%
Asia-Pacific	52	71	97	130	170	214	274	31%
Japan	8	11	17	23	31	41	52	36%
Latin America	1	1	1	2	3	4	5	43%
Central Eastern Europe	1	1	2	3	4	5	6	46%
Middle East and Africa	0	0	1	1	2	2	3	48%
Total (PB per Month)								
Consumer gaming	91	131	187	252	324	399	490	30%

Source: Cisco, 2008

Cross-check: World of Warcraft announced in early 2008 that they had reached 10 million active subscribers, up from 8 million in early 2007. Other massive multiplayer online role-playing games (MMORPGs) have a total of approximately 7 million subscribers.[1] If the average MMORPG gamer plays 80 hours per month[2] per game, at 20 MB per hour, the total monthly MMORPG gaming traffic in late 2007 would be 27 PB per month. This would mean our estimate for 2007, which includes casual gaming, first-person shooters, and online console gaming, is approximately five times MMORPG traffic, which is within reason.

[1] Source: Woodcock, Bruce Sterling. "An Analysis of MMOG Subscription Growth," MMOGCHART.COM 23.0. April 2008. http://www.mmogchart.com.

[2] According to a survey conduced by Nick Yee at Stanford, MMORPG players spent 22 hours per week in gameplay. Yee, N. (2006). "The Demographics, Motivations and Derived Experiences of Users of Massively-Multiuser Online Graphical Environments." PRESENCE: Teleoperators and Virtual Environments 15, 309–329.

Figure B-3 shows a simplified illustration of the methodology behind the gaming forecast.

Figure B-3 *Methodology for Consumer Internet Gaming Traffic Forecast*

This methodology was applied separately to casual gaming, MMO gaming, and console gaming.

Voice over IP

This category includes phone-based Voice over IP (VoIP) services direct from a service provider, phone-based VoIP services offered by a third-party but transported by a service provider, and softphone-based Internet VoIP applications such as Skype. Table B-7 shows the global forecast for consumer VoIP to 2012.

Table B-7 *Global Consumer VoIP Traffic 2006–2012*

Consumer VoIP Traffic, 2006–2012	2006	2007	2008	2009	2010	2011	2012	CAGR 2007–2012
By Geography (PB per Month)								
North America	4	6	8	10	12	13	14	17%
Western Europe	6	10	15	19	23	27	30	24%
Asia-Pacific	7	14	20	27	34	41	48	28%
Japan	5	6	8	9	10	11	12	14%

continues

Table B-7   *Global Consumer VoIP Traffic 2006–2012 (Continued)*

Consumer VoIP Traffic, 2006–2012	2006	2007	2008	2009	2010	2011	2012	CAGR 2007–2012
Latin America	0	1	1	2	3	3	4	36%
Central Eastern Europe	1	1	2	2	3	4	4	33%
Middle East and Africa	0	1	1	1	2	2	3	37%
Total (PB per Month)								
Consumer VoIP	23	39	56	72	87	101	114	24%

Source: Cisco, 2008

Figure B-4 shows a simplified illustration of the methodology behind the VoIP forecast.

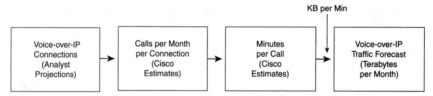

Figure B-4   *Methodology for Consumer VoIP Traffic Forecast*

Video Communications

The Video Communications category includes Internet video calling, video instant messaging, video monitoring, and webcam traffic. This segment is relatively small for the forecast period, but is included for tracking purposes because it is expected to experience substantial long-term growth in the 2012 to 2017 timeframe. Table B-8 shows the global forecast for consumer Internet video communications through 2012.

Table B-8   *Global Consumer Internet Video Communications 2006–2012*

Consumer Internet Video Communications 2006–2012	2006	2007	2008	2009	2010	2011	2012	CAGR 2007–2012
By Geography (PB per Month)								
North America	3	4	5	6	8	11	13	29%
Western Europe	5	7	10	13	17	27	53	50%
Asia-Pacific	6	12	20	25	40	58	79	46%
Japan	1	1	1	1	1	2	2	28%
Latin America	1	1	1	1	1	2	2	28%
Central Eastern Europe	0	1	1	1	2	2	2	30%
Middle East and Africa	0	0	0	0	1	1	1	35%
Total (PB per Month)								
Consumer video communications	16	25	37	49	70	103	154	44%

Source: Cisco, 2008

Figure B-5 shows a simplified illustration of the methodology behind the video communications forecast.

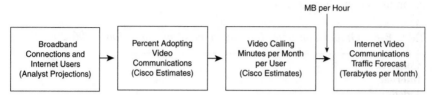

Figure B-5 *Methodology for Consumer Internet Video Communications Traffic Forecast*

Internet Video to PC

Internet Video to PC refers to online video that is downloaded or streamed for viewing on a PC screen. It excludes P2P downloads, and is distinct from Internet delivery of video to a TV screen through a set-top box or equivalent device. Much of the video viewed on PC is short-form content, and the bulk is made up of free clips, episodes, and other content offered by traditional content producers such as movie studios and television networks. Table B-9 shows the global forecast for consumer Internet video to PC traffic through 2012.

Table B-9 *Global Consumer Internet Video to PC Traffic from 2006–2012*

Consumer Internet Video to PC 2006–2012	2006	2007	2008	2009	2010	2011	2012	CAGR 2007–2012
By Geography (PB per Month)								
North America	59	156	270	389	505	635	771	38%
Western Europe	83	227	571	975	1459	2062	2852	66%
Asia-Pacific	99	210	414	686	1028	1469	2137	59%

Table B-9   *Global Consumer Internet Video to PC Traffic*
            from 2006–2012 (Continued)

Consumer Internet Video to PC 2006–2012	2006	2007	2008	2009	2010	2011	2012	CAGR 2007–2012
Japan	13	25	36	53	73	100	121	37%
Latin America	9	14	29	50	77	115	161	64%
Central Eastern Europe	4	9	16	30	53	91	138	74%
Middle East and Africa	2	6	9	14	20	28	35	42%
Total (PB per Month)								
Consumer Internet video to PC	269	647	1346	2196	3215	4501	6216	57%

Source: Cisco, 2008

Cross-check: Global YouTube traffic is estimated to have generated 15 to 20 PB per month at the end of 2006. Our estimate for user-generated content viewing traffic in that year is approximately 27 PB per month.

Cross-check: comScore estimates that in the United States, 10.2 billion online video streams were initiated in December 2007. If each stream generated 10 MB of traffic, the total for the United States would be 102 PB for the month of September, up from approximately 43 PB for the month of March 2007. Compare this to our North American estimate of 163 PB per month of Internet video to PC traffic by year-end 2007. Cisco's Internet Video to PC category includes a certain amount of traffic that is excluded from the comScore estimates, such as videos from government websites and certain Internet television applications such as Joost.

Figure B-6 shows a simplified illustration of the methodology behind the video to PC forecast.

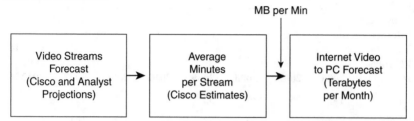

Figure B-6 *Methodology for Consumer Internet Video to PC Traffic Forecast*

Internet Video to TV

Internet Video to TV includes video delivered via the Internet to a TV screen, by way of an Internet-enabled set-top box or equivalent device. Examples of devices now available include Apple TV, Tivo Series 3, and Microsoft Xbox 360, through which users can download film and television content. Table B-10 shows the global forecast for consumer Internet video to TV traffic through 2012.

Table B-10 *Global Consumer Internet Video to TV Traffic 2006–2012*

Consumer Internet Video to TV 2006–2012	2006	2007	2008	2009	2010	2011	2012	CAGR 2007–2012
By Geography (PB per Month)								
North America	4	54	174	338	553	765	968	78%
Western Europe	3	14	61	236	561	1118	1848	167%
Asia-Pacific	2	19	67	125	217	336	544	96%
Japan	5	10	22	43	68	95	120	64%

Table B-10 *Global Consumer Internet Video to TV Traffic 2006–2012 (Continued)*

Consumer Internet Video to TV 2006–2012	2006	2007	2008	2009	2010	2011	2012	CAGR 2007–2012
Latin America	0	1	3	7	11	16	22	101%
Central Eastern Europe	0	1	2	5	8	13	20	84%
Middle East and Africa	0	0	1	2	3	5	6	87%
Total (PB per Month)								
Consumer video to TV	14	99	330	756	1422	2348	3529	104%

Source: Cisco, 2008

Cross-check: At the end of 2007, there were approximately 10 million Xbox consoles in North America capable of downloading video. If 30 percent of those consoles downloaded 5 hours of content per month, that would generate approximately 30 PB per month. Our estimate for Internet to TV in North America for 2007 is 54 PB, the remainder made up by Internet-enabled STBs and other gaming consoles.

Figure B-7 shows a simplified illustration of the methodology behind the video to TV. Analyst projections were used for networked consoles, IPTV set-top boxes (STBs), and non-service-provider Internet STBs. For cable Internet-enabled STBs, Cisco's own forecast was used.

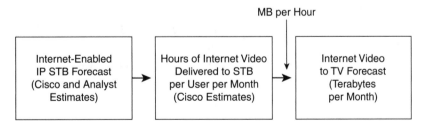

Figure B-7 *Methodology for Consumer Internet Video to TV Traffic Forecast*

Consumer Non-Internet IP Traffic 2006–2011

Non-Internet IP Video refers to IP traffic generated by traditional commercial TV services. This traffic remains within the footprint of a single service provider, so it is not considered Internet traffic. (For Internet video delivered to the STB, see Internet Video to TV in the previous section.) Table B-11 shows the global forecast for consumer non-Internet IP traffic through 2012.

Table B-11 *Global Consumer Non-Internet IP Traffic 2006–2012*

Consumer Non-Internet IP Traffic 2006–2012	2006	2007	2008	2009	2010	2011	2012	CAGR 2007–2012
By Subsegment (PB per Month)								
Cable VoD	334	883	2078	3535	5655	6996	7565	54%
Cable IP VoD	0	3	48	198	635	1277	2144	269%
IPTV VoD	25	73	230	531	1083	1532	2138	97%
Broadcast	3	3	3	4	4	5	5	12%
By Geography (PB per Month)								
North America	243	709	1611	2666	4226	5048	7070	58%
Western Europe	59	126	309	612	1129	1378	2092	75%
Asia-Pacific	27	64	244	569	1218	2141	1222	80%
Japan	17	32	95	191	337	463	507	74%
Latin America	7	16	54	120	233	383	461	95%
Central Eastern Europe	2	7	29	81	190	339	426	125%

Table B-11   *Global Consumer Non-Internet IP Traffic 2006–2012 (Continued)*

Consumer Non-Internet IP Traffic 2006–2012	2006	2007	2008	2009	2010	2011	2012	CAGR 2007–2012
Middle East and Africa	5	7	17	29	44	58	74	60%
Total (PB per Month)								
Non-Internet IP video traffic	361	962	2359	4268	7378	9810	11,852	65%

Source: Cisco, 2008

Cross-check: In mid-2008, Comcast's VoD views were approximately 300 million per month, up from 150 million per month in mid-2006. Time Warner's VoD views were 110 million per month, and the other cable operators are estimated to generate another 250 million, for a total of 660 million VoD views per month in North America at the end of 2007. Assuming each view is approximately 30 minutes, this would amount to approximately 330 million hours per month, which is very close to Cisco's estimate. (Source: Comcast, Time Warner, Kagan, 2008.) Our model assumes that VoD's share of overall household viewing hours will increase gradually, reaching approximately 12 percent of viewing hours in 2012.

Percent of VoD that is transported over IP in the metro: It was assumed that in most regions, once a VoD-enabled STB is deployed, the cable operator is transporting the VoD traffic over IP in the metro. All IPTV VoD traffic is assumed to travel over IP in both the metro and core.

MB per hour: The bandwidth consumed per hour is expected to grow with the availability of high-definition content and the penetration of high-definition STBs. In addition, the model factored in the bandwidth savings that will accompany DOCSIS 3.0 (MPEG-4) and switched digital video. Other means of bandwidth recovery were not considered in this version of the forecast.

Figure B-8 shows a simplified illustration of the methodology behind the VoD portion of the non-Internet IP traffic forecast.

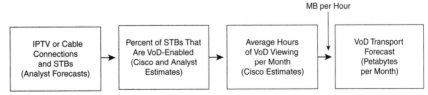

Figure B-8   *Methodology for VoD Transport Traffic Forecast*

Given the importance of this forecast to the top-line amount of traffic, more details on the assumptions follow:

- **IPTV or cable connections and STBs**: Trusted analyst sources for this data were Kagan, MRG, and Gartner.

- **Percent of STBs that are VoD enabled**: The percentage of digital STBs that are VoD enabled varies by region. In North America, nearly all digital STBs are VoD enabled. In other regions, the percentage is lower. Trusted analyst sources for this were Kagan and ABI.

- **Average hours of VoD viewing per month**: We adopted a conservative estimate of VoD views per STB per month to compensate for (1) users who are VoD enabled but do not use VoD and (2) VoD streams that are terminated before completion (believed to constitute 25 percent of all VoD views). In 2007, we assumed that 4 percent of total household viewing hours per month were VoD. In North America, where the average household views 8 hours of television per day, this would amount to 342 million hours per month.

Business IP Traffic

The enterprise forecast is based on the number of network-connected computers worldwide. In our experience, this provides the most accurate measure of enterprise data usage. An average business user might generate 4 GB per month of Internet and WAN traffic. A large enterprise user would generate significantly more traffic, 8 to 10 GB per month. Table B-12 shows the global forecast for business IP traffic through 2012.

Table B-12   *Business IP Traffic 2006–2012*

Business IP Traffic 2006–2012	2006	2007	2008	2009	2010	2011	2012	CAGR 2007–2012
By Subsegment (PB per Month)								
Business Internet traffic	1055	1469	2031	2811	3818	5076	6677	35%
Business IP WAN traffic	531	723	977	1329	1804	2404	3162	34%
By Geography (PB per Month)								
North America	620	840	1115	1492	1991	2624	3409	32%
Western Europe	295	405	554	747	989	1284	1642	32%
Asia-Pacific	389	553	784	1112	1543	2076	2755	38%
Japan	134	175	233	311	412	541	705	32%
Latin America	50	74	112	180	274	395	568	50%
Central Eastern Europe	49	73	105	149	206	280	380	39%
Middle East and Africa	49	73	105	149	206	280	380	39%
Total (PB per month)								
Business IP Traffic	2279	3417	5383	7806	10,939	14,988	20,341	35%

Source: Cisco, 2008

Business Internet Traffic includes all business traffic that crosses the public Internet.

Business IP WAN includes all business traffic that is transported over IP but remains within the corporate WAN, excluding storage or backup transfer.

Figure B-9 shows a simplified illustration of the methodology behind the business IP traffic forecast.

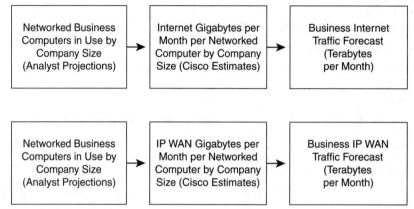

Figure B-9 *Methodology for Business IP Traffic Forecast*

Mobile Data and Internet Traffic

Mobile data traffic includes handset-based data traffic, such as text messaging, multimedia messaging, and handset video services. Mobile Internet traffic is generated by wireless cards for portable computers, WiFi hotspots, and handset-based mobile Internet usage. Table B-13 shows the global forecast for mobile data and Internet traffic through 2012.

Table B-13 *Mobile Data and Internet Traffic 2006–2012*

Mobile Data and Internet Traffic 2006–2012	2006	2007	2008	2009	2010	2011	2012	CAGR 2007–2012
By Subsegment (PB per Month)								
Mobile Internet	7	26	65	153	345	744	1496	125%
By Geography (PB per Month)								
North America	2	8	21	48	105	203	378	116%

Table B-13   *Mobile Data and Internet Traffic 2006–2012*

Mobile Data and Internet Traffic 2006–2012	2006	2007	2008	2009	2010	2011	2012	CAGR 2007–2012
Western Europe	1	2	10	28	77	171	357	171%
Asia-Pacific	1	4	10	25	56	118	241	125%
Japan	2	8	17	34	62	107	165	82%
Latin America	0	1	3	8	21	96	271	199%
Central Eastern Europe	0	1	3	6	13	24	38	99%
Middle East and Africa	0	1	2	5	11	25	45	133%
Total (PB per Month)								
Mobile data and Internet	7	26	65	153	345	744	1496	125%

Source: Cisco, 2008

Figure B-10 shows a simplified illustration of the methodology behind the mobile data and Internet traffic forecast.

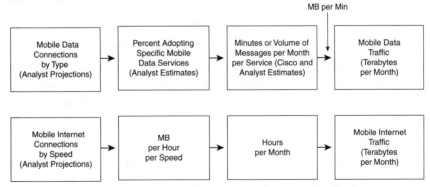

Figure B-10   *Methodology for Mobile Data and Internet Traffic Forecast*

Frequently Asked Questions

Q: Have there been any methodological changes in the latest forecast update?

A: The only methodological change since the January 2008 forecast is that the Multinationals category of business traffic was eliminated. Instead of treating multinationals separately, traffic from offices of multinationals is now counted in the respective regions where the offices are located.

Q: The growth rate seems high. I have heard that Internet traffic growth is slowing. Is this accurate?

A: The model estimates that Internet traffic grew 46 percent from 2006 to 2007. This growth rate is in line with estimates from Andrew Odlyzko at the University of Minnesota, widely recognized as an authority on Internet traffic. Cisco does project a slight increase in the growth from 2007 to 2008 of 51 percent, followed by 44 percent for 2009 and 40 percent for 2010, and continuing to decline in subsequent years. Cisco's forecast is considered conservative by most industry analysts.

Q: The growth rate seems low, given the rapid adoption of video. Is this accurate?

A: There is no question that video is driving a substantial amount of traffic. However, the volumes are so large that sustaining high growth rates becomes increasingly difficult. For instance, despite a declining growth rate, Cisco is projecting that global Internet traffic in 2012 will be over a thousand times greater than all the traffic traversing the U.S. Internet backbone in 2000.

Q: Why is VoIP traffic so low?

A: Although immensely popular, VoIP is very lightweight in terms of bandwidth. However, it is an important consideration for service providers in that quality of service (QoS) is important for voice, and one strategy for improving QoS is to increase capacity so that there is always sufficient bandwidth for the speedy transport of time-sensitive voice and video traffic.

Q: Does this forecast include signaling traffic?

A: No, signaling traffic is not included. However, an estimate can be made using the standard rule that IP signaling traffic is approximately 3 percent of bearer traffic.

Q: Why is broadcast TV traffic so low in comparison to VoD traffic?

A: Broadcast traffic is low because it is a one-to-many service rather than a one-to-one service, like VoD. For each VoD request, a new stream must be served, whereas when hundreds of people tune in to the same television show, only one copy of this show needs to cross most of the network, until close to the edge where it is split and sent over each access line. In this forecast, the access-line traffic for broadcast TV is not included.

Q: What about satellite video traffic?

A: Because satellite is similar to broadcast in that it is one to many, the exclusion of satellite from the forecast is not expected to make any significant difference. However, many analysts believe that direct broadcast satellite (DBS) providers will move to establish a broadband connection to the home (possibly through WiMAX), to be able to offer on-demand content, Internet content, and interactive content. This scenario has not been included in this forecast, but has been considered by the analyst whose WiMAX connections forecast has been incorporated into our assumptions.

Q: What about digital terrestrial video traffic?

A: Like satellite, digital terrestrial television (DTT) is a one-to-many service, so the exclusion of DTT is not expected to materially impact the accuracy of the forecast. Also similar to satellite, Pay-DTT providers may move to establish a broadband connection to the home to be able to offer on-demand content, Internet content, and interactive content. This scenario has not been included in this forecast because the penetration of DTT remains low throughout the forecast period. This may be included in future versions of the forecast.

Q: Why isn't Internet gaming traffic more significant in 2012?

A: First-person shooters (FPS) are the most bandwidth-intensive games at over 50 MB per hour of play. However, FPSs are played by a minority of gamers. The most popular games, such as casual online games, nonshooter console games, and multiplayer virtual worlds, are surprisingly lightweight in terms of traffic, partly because much of the graphical processing and rendering occurs on the client side, which is downloaded once and then does not cross the network again after download. There is a possibility that multiplayer games will break into the mainstream, whereas we assume that online gamers constitute a maximum of approximately 40 percent of the online population, and that multiplayer gamers are a maximum of approximately 40 percent of the gaming population. Refer to the companion paper, "Approaching the Zettabyte Era," at Cisco.com for consideration of this and other alternative scenarios.

For More Information

For more information, refer to the companion paper, "Approaching the Zettabyte Era," at Cisco.com or by entering the following URL: http://tinyurl.com/4wucvf. Inquiries can be directed to Arielle Sumits and Jaak Defour at traffic-inquiries@cisco.com.

Numerics

A

B

C

X-Y-Z

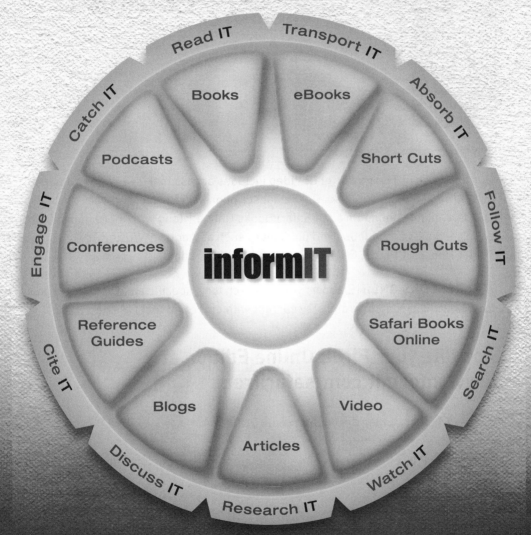

FREE Online Edition

Your purchase of **The Power of IP Video** includes access to a free online edition for 45 days through the Safari Books Online subscription service. Nearly every Cisco Press book is available online through Safari Books Online, along with more than 5,000 other technical books and videos from publishers such as Addison-Wesley Professional, Exam Cram, IBM Press, O'Reilly, Prentice Hall, Que, and Sams.

SAFARI BOOKS ONLINE allows you to search for a specific answer, cut and paste code, download chapters, and stay current with emerging technologies.

Activate your FREE Online Edition at
www.informit.com/safarifree

> **STEP 1:** Enter the coupon code: OUCVJGA.

> **STEP 2:** New Safari users, complete the brief registration form.
> Safari subscribers, just log in.